More about Heather Wokusch and ~~The Progressives' Handbooks...~~

"I suggest you check out Wokusch's books. They are part encyclopedia and part self-defense manual. The books provide the basic background information and pithy quotes about U.S. weapons of mass destruction, women's issues, education, mainstream media, elections and voting, the environment, and foreign policy.

"What sets the books above the heap of other politically-inspired manuals is Wokusch's writing style. She is punchy but not preachy and her ability to synthesize information, giving readers everything they need to know and leaving out the rest, is invaluable.

"The best part of *The Progressives' Handbook* is that it aims to make you a better progressive -- which is the point of handbooks, right? If you've read the books and happen to find yourself visiting your conservative relatives or seated at a dinner party next to a right-winger who wants to talk shop, you will be armed with the best ammunition.

"You may feel strongly about one or many of the issues covered in *The Progressives' Handbook*, but after reading Wokusch you will actually be able to talk your walk." **– Tara Lohan, AlterNet.org**

'Heather Wokusch is a curative force for anyone in despair about Bush/Cheney doctrine and Neocon dreams of empire... I highly recommend her powerful voice to all who long for the facts and information on what to do with them." - **Dori Smith, host of Talk Nation Radio.**

'Heather Wokusch stands in a fine - though scarcely flourishing - tradition of American journalism: she's committed to serving the people for whom she writes, to giving a voice to the voiceless and not taking buzzwords for an answer. If you want to know what's at stake in today's politics, don't rely on the corporate-controlled media: read *The Progressives' Handbook*." - **Steven P. McGiffen, author of *Biotechnology: Corporate Power Versus The Public Interest***

'Wokusch's exceptionally intelligent, witty, and passionate work beckons us to action." - **Sunil K. Sharma, Dissident Voice.org Editor and Publisher**

The Progressives' Handbook:
Get the Facts and Make a Difference Now (Volume 1)
Everything you need to know about the Bush administration's
record on:
US Weapons of Mass Destruction
Women's Issues
Education
Mainstream Media
... and what you can do about it!

By Heather Wokusch

This book would never have been possible without the help of two great men in my life. To my father, Donald Gene Sutherland, thank you for your critical support at the perfect time. And to my husband, Norbert Wokusch, thank you for your patience during the endless late nights and weekends I've spent working on this project; your profound wisdom and integrity are a constant source of inspiration.

ISBN-13: 9780978 784201
ISBN-10: 0-9787842-0-0

Library of Congress Control Number: 2006907057

Cover designed by Yuko Kodama
ykodama@earthlink.net

Also by Heather Wokusch

The Progressives' Handbook:
Get the Facts and Make a Difference Now (Volume 2)
Everything you need to know about the Bush administration's record on:
Elections & Voting
Environment
Foreign Policy
... and what you can do about it!

Sign up for Heather's blog and podcast:
www.heatherwokusch.com

Visit The Progressives' Handbook Action Center:
www.progressiveshandbook.com

Contents

Mainstream Media

Introduction

"The reality-based community [believes] that solutions emerge from your judicious study of discernible reality ... That's not the way the world really works anymore. We're an empire now, and when we act, we create our own reality." – an aide to George W. Bush, October 2004 [1]

It's not easy these days for "reality-based" Americans. Unemployment is up, living wages are down, over 36 million of us struggle with poverty and 47 million languish without health insurance.[2] Thousands of service members and countless civilians have died in pointless quagmires in Afghanistan and Iraq, while the administration's $670 billion so-called war on terror ravages America's reputation and threatens national security.

Yet Bush tells us to "stay the course."

Only fools stay the course when it's heading over a cliff, and that's why I wrote **The Progressives' Handbook: Get the Facts and Make a Difference Now**.

Volume 1 of the series details the Bush administration's record and provides focused action tips on US Weapons of Mass Destruction, Women's Issues, Education and Mainstream Media, while **Volume 2** covers the Environment, Elections & Voting and Foreign Policy.

As the US approaches a critical presidential election, it's more important than ever to face Bush's legacy. This updated version of **Volume 1** aims to fuel the debate.

Now more than ever, informed and inspired grassroots activism is essential. And in that spirit, welcome to **The Progressives' Handbook -**

Heather Wokusch
November 2007

US Weapons of Mass Destruction

"See, free nations do not develop weapons of mass destruction." - George W. Bush, October 2003 [1]

While Bush uses the specter of 9/11 to justify America's weapons of mass destruction (WMD) build-up, it's not clear how fresh billions spent on developing nuclear bombs or biological nerve agents will help the US protect itself, let alone spread democracy abroad.

Thankfully, the average US citizen is light years ahead of the Bush administration when it comes to homegrown WMD. An April 2004 PIPA/Knowledge Network Poll [2] showed that Americans oppose the invention of new infectious diseases, and don't want the US to use nuclear weapons first. Instead, Americans favor:

- inspections of biological research laboratories, including those in the USA
- reducing the number of nuclear weapons on high alert
- US participation in the treaty banning all nuclear weapons testing

In contrast, the Bush administration has worked overtime to break international WMD agreements and fund ever more clandestine and destructive WMD programs. Put it together and you get:

Should the US...

	American public	Bush & Co.
1. use nuclear weapons first?	No	Yes
2. invent new infectious diseases?	No	Yes
3. forbid inspections of its biological research labs?	No	Yes
4. disregard the nuclear test ban treaty?	No	Yes
5. maintain its number of weapons on high alert?	No	Yes

The discrepancy between US public opinion and the administration's actions is disturbing enough, but becomes even more urgent given the profligate spending and complete lack of oversight around homegrown WMD.

Chemical and Biological Weapons

"But you're not gonna go out and get those entrepreneurial bad guys out there to sign the chemical weapons treaty, and even if they do

they don't mean it ... like the Russians, how many times did they violate nuclear treaties? This is an exercise in liberal symbolism, liberal feel good-ism, but in terms of – it's like any other law – we have laws against murder but it didn't stop Pedro Medina, but old Sparky did." – conservative commentator Rush Limbaugh criticizing a proposed ban on chemical weapons, while simultaneously praising an electric chair nicknamed "Old Sparky," April 1997. [3]

In January 2005, former US Senate Majority leader Bill Frist told an audience at the World Economic Forum,"The greatest existential threat we have in the world today is biological."

What nonsense. As Milton Leitenberg, senior research scholar at the University of Maryland, observed in a February 2006 *Los Angeles Times* article, "Is bioterrorism a greater existential threat than global climate change, global poverty levels, wars and conflicts, nuclear proliferation, ocean-quality deterioration, deforestation, desertification, depletion of freshwater aquifers or the balancing of population growth and food production? Is it likely to kill more people than the more mundane scourges of AIDS, tuberculosis, malaria, measles and cholera, which kill more than 11 million people each year?"[4]

Since 2002, the Bush administration has spent over $30 billion on biological defense, even though the odds of an American dying in a bioterrorism attack are one in 56 million (compared to one in 322 for heart disease). Put differently, since 2001, federal grants for biowarfare-agent research have shot up 2000%, while funding for researching commonplace diseases such as tuberculosis and hepatitis has actually declined.[5]

Misguided priorities.

Risky weapons labs[6]

A whopping $6 billion went up for grabs in 2004 for federal biodefense programs, and laboratories across the country went ballistic trying to get their hands on some of that cash.

This dangerous situation was exacerbated by the Bush administration's nose-thumbing of the Biological Weapons Convention. In short, reduced pressure on weapons labs to issue declarations and allow inspections has meant less accountability – and more opportunities for secrecy and abuse.

You might recall that in February 2003, the University of California at Davis (UCD) took a full ten days to inform nearby communities that a rhesus monkey had escaped from its primate-breeding facility. Coincidentally, UCD had been vying for government funds to set up its own "hot zone" biodefense lab which could use primates for biological weapons testing. What if that monkey had been infected with ebola, or some other virus? Would the public have ever been informed?

At roughly the same time, the Pentagon unearthed over 2,000 tons of hazardous biological waste in Maryland, much of it undocumented leftovers of an abandoned germ warfare program.[7] Nearby, the FBI was draining a pond for clues into 2001's deadly anthrax attacks.

Doesn't inspire much trust in the transparency of US biological weapons programs. And things appear to be getting worse.

In June 2004, the Army was caught shirking inspections at a major biodefense lab under its domain. The scandal went back to 1999, when the Army commissioned a biological and chemical weapons-agent lab at Tennessee's Oak Ridge National Laboratory. Oversight regulations obligated the Army to inspect the lab each year thereafter, and the Centers for Disease Control (CDC) were supposed to have inspected the lab on a regular basis too.

Everything seemed to be running smoothly; in December 2003, the committee in charge of safety at the Oak Ridge lab announced that it "remains comfortable of the review and inspections of the Chem/Bio Facility conducted by the CDC and the Army."[8]

Small problem. In 2004, the Department of Energy's Inspector General discovered that the Army actually hadn't inspected the Oak Ridge biodefense lab for the previous **three years**, and that the CDC hadn't been there for **four years**. Yet the lab's safety committee said it was "comfortable" with the imaginary inspections.

Oversight of our dangerous weapons programs? What oversight?

Another egregious 2004 case involved Southern Research, a military biodefense contractor which landed in hot water by accidentally sending live anthrax across the country from Frederick, Maryland to the Children's Hospital of Oakland (California). **Live anthrax.** Laboratory workers in Oakland who received the virulent anthrax were unnecessarily put at grave risk, as were those who provided transport. To make matters worse, it turns out Southern Research's lab in Frederick, Maryland didn't even maintain the institutional biosafety committee required by federal research rules. The punishment for these acts of gross incompetence and irresponsibility? The

Bush administration gave Southern Research the task of safeguarding a $30 million biodefense facility being built near Chicago.[9]

Worried about these stunning breaches of accountability, the National Academy of Sciences has suggested screening plans for "certain types of experiments before they are conducted."[10] The Academy says that since scientists "cannot guarantee that the knowledge they generate will not play a role in advancing biowarfare or bioterrorism," a new oversight system is needed.

Characteristically, the Bush administration has so far failed to show much interest in calls for better oversight.

The White House says that dangers abroad justify the increase in stateside biological weapons labs, but it doesn't take a genius to figure out that the labs themselves are putting Americans at risk. For example, in September 2004, three lab workers at the Boston University Medical Center were accidentally exposed to a potentially lethal biowarfare agent called tularaemia bacterium. The lab didn't report the tularemia infections until months later though – after it had won a contract to build a new, $178 million biodefense laboratory.[11]

That same month, the College of American Pathologists accidentally sent over 4,000 laboratories worldwide a virus that had killed one million people in the late 1950s; it wasn't until six months later that a lab in Canada caught the error, and it wasn't until April 2005 that the public was informed. In September 2005, three mice infected with the bubonic plague disappeared from a research laboratory in New Jersey, and just weeks later, a cargo plane carrying influenza and herpes viruses crashed in Canada.

The surge in funding for biological weapons has been accompanied by an increase in corresponding dangers. As of August 2007, laboratories across the country had reported 36 lost shipments and accidents for that year, almost double the number for all of 2004. For example, a technician in Maryland was bitten by a ferret inoculated with the bird flu virus in July 2007, a worker in New Mexico was bitten by a monkey infected with the bacteria that causes plague in September 2006 and a dead mouse inoculated with a dangerous bacteria could not be located in an Oklahoma lab in December 2006. And these are just the reported cases.[12]

This ongoing series of blunders doesn't speak well for the billions of dollars the administration has invested in counteracting bioterrorism. For the record, Bush's 2007 budget earmarked almost $2 billion for biodefense research and development via the National Institutes of Health, not to mention further fortunes funnelled through other agencies.[13]

A new arms race

Bush has shown little patience with international arms control treaties in general, and seems especially determined to turn the Biological Weapons Convention on its head. While this may profit stateside WMD manufacturers, it spells collective suicide.

Take the $200 million set aside for Maryland's National Biodefense Analysis and Countermeasures Center, which among other productive pursuits, will study how to spread genetically-engineered germs in an aerosol spray. Barbara Hatch Rosenberg of the State University of New York told *Gulf News*, "It sounds like they're poised for multiple challenges to the Biological Weapons Convention that could provoke a biological arms race, and for activities that could endanger public health."[14]

Your tax dollars hard at work.

Yet the Bush administration has much more planned; there's also the new Homeland Security Department Biothreat Characterization Center (BTCC), slated to focus on packaging bioweapons agents, creating dangerous new pathogens and other activities. No doubt the inevitable cuts to domestic social services necessary to fund BTCC will be worth it.

Another contentious issue is "dual-use" research projects with potential biological weaponry applications. The National Institutes of Health (NIH) guidelines for such projects require only voluntary compliance, which usually translates to no compliance at all. For example, in April 2007, the watchdog group Sunshine Project reported a full 18 out of the top 20 US biotech companies do not comply with NIH guidelines on dual-use biotech research, leading Sunshine Project Director Edward Hammond to conclude, "Effective federal management of dual-use risks requires making safety and security oversight truly mandatory and subject to the sobering light of public scrutiny. We shouldn't wait for a bioweapons disaster to protect ourselves from ourselves."[15]

The White House claims that its biological weapons programs are strictly for defensive purposes, and therefore within the framework of arms control treaties; if other countries were to set up similar programs, however, you can bet your sweet anthrax the Bush administration would judge them in a different light. It can also be assumed that other countries are eyeing the US bioweapons buildup – and planning their military R&D budgets accordingly.

Poisoning ourselves

In 2003, the Pentagon admitted to using biological/chemical agents on 5,842 service members in secret tests conducted over a ten-year period (1962-73).[16]

In operations called Project 112 and Project SHAD, the Defense Department tested homegrown WMD capabilities on service members aboard Navy ships, and in all sorts of other despicable ways – such as spraying a Hawaiian rainforest and parts of Oahu. All in all, tests were conducted in six states (Alaska, Florida, Georgia, Hawaii, Maryland, Utah) Canada and Britain.

Many military personnel were not even informed when the toxic agents were being tested on them. Only decades later, as crucial documents slowly become declassified, have the veterans' health complaints been acknow-ledged.

"Could never happen today," you might think, "too many legal protections for citizens in place." Think again.

There's a tricky clause in Chapter 32/Title 50 of the United States Code (the aggregation of US general and permanent laws). Specifically, Section 1520a lists the following cases in which the Secretary of Defense can conduct a chemical or biological agent test or experiment on humans *if informed consent has been obtained*.[17]

> (1) Any peaceful purpose that is related to a medical, therapeutic, pharmaceutical, agricultural, industrial, or research activity.
> (2) Any purpose that is directly related to protection against toxic chemicals or biological weapons and agents.
> (3) Any law enforcement purpose, including any purpose related to riot control.

The definition is a little too open-ended for comfort; apparently there are a lot of circumstances under which the Secretary of Defense can test chemical or biological agents on human beings, but at least informed consent has to be obtained in advance.

Or does it. Get a load of Section 1515, another part of Chapter 32, this one entitled "Suspension; Presidential authorization":[18]

> After November 19, 1969, the operation of this chapter, or any portion thereof, may be suspended by the President during the period of any war declared by Congress and during the period of any national emergency declared by Congress or by the President.

You got it. If the President or Congress decides we're at war then the Secretary of Defense doesn't need anybody's consent to test chemical or biological agents on human beings. Gives one pause during these days of a perpetual "war on terror."

It's not a stretch to wonder what kind of clandestine WMD tests the Defense Department could be conducting in the US right now, on military or civilian populations, without consent, let alone on populations abroad.

An ominous sign: In June 2007, National Intelligence Director Mike McConnell gained White House approval to update a 1981 presidential order on how US spy agencies operate. Potentially up for review in the highly secretive overhaul, referred to as Order 12333, is the topic of human experimentation.[19]

Napalm returns

Remember the 1972 photograph of the naked Vietnamese girl running from a napalm attack? The sheer horror depicted in that image was enough to mobilize the US anti-war movement, and prompt the United Nations later to ban the use of napalm gas against civilians.

Significantly, the United States chose not to support the napalm ban, which means that it has the dubious distinction of being one of the few nations on earth to condone napalm's use.

But that photograph: five terrified Vietnamese children running from the deadly blast behind them, a naked little girl in the middle with part of her skin burned off.

Very few weapons are as hellish and inhumane as napalm, a polystyrene and jet fuel concoction which ignites on impact and literally melts flesh. In a civilized world, there's no excuse for such a weapon. Period.

So how do you feel knowing that the US military is reported to have used napalm-like weapons in Iraq?

The Vietnam-era napalm bomb was called Mark 47, and its contemporary equivalent is Mark 77, a 750-lb incendiary bomb that is said to be even harder to extinguish. While the chemical composition of both bombs is different, the end result is equally gruesome, so they're often confused.

Military spokespeople at first denied Mark 77 had been used by US forces in Iraq, then reneged, saying it had been used only in March/April 2003. Colonel James Alles, commander of Marine Air Group 11, admitted in August 2003 that during the initial push for Baghdad: "We napalmed both those [bridge] approaches. Unfortunately there were people there ... you could see them in the cockpit video. They were Iraqi soldiers. It's no great way to die. The generals love napalm. It has a big psychological effect."[20]

The same "big psychological effect" apparently also was used in the November 2004 attack on Fallujah by US forces, which killed an estimated 4,000-6,000 Iraqis. Eyewitnesses talked about "weird" bombs that exploded into fires that burned the skin despite water being thrown on the burns.[21]

UK reaction to the revelation of incendiary-weapons use was swift and strong, with demands that Prime Minister Blair remove British troops from Iraq until the US ceased from using such weaponry. In late November 2004, Labor MP Alice Mahon called on Blair to make "an emergency statement to the Commons to explain why this is happening. It begs the question: 'Did we know about this hideous weapon's use in Iraq?'"

No similar outrage in Congress. In fact, no comment at all.

And no heart-wrenching photographs in Sunday newspapers either. While Fallujan residents were reportedly being gassed and having their skin melted by US weapons, embedded journalists were safely ensconced far away from the carnage. Even the Iraqi Red Crescent, eager to help wounded civilians and assist refugees, was forbidden by US military officials from entering the city for weeks afterwards.[22]

Questions about the November 2004 attack on Falluja resurfaced one year later, when the Italian network RAI ran a documentary accusing US forces of having used white-phosphorus munitions in the assault; white phosphorus is a particularly barbaric incendiary agent which can burn victims to the bone.

While the US State Department initially denied the report, claiming that white phosphorous had only been used for "illumination purposes," it was forced to change its story when the March/April 2005 issue of the US Army's *Field Artillery* magazine ran an article written by Fallujah veterans who said: "WP [white phosphorus] proved to be an effective and versatile munition. We used it for screening missions at two breeches and, later in the fight, as a potent psychological weapon against the insurgents in trench lines and spider holes where we could not get effects on them with HE [High Explosive]. We fired 'shake and bake' missions at the insurgents, using WP to flush them out and HE to take them out."[23]

The RAI documentary showed graphic images of Fallujah residents with their skin melted, and accused the US of using white phosphorous shells in a "massive and indiscriminate way" against civilians during the 2004 offensive.

The complete inhumanity of deploying such inhumane weaponry aside, it's especially glaring that the Bush administration justified the invasion of Iraq in part based on Hussein's use of unconventional weapons, then turned around and apparently did the same thing in Fallujah.

To make matters worse, the Pentagon tried to downplay the outrage over white phosphorus being used as munitions in Fallujah by dismissing it as an incendiary weapon, further claiming that since the US is not a signatory to the protocol of the Convention on Conventional Weapons, the US can use white phosphorus with impunity.

Tell that to the civilians with their skin burned off.

Anthrax hits home

On September 18 2001, letters containing anthrax were sent to "Editor, NY Post" and "Tom Brokaw, NBC TV," and less than a month later, two more anthrax-laced letters were sent to "Senator (Tom) Daschle" and "Senator (Patrick) Leahy." Five died as a result of the letters, and many others, including a seven-month-old baby, were infected.

The nation panicked. Governmental and postal services ground to a halt, businesses faltered and the American public approached their mailboxes with suspicion. Accusations flew and of course Al Qaeda and Iraq were the prime suspects.

It's worth looking at what happened next.

Less than two weeks after the letters were discovered, US government officials realized the anthrax source was domestic. Of course, that didn't stop Vice President Dick Cheney from commenting on CNN that it was "reasonable" to assume the anthrax attacks were linked to 9/11 because Osama bin Laden's terrorist training manuals teach "how to deploy these kinds of substances."[24]

Most media dropped the anthrax story quite quickly, only glossing over the FBI's fumbling of the case, and while former US Army scientist Steven Hatfill was temporarily a prime suspect, nothing ever came of the investigation.

The big story behind the anthrax attacks, however, was never properly covered: reports that White House staff started taking Cipro, an anthrax-treatment drug, weeks before the attacks occurred.

According to Judicial Watch Chairman and General Counsel Larry Klayman, "One doesn't simply start taking a powerful antibiotic for no good reason. The American people are entitled to know what the White House staffers knew."[25]

Coincidentally, while Bush claimed to be "working to protect" the American public after the anthrax attacks, he actually was working hard to protect the corporate profits of Bayer AG, the large pharmaceutical company which produces Cipro.[26] After the attacks, demand for Cipro skyrocketed and five drug companies (approved to produce the drug when Bayer's patent expired in 2003) said they could produce the nation's emergency stock of Cipro at a fraction of the time and cost Bayer demanded. Considering national interest, Bush might have been expected to support breaking the patent, but instead he supported Bayer's monopoly over Cipro.[27]

While serious questions behind the anthrax incidents may never be answered, it's clear the attacks were phenomenally successful in two ways: providing justification for the Bush administration to rev up spending on biodefense and adding more fuel to the fire for an invasion of Iraq.

Courting doomsday

So what did the Bush administration learn from the anthrax fiasco? Did it wake up to the insanity of homegrown WMD? Did it destroy existing WMD stockpiles and decide never to produce more chemical/biological weapons?

Hardly. Instead, it has been funneling US tax dollars into more and more destructive weaponry, including a secretive program called Project Jefferson, the Pentagon's attempt to genetically engineer a super-resistant, even more deadly version of the anthrax bacteria.

Feeling safer?

After the Project Jefferson program was revealed in 2001, the Pentagon dismissed public outrage by announcing it would not only complete the dangerous project, but keep the results classified too.

Unfortunately, Project Jefferson has good company. In October 2005, US scientists resurrected the 1918 Spanish flu, a virus which killed almost 50 million people. And a virologist in St. Louis has been working on a more lethal form of mousepox (related to smallpox) just to try stopping the virus once it's been created.

As Richard H. Ebright, professor of chemistry at Rutgers University, told *Mother Jones* magazine, this work "creates a new vulnerability for the United States and the world. It's like the National Institutes of Health was funding a research and development arm of Al Quaeda."[28]

It's uncertain how many other chemical/biological weapons research programs are taking place all over the country right now – out of control funding and top secrecy mean a toxic WMD program could be in your own backyard right now, or else coming soon.

Former US Senate Majority Leader Bill Frist didn't help matters either. In January 2005, the Republican senator from Tennessee called for a new Manhattan Project (referring to the WWII-era nuclear weapons bonanza) for biological weapons.[29] Yet while Frist cited the 2001 US anthrax attacks as proof more biological weapons research was necessary, he failed to mention that those incidents involved anthrax produced right in the good 'ole USA - or that the primary suspect in the attacks was a US Army scientist. Frist also didn't clarify how developing even more biological warfare agents would make the world safer.

But as biotechnology expert Edward Hammond noted in a January 2005 *Sunshine Project* newsletter, Frist had already gotten his wish: "the Senator is apparently unaware that the US biodefense budget **IS** larger than that of the Manhattan Project (after adjusting up for inflation)."

The original Manhattan Project ultimately led to US forces dropping atom bombs on Hiroshima and Nagasaki, with the resulting slaughter of hundreds of thousands of people. It's terrifying to consider the potential repercussions of today's biological weapons Manhattan Project.

Nuclear Weapons

"The country with the largest number of weapons of mass destruction is America. Of the nearly 30,000 nuclear weapons in the world, Russia and America own 95 percent. No one else can destroy all life on earth except Russia and America. The two rogue nations are Russia and America, holding the world at nuclear ransom. Period." – physician, author, anti-nuclear activist Helen Caldicott, May 2005 [30]

Despite America's arsenal of over 10,000 nuclear warheads, the Bush administration is flooding tax dollars into even more destructive nuclear weaponry. After all, Armageddon is big business. The US budget for nuclear-weapon activities in fiscal 2004 topped $6 billion, over half a billion more than in 2003. Expenditures for nuclear-test readiness alone surged by 39% in the same period.[31]

Even worse, a 2004 report entitled "Weaponeers of Waste" by the National Resources Defense Council (NRDC) found that much of that funding had gone to projects "irrelevant to the defense and security challenges" of the United States. According to NRDC senior policy analyst Christopher Paine, "Spending billions to extend the life of thousands of Cold War nuclear warheads is a colossal waste of taxpayer dollars. The government could keep a small fraction of those weapons in the stockpile and spend the rest of the money to make to world safer by eliminating nuclear warheads."[32]

No such enlightened thinking in the Bush administration, which is steadily marching us towards nuclear Armageddon. The Department of Energy's (DoE) budget for FY 2006 requested over $6.6 billion for nuclear "Weapons activities," including development of the infamous nuclear bunker-buster, which was rejected by Congress in 2005. Meanwhile, funds for "Nuclear waste disposal" were to be slashed by over 12%.[33]

New Mexico, for example, was targeted to receive over 40% of the nation's spending on nuclear weapons in 2006; while a full 67% of the DoE's $4.1 billion was geared towards nuclear weapons programs, however, only 9% was slated for cleanup and a paltry 1% for renewable energy.[34]

Same sorry story across the country. The administration's FY 2007 budget request for nuclear "Weapons activities" was $6.4 billion. A grand total of $107 million (or a miniscule fraction of one percent) was slated to go towards expanded efforts to secure and/or remove "at risk nuclear or radioactive material worldwide."[35] Billions for Armageddon and pittance for environmental protection or self-preservation.

Poor oversight

Sloppiness characterizes the running of many of the nation's nuclear-weapons plants, and government security contractors have been lax in monitoring worker effectiveness.

The Y-12 nuclear weapons plant in Tennessee, for example, made headlines in March 2004 when it reported missing 200 keys to protected areas. This discovery followed reports of missing master keys in both the Sandia

National Laboratory in New Mexico and the Lawrence Livermore National Laboratory in California.[36]

In early 2004, news also surfaced that security personnel guarding the nation's nuclear stockpiles, including tons of enriched uranium at Y-12, had been cheating on their antiterrorism drills.[37] An Energy Department investigation discovered that contract security guards at the Y-12 plant had been given access to computer models of antiterrorism drill strikes *in advance*, thus rendering the tests useless. Amazingly, a representative from the longtime government contractor charged with securing the facility, Wackenhut, still had the audacity to claim that security at Y-12 was "better than it's ever been." Few were convinced.

Then in July 2004, all classified work at Los Alamos National Laboratory in New Mexico was temporarily stopped due to a security breach; two "removable data storage devices" with top-secret information couldn't be located.[38] Arguably even more troubling, in June 2006, it was revealed that the National Nuclear Safety Administration (NNSA) database had been hacked and the personal records of at least 1,500 employees and contractors stolen. The NNSA amazingly took over seven months to report the theft to the Energy Department.[39]

More recently, a B52 bomber was armed with six nuclear warheads and flown from an Air Force base in North Dakota to another in Louisiana. The August 2007 incident not only presented unthinkable security risks but also violated a Cold War treaty against flying nuclear weapons. Air Force officials were at a loss to explain how the incident could have happened, while bloggers buzzed that the weapons were actually meant for an aborted attack on Iran.

And on and on.

With the fresh billions flooding into nuclear-weapons programs and oversight crumbling under secrecy demands, the likelihood of an accident or terrorism attack involving a nuclear-weapons plant or storage facility increases exponentially.

But there's some good news. In February 2006, a federal grand jury ruled that two Department of Energy contractors were negligent in allowing plutonium from a nuclear weapons plant to contaminate surrounding areas. The contractors, Dow Chemical and former Rockwell Intl. were ordered to pay a group of 13,000 plaintiffs $553.9 million in damages.

If payout ever happens, however, it will probably be covered by US taxpayers as Uncle Sam is contractually bound to indemnify the negligent contractors.[40]

Depleted uranium[41]

One of the legacies of the Vietnam War is the quote, "we had to destroy the village in order to save it." Rings some bells these days. In the name of fighting "terror," WMD are being used against civilians in order to prevent WMD from being used against civilians.

Case in point: the American military's ongoing use of depleted uranium (DU), despite numerous independent studies warning of DU's toxic-radioactive effects. Research conducted before the Gulf War by the US-based Science Applications International Corporation found that short-term high doses of DU could result in death, and long-term low doses could lead to cancer.[42] Regardless, American forces used DU weapons in the 1991 Gulf war, the 1999 Balkan conflict, the 2001 invasion of Afghanistan, and the 2003 invasion of Iraq.

The implications are staggering. The Geneva Conventions clearly ban weapons that continue to kill or cause genetic effects after the fighting ends, not to mention weapons that unduly damage the natural environment. DU fails miserably on each count. And DU makes no distinction between friend and foe - its victims include civilians abroad as well as service members sent overseas to fight.

Hundreds of thousands of US and allied troops entered areas heavily contaminated by DU dust and debris in the Gulf War, and roughly 11 tons of DU was used by NATO forces in the Balkans.[43] In Afghan cities subjected to allied bombing, uranium concentrations were recorded at 400% to 2000% above normal, with birth defects sharply on the rise.[44]

In July 2007, Iraq's Environment Minister told a meeting of the Arab League that the DU weaponry used by US forces in 2003's invasion had led to a surge of cancer cases in Iraq. She said that "at least 350" sites had been contaminated with DU and that Iraq was facing 7,000-8,000 new cancer cases each year.[45]

These facts would indicate an urgent push to unravel DU's deadly legacy and prevent further harm; instead, there seems to have been an urgent push to cover up the facts.

In an ominous 1991 memo, US Lt. Col. Ziehmn said that despite concerns over their toxic effects, if DU weapons "proved their worth during our recent combat activities, then we should assure their future existence ... I believe we should keep this sensitive issue at mind when after-action reports are written."[46]

This institutionalized denial could explain why governmental studies into the health effects of DU on Gulf war veterans have included flaws and omissions, such as lengthy delays ensuring that many DU acute exposure victims have been dead too long for autopsies to be performed. It may also explain why the United Nations Environment Program took a over a year after the Balkan conflict to begin investigating post-war uranium contamination, and why the US government vetoed a proposed World Health Organization study into the health effects of DU on Iraqi civilians.[47]

DU's ability to penetrate hard targets is desirable militarily, but alternatives such as Tungsten can achieve similar results without the radiation hazards. What then justifies the continued use of DU?

One answer might lie in a powerful corporate lobby: DU is a waste byproduct of the enrichment of natural uranium for use in nuclear reactors/weapons. In other words, by providing DU for weaponry, the nuclear industry can effectively dump its toxic garbage in other countries, and avoid the expensive hassle of storing nuclear waste.

Double-speak, denial and winning a nuclear war

Bush has been a friend to the nuclear industry from the start, by opposing the Comprehensive Test Ban Treaty and by thumbing his nose at the Nuclear Non-Proliferation Treaty.

With 2002's Nuclear Posture Review (NPR), however, the Bush administration entered Dr. Strangelove territory big time. Among other proposals, NPR says that the US should develop "nuclear strike capabilities" against countries such as Russia, China, Iraq, North Korea, Syria, Iran and Libya, and that the US could use nuclear weapons in the vaguely worded "event of surprising military developments."[48]

In tandem with NPR, the Bush administration has publicly euphemized nuclear weapons as "low-yield," "tactical," and "user-friendly." (How significant that one of the brains behind current US nuclear policy, Dr. Keith Payne, is well known for his 1980's essay "Victory is Possible," an optimistic approach to all-out nuclear war.)

Meanwhile, former Secretary of Defense Donald Rumsfeld continually warned of rogue states holding "America hostage to nuclear blackmail," but failed to mention his own contribution: Rumsfeld was on the board of ABB, a company that sold hundreds of millions of dollars of equipment and services to North Korean nuclear plants.[49] It's another intriguing coincidence that despite his administration's slamming "axis of evil" nukes, in 2003 Bush requested $3.5 million for a consortium building nuclear reactors in North Korea.

But the administration can't shoulder all of the blame for the country's embrace of nuclear weapons; a Gallup poll released in March 2005 found that over one in four Americans (a full 27%) believed that using nuclear weapons to fight terrorism is acceptable.[50]

And US elected leaders often don't help set the record straight: Rep. Sam Johnson (R-TX) told a church group in early 2005, "Syria is the problem. Syria is where those weapons of mass destruction are, in my view. You know, I can fly an F-15, put two nukes on 'em and I'll make one pass. We won't have to worry about Syria anymore."[51]

The congressional Representative said that to a church group: Just nuke Syria, and we won't have to worry anymore.

Condoning genocide by nuclear attack has no place in civil society – anywhere. Yet coming from a politician representing a country with the dubious distinction of having deployed atomic weapons in the past (and having killed hundreds of thousands of people in Hiroshima and Nagasaki as a result) the attitude is even more disgraceful.

Discarding non-proliferation agreements

The US has always been somewhat impatient with international non-proliferation agreements. Despite a 1992 self-imposed moratorium, the country has conducted 23 nuclear tests since 1997 (the most recent in August 2006) dismissing them as subcritical and therefore acceptable.

But the Bush administration has upped the nuclear ante considerably, by announcing plans for further sub-critical nuclear tests, and by authorizing the nation's weapons labs to resume full-on nuclear testing with as little as six-months' notice.[52]

These moves fly in the face of the Comprehensive Test Ban Treaty (CTBT), aimed at banning all nuclear explosions. Signed by President Clinton in 1996 but rejected by the Senate in 1999, the CTBT can't enter into force until it's ratified by the "dirty dozen" holdouts (including the US, Iran, China, North Korea and Israel, among others) from the original group of 44 nuclear-capable signatories.

Bush rejected the CTBT in his first days as president, and other countries have followed his lead in withdrawing their support as well. Iran, for example, one of the original signatories, had permitted five monitoring stations to be built on its soil; soon after the US began withholding funds from the CTBT's on-site inspection program in January 2002, however, Iran began withholding monitoring data from the international community, thus rendering its stations useless.

As Daryl Kimball of the US-based Arms Control Association noted, "There is a risk that states like China and Iran will begin to withdraw their support from implementation of the treaty, and these are signs of the problems that may occur ... The US is risking that possibility and that may indeed be what the US wants."[53]

Closely connected to the issue of non-proliferation is the funding of domestic nuclear-weapons programs. In November 2004, Congress showed signs of intelligent life when it rejected many of the administration's funding requests; denied, for example, was $9 million for the development of low-yield nuclear weapons (also called "mini-nukes") and $30 million to speed up the possibility of resuming nuclear testing in Nevada.

Also turned down was $27.6 million for the so-called bunker buster, officially known as the Robust Nuclear Earth Penetrator (RNEP). Billed as a research project on destroying underground bunkers, RNEP has seen its proposed budget quadruple in recent years: Bush requested $6.1 million for the project in FY 2003, but then a full $27.6 million in FY 2005. Quite a hefty increase, and makes you wonder if only research is involved, or if it's actually a full-blown weapons-development program.

The secrecy surrounding US nuclear weapons programs, not to mention the unchecked millions available in administration discretionary funds, makes it likely that at least some of the nuclear weapons programs Congress rejected will get back-door funding one way or another. For example, while no funding was provided for the nuclear bunker buster in the FY 2006 budget, a full $25 million was granted for the Reliable Replacement Warhead, a program which potentially could include designing a new nuclear weapon. Accordingly, the administration's FY 2007 budget requested an increase to $27.7 million for the Reliable Replacement Warhead program.[54]

Arming the Heavens

> *"In fact, this system will provide no real defense... Do not allow the American public to be deceived. The 'initial defensive capability' being advertised by the Missile Defense Agency is a sham."* – Thirty-one distinguished former government officials (who had served under eight different presidents and in areas ranging from the Pentagon to the State Department) warning Bush against missile defense deployment, May 2004 [55]

Missile "defense" mania

The Bush administration requested over ten billion dollars in its fiscal 2005 budget for the Star Wars missile "defense" program it had hoped to roll out in Alaska and California by late 2004.

Can you imagine if those funds had been spent on our communities instead? Look at that 10 billion dollars again. In comparison, Bush's fiscal year 2005 discretionary budget requested a total of:[56]
- 3 billion dollars for energy
- 5 billion dollars for agriculture
- 8 billion dollars for Social Security and Medicare

In other words, energy, agriculture, Social Security and Medicare each had less value for Bush than a Star War missile "defense" boondoggle. Unbelievable.

Put another way, Bush's proposed 2005 expenditure on missile "defense" was almost double what the Department of Homeland Security was shelling out for customs and border patrol at the time. Hmm, which investment would have more effectively protected the US?

For FY 2006, the administration requested roughly $10 billion for missile defense, and a further $10.4 billion for FY 2007. A Congressional Budget Office report estimated that spending could reach $19 billion by 2013.[57]

At least our neighbors to the north have provided some welcome sanity in refusing to go along with Bush's missile folly. Former Canadian Prime Minister Paul Martin flatly stated in December 2004 that he didn't believe the US missile defense program would actually be able to shoot down incoming rockets, and that he would not provide any money for Bush's pet project. Martin also said that he wouldn't allow rockets to be stationed on Canadian soil, adding, "I don't believe space belongs to any country. We will not engage in the weaponization of space."[58]

Former Prime Minister Martin was vindicated just days later when a major test of Bush's prized missile "defense" system ended up an embarrassing flop: the so-called "kill vehicle" (a missile to shoot down enemy missiles) never even managed to leave the ground.

There was heightened pressure for the late-December test to succeed, since the administration's previous missile "defense" test, in December 2002, had also failed when the warhead didn't separate from its booster rocket. After all, the program was already estimated to have cost taxpayers $130 billion, with an additional $50 billion slated to be spent in the following five years. Meanwhile, service members didn't have proper gear, veterans were seeing their benefits cut, and the threat of a ballistic missile attack on the United States had grown relatively unlikely anyway.

Even if the test had gone according to plan, however, the Government Accountability Office, Congress' auditing arm, claims that the tests conducted so far lack validity because they are "repetitive and scripted." Crucial parts of the system haven't been tested together, and the test conditions are so artificial that the results are almost meaningless.

Nonetheless, in February 2005, yet another test fizzled out when the interceptor missile failed to launch. More tens of millions down the drain that could have been spent on something productive.

Weather warfare

It may sound like something out of a James Bond movie, but a weapon capable of triggering climate change is in the works – and may already be fully operational.[59]

A 1996 report commissioned by the Air Force predicts:[60]
> "In 2025, US forces can 'own the weather' by capitalizing on emerging technologies and focusing development of those technologies to war-fighting applications. Such capabilities offers the war fighter tools to shape the battlespace in ways never before possible ... In the future, such operations will enhance air and space superiority and provide new options for battlespace shaping and battlespace awareness. The technology is there, waiting for us to pull it all together; in 2025 we can 'Own the Weather.'"

The technology is there alright – on a Defense Department site near Gakona, Alaska. It's called The High-frequency Active Auroral Research Program (HAARP) and is run by the US Air Force and US Navy, among others.

HAARP works by heating up parts of the ionosphere, the electrically charged layer just above the ozone layer, through radio frequency beams. The radiation bounces back to earth, and is thought to disrupt weather, communications and human health as a result.

HAARP's homepage sells it as "Arctic research to ensure the development of the knowledge, understanding and capability to meet national defense needs in the Arctic."[61] But just how many national defense needs does the Arctic region really have?

Speaking to a group of Alaskan lawmakers in 1996, Richard Williams of Princeton University called HAARP "a global threat to the atmosphere," and added, "The project's internal documents indicate that plans include the eventual use of power levels up to ten billion watts. This is an enormous power level, more than 200 times the total electrical power level used by the city of Juneau. There could be a serious impact in the atmosphere that might result from energies of this magnitude."[62]

Secrecy and mystery shroud the HAARP program, but one thing is clear: the Defense Department intends to complete its 180 massive towers equipped with antennas at Gakona. Whether this massive and costly undertaking is truly for national defense needs in the Arctic or something more sinister remains to be seen.

FALCON

International agreements and treaties could become a thing of the past once the FALCON has landed.

The Pentagon's ultimate jeans-creaming weapon is just years, and billions of your tax dollars, away. Made public in July 2003, The Force Application and Launch from Continental US program (FALCON) will enable the US government to bomb "anywhere on Earth in less than two hours."

What a way to win friends and influence people.

A mini-FALCON, with the ability to carry a payload of 1,000 pounds of munitions, is scheduled for release in 2010. Then in 2025, the super-duper "reusable Hypersonic Cruise Vehicle" FALCON is slated to hit the skies complete with a 12,000 pound payload.

Let's take a closer look at the Pentagon's idea of future warfare. The following are quotes from the US government's *FALCON Technology Demonstration Program Fact Sheet:* [63]

- "Recent military engagements in Bosnia, Afghanistan and Iraq have underscored both the capabilities and limitations of U.S air forces in terms of placing ordnance on military targets."
- "Moreover, the current and future international political environment severely constrains this country's ability to conduct long-range strike missions on high-value, time critical targets from outside ... the continental US."

In other words, the US has alienated so many former allies that it can't depend on the use of overseas bases from which to conduct bombing raids. The Pentagon's solution? Get farther-reaching bombs.

The FALCON Fact sheet ominously adds, "The intent is to hold adversary vital interests at risk at all times." Makes you wonder when global military domination became synonymous with spreading democracy.

No Damn Excuse

> *"The noble task of arms control and disarmament cannot be accomplished by confrontation and condemnation. Hostile attitudes only serve to heat up the situation, whereas a true sense of respect gradually cools down what otherwise could become explosive." – the Dalai Lama*

US landmines litter countries abroad, dangerous weapons caches are missing in Iraq, defense contractors are imposed on everyday US civilian life – and the Bush administration claims to be making the world a safer place.

Landmines

Princess Diana worked tirelessly to publicize the dangers of landmines, saying the world was "too little aware of the waste of life, limb and land which anti-personnel landmines are causing among some of the poorest people on earth." In a 1997 speech to landmine advisory groups, she noted:

> "For the mine is a stealthy killer. Long after conflict is ended, its innocent victims die or are wounded singly, in countries of which we hear little. Their lonely fate is never reported. The world, with its many other preoccupations, remains largely unmoved by a death roll of something like 800 people every month - many of them women and children. Those who are not killed outright - and they number

another 1,200 a month - suffer terrible injuries and are handicapped for life."[64]

Compare Princess Diana's compassion to the Bush administration's actions.

In February 2004, the White House unveiled its new policy on landmines, reversing almost all of the gains made during the Clinton years. Bush's scandalous policy rejects the 1997 Mine Ban Treaty (an international agreement ratified by 144 countries) insisting instead that the US continue developing non-persistent anti-personnel and anti-vehicle landmines.

Keep in mind that the United States already stockpiles 7.5 million anti-vehicle mines and over 10 million anti-personnel mines. Why on earth are more needed?

And how hypocritical that an administration which touts family values and calls itself moral doesn't do everything in its power to stop the scourge of landmines. *The International Campaign to Ban Landmines'* web site lists these tragic facts:[65]

- It is estimated that there are between 15,000 and 20,000 new casualties caused by landmines and unexploded ordnance each year. That means there are some 1,500 new casualties each month, more than 40 new casualties a day, at least two new casualties per hour.
- Most of the casualties are civilians and most live in countries that are now at peace.
- A landmine blast causes injuries like blindness, burns, destroyed limbs and shrapnel wounds.
- Those who survive and receive medical treatment often require amputations, long hospital stays and extensive rehabilitation.
- The injuries are no accident, since landmines are designed to maim rather than kill their victims.
- Landmines deprive people in some of the poorest countries of land and infrastructure.

Predictably, the administration has tried to package its disgraceful landmine policy in rosy terms. A March 2004 Department of Defense press release claimed the Bush administration's approach "will help reduce humanitarian risk and save the lives of U.S. military personnel and civilians," but if that's really the goal, you'd think that getting rid of landmines altogether would be more effective than developing even more of them. The press release went on to say that so-called "non-persistent" landmines have been "rigorously tested and have never failed to destroy themselves or become inert within a set time."[66] Sure.

There are two categories of landmines: non-persistent and long-lived. Non-persistent landmines, the kind the Bush administration has announced it will develop, are meant to either detonate or self-deactivate within roughly nineteen weeks, thus supposedly eliminating ongoing danger to civilians. But as *Human Rights Watch* notes, "Assurances that U.S. landmines are unquestionably reliable are inconsistent with the cautions contained in Army field manuals, the findings of ammunition surveillance testing data, and experiences in the 1991 Gulf War." While in "theoretically perfect conditions" the mines should destroy themselves, in reality, 2-5% of the self-destruct mechanisms don't work and up to 10% of the mines don't arm properly.[67]

The bottom line: if there were a meadow filled with US non-persistent landmines, that according to the government "have never failed to destroy themselves or become inert within a set time," would you walk across that meadow after the allotted time period? Would you let your child play there? If not, then how can the US government ask anyone else to risk exposure?

In late November 2004, the world community met in Nairobi, Kenya to tackle the global landmine dilemma, and even countries which hadn't joined the Mine Ban Treaty showed up in Nairobi to lend a hand. Russia was there. China was there. Israel was there. And the United States? A big, fat, flaming no-show.

Acting as a goodwill ambassador the UN Children's Fund (UNICEF), the actor and activist Danny Glover attended the Nairobi landmine meeting. Glover's assessment of his government's no-show: "As a citizen of the U.S., I feel embarrassed and angry."[68]

Down with arms control

From the very start, the Bush administration has thumbed its nose at international arms control agreements. Here's a partial list:

Comprehensive Test Ban Treaty (CTBT):
The UN-sponsored organization was set up in 1996 to ban nuclear-test explosions and to establish a corresponding global monitoring system. But there's a catch - the treaty can't go into effect until all 44 of the nuclear-capable countries that joined in 1996 have ratified it.

> Bush dismissed the CTBT as "unenforceable" right after assuming office, and then cut funding for inspections research. By doing so, he encouraged other holdouts (such as North Korea) to use US intransigence as justification for building up their own nuclear-weapon programs.

Nuclear Non-Proliferation Treaty (NPT):
In force since the USA ratified it in 1970, the NPT obliges five nuclear countries (China, France, Russia, USA and UK) not to acquire or transfer nuclear weapons or use them against NPT countries that don't have nuclear weapons. In turn, countries without nuclear weapons should not acquire or build them. With over 185 member countries, the NPT is the world's most widely-accepted arms control agreement.

> The administration hasn't actually pulled out of the treaty yet, but has ignored it by pumping funding into nuclear weapons programs, and by repealing the ban on low-yield nuclear weapons. Bush has also pushed development of the Robust Nuclear Earth Penetrator, which although sold to the American public as a "bunker buster," is in fact a nuclear weapon. Even worse, the Pentagon's 2002 Nuclear Posture Review lists various cases in which a US nuclear strike would be justified. In July 2004, the administration further negated the NPT by pledging to fight against its provisions for inspections and verification.

Anti-Ballistic Missile Treaty (ABM):
Ballistic missiles are especially dangerous because they can carry nuclear (and other WMD) warheads and can travel great distances in minutes. To stop the endless build up of ballistic missiles and the anti-ballistic missiles meant to shoot them down, this treaty has limited the United States and Soviet Union to only two ABM deployment areas each since 1972. Here's the logic: there won't be adequate defense against an incoming ballistic missile, so each country will think twice before using one first.

> The Bush administration withdrew from the treaty in 2001, and requested billions for a boondoggle missile "defense" program instead. In other words, while tax dollars are being splurged on a wasteful sham, the US has become more vulnerable because other countries have more reason to build ballistic missiles.

Biological Weapon Convention (BWC) draft Protocol:
Since 1972, BWC has banned the development, stockpiling, transfer, and use of biological weapons worldwide. The catch is that BWC doesn't have an enforcement mechanism so is prone to systematic violations. To ensure compliance by the 144 member states, ten years of negotiations led to a 2001 draft Protocol which would have increased transparency, and thereby helped prevent cheating.

> The Bush administration abandoned the Protocol as being too weak, but didn't come up with a better option. Of course, that conveniently allowed the US biological weapons program to remain shrouded in secrecy indefinitely. It's worth noting that when former United Nations Ambassador John R. Bolton (then Under Secretary for Arms

Control and International Security) addressed a BWC meeting in late 2001 to explain why the US hadn't supported the Protocol, he cited the familiar Hussein-as-boogeyman threat: "The United States strongly suspects that Iraq has taken advantage of three years of no UN inspections to improve all phases of its offensive BW program. The existence of Iraq's program is beyond dispute, in complete contravention of the BWC."[69]

Conference on the Illicit Trade in Small Arms and Light Weapons in All Its Aspects:
At a United Nations conference in July 2001, a program of action was put forward to deal with the "illegal manufacture, trade, stockpiling, transfer, possession as well as financing for acquisition of illicit [small arms and light weapons] SALW, and take action under appropriate international law against such groups and individuals." Of course, the Bush administration balked at the concept of restricting gun ownership, even the ownership of illegal weapons.

The National Rifle Association is happy. Gun manufacturers are happy. Drug cartels and terrorists are happy too. But the rest of us face increased danger from illicit guns.

Gee, now where did I put that stinger missile?

Sure, all of us misplace things every now and then, but the US government has developed the increasingly nasty habit of losing deadly weapons.

Case in point: the Pentagon can't seem to locate hundreds of its Stinger shoulder-fired anti-aircraft missiles. While the Army says it transferred 7,551 Stingers abroad from 1982 to 2004, a June 2004 report by the congressional Government Accountability Office (GAO) found that the true number was at least 8,331. The GAO also noted that "the Pentagon's process for inspecting the missiles provided to foreign governments is faulty and does not guarantee that the missiles are where they are supposed to be."[70] For example, some US officials overseas just counted the Stinger cases, without even opening up the containers to see if the missiles were inside.

Keep that sloppy record-keeping in mind the next time a US military or civilian aircraft is shot down with a Stinger missile.

Then in July 2007, the GAO found that the Pentagon couldn't locate 190,000 AK47 rifles and pistols which had been distributed to Iraqi security forces in 2004 and 2005. The "lost" items represented over half of the weapons allocated and raised concerns that they were being used against US troops.

Similarly aggravating was the summer-2004 debacle in which hundreds of tons of high-grade explosives went missing from previously monitored bunkers at Al Qaqaa, Iraq.

Al Qaqaa had for many years housed explosives powerful enough to detonate nuclear weapons or blow up buildings, but the site was sealed off by the International Atomic Energy Agency (IAEA) just before the 2003 invasion.

When it was later discovered that the massive weapons cache at Al Qaqaa had been looted, critics therefore accused the administration of incompetence for not having secured the site; Bush predictably shot back against those "wild charges," suggesting instead that the theft had taken place before US forces had arrived.

In late October 2004, however, an ABC film crew released footage taken the previous April 18th, nine days *after* the "fall" of Baghdad, showing US troops entering what looks like the Al Qaqaa facility – and the munitions are still there. The ABC footage shows one container labeled "Al Qaqaa State Establishment," others marked "explosive," and the videotape perfectly matches the IAEA's own photographs of the facility taken previously.[71]

In other words, the "wild charges" don't seem very unfounded after all: it's quite probable that because US forces were diverted elsewhere, perhaps to guard Iraq's oil fields, the huge cache of deadly weapons at Al Qaqaa was raided. Doesn't do much to support the claim that the invasion of Iraq was to secure WMD, rather than to secure oil profits.

The issue remains, however, what happened to the nearly 380 tons of extremely powerful explosives that had been stored at Al Qaqaa. It isn't out of the question that those very weapons have since been used against US forces in Iraq.

What an irony that the invasion was billed as a way to save the world from Iraq's WMD, yet the administration's incompetence at Al Qaqaa actually made the world a much more dangerous place.

And the looted munitions facility at Al Qaqaa is apparently just the tip of the iceberg; a United Nations agency reported that around 90 critical sites across Iraq had been looted during the weeks after the invasion.

In a letter to the United Nations' Security Council, the IAEA's director general, Mohamed ElBaradei, said his inspectors had "been able to identify quantities of industrial items, some radioactively contaminated, that had been transferred out of Iraq from sites [previously] monitored by the IAEA," and that his group "continues to be concerned about the widespread and apparently systematic dismantlement that has taken place at sites previously relevant to Iraq's nuclear programme."[72] Tough talk from ElBaradei; no wonder the White House has pushed for his resignation.

Pre-invasion, the administration consistently ridiculed the weapons inspections (which in hindsight turned out to have worked remarkably well), and after the fall of Hussein, the US government has severely curtailed the IAEA's ability to monitor Iraq's nuclear facilities and stockpiles. You've got to wonder why. Wasn't the whole point of the Iraq invasion to secure loose WMD? You'd think the IAEA's expertise would be invited, not feared.

You'd also think that the Bush administration would avoid allying itself on the international stage with dubious regimes dealing in illicit weapons. Pakistan, for example. After the nuclear weapons ring run by the "father" of Pakistan's nuclear bomb program, Abdul Qadeer Khan, was exposed, at minimum you'd expect tough words from the White House. Didn't happen.

And after Pakistan's President Musharraf pardoned Khan and decided to shield him from foreign investigators indefinitely, you'd expect tough actions from the administration. Didn't happen either. Instead, Bush called military dictator Musharraf a "courageous leader" for his support in the so-called war on terror, even though the pardoned weapons-dealer Khan has admitted to transferring nuclear technology to Iran and Libya.

The Bush administration sure has some odd priorities.

I pledge allegiance to Lockheed Martin

You might wonder about the proliferation of homegrown WMD. Americans are peace-loving people; so why is the government acting like it's controlled by weapons manufacturers?

Because to a large extent it is. In recent years, military contractors have diversified into both the public arena and the average consumer's daily life. For example, Lockheed Martin is the US government's biggest provider of IT services, systems integration, and training; in fact, almost 80% of Lockheed Martin's business (which the company's web site says topped $39.6 billion in 2006) is with the Department of Defense and US federal government agencies.

A November 2004 *New York Times* article noted that Lockheed Martin's influence "now stretches from the Pentagon to the post office. It sorts your mail and totals your taxes. It cuts Social Security checks and counts the United States census. It runs space flights and monitors air traffic. To make all that happen, Lockheed writes more computer code than Microsoft."[73]

And of course, the company's business has boomed under Bush. The US national security budget now tops $500 billion annually, and Lockheed is among a handful of companies reaping the benefits. Bush's drive for perpetual war is also profitable for the company, which in fiscal 2003 was the top recipient ($21.9 billion) of Pentagon primary contracts.

So what's wrong with this picture? Plenty.

As might be expected, former Lockheed Martin executives, lawyers and lobbyists have received plum appointments within the Bush administration - including the Director of the National Nuclear Weapons Complex, the Director of the National Spy Satellite Agency, the Secretary of the Navy as well as members of the Defense Policy Board, the Defense Science Board and the Homeland Security Council, just to name a few.[74] While technically legal, these appointments present conflict-of-interest possibilities galore. Why pursue peace and harmony overseas when your former company (which might provide you with a cushy position after your short stint in government) will make billions from weapons deals?

Then there's the related matter providing deadly arms to countries abroad (often at US taxpayer expense) despite obvious risks to global security. In August 2007, for example, the Bush administration announced a $20 billion weapons deal for Saudi Arabia, despite concerns that the country had been working against US interests in Iraq. The Saudi arms sale corresponded with a projected increase of $30 billion in US weapons to Israel over the next ten years.

No doubt Egypt, Jordan and other US allies in the region will receive more weapons from Uncle Sam as well.

While promoting a Middle East arms race may please "Left Behind" Christians hoping for a fiery apocalypse, it denies the sleazy business and deadly consequences associated with such weapons sales. As Frieda Berrigan, senior research associate at the World Policy Institute's Arms Trade Resource Center, observed in a May 2007 *Los Angeles Times* opinion piece, "The connection between the factory that makes a weapons system and the community where that weapon 'does its duty' is invariably missing in action, as are the relationships among the companies making the weapons and the generals (on-duty and retired) and politicians making the deals, or raking in their own cuts of the profits for themselves and/or their constituencies. In other words, our most successful (and most deadly) export remains our most invisible one."[75]

Remember that US taxpayers fund the bulk of many military contractors' sales, but receive no financial gain in return. In essence, Lockheed Martin, General Dynamics, Northrop Grumman, Boeing and the other biggies are publicly subsidized, but the profits remain private. How fair is that?

There's also the shady issue of oversight. Who makes sure that these massive million-dollar, if not billion-dollar weapons sales to the Pentagon are handled without waste or corruption? Well, usually the Pentagon. Not comforting.

And what if those billions in US taxpayer dollars had been earmarked for peaceful purposes abroad instead? Rather than bombs and warplanes, what if the US supplied other countries with funds for community building, agricultural programs, conflict mediation, projects to empower women... the world would be a much better and safer place.

Coming soon to a protest rally near you

It's naïve to think that once developed, US military weapons will only be used against foreign populations. The Bush administration's "you're with us or against us" mentality leaves little room for domestic dissent, and as the line blurs between military and national security technologies, folks back home may find themselves targeted. As Jondavid Black of Lockheed told the *New York Times* in November 2004, what his company does "for the military in downtown Falluja, they can do for the police in downtown Reno."[76]

One domestic crowd-control device possibly coming to your hometown is Raytheon's "Active Denial System" heat-beam, which a US Air Force fact sheet describes as a "focused speed-of-light millimeter wave energy beam to induce an intolerable heating sensation." The weapon cost $50 million to develop, and according to Doug Johnson, Executive Director of the Minneapolis-based Center for Torture Victims, could easily end up being used as a torture device. Johnson told *The Sacramento Bee*.[77]

> "It seems fundamentally a weapon that's designed to create a great deal of pain and fear. The concern I would have is ... once this kind of technology is available and there's a perception that it's safe and nonlethal, it seems like a natural device to be used in interrogations.

> "Is it torture if it only creates a sensation of pain, but leaves no marks and no long-term damage? I would say yes. Torture is primarily a psychological device, and finding different ways to use

the body against the mind has been the struggle of torture technologies for thousands of years."

The US military tested a heat-beam prototype in the first half of 2005, and as Charles "Sid" Heal, commander of the Los Angeles Sheriff's Department, told *Bloomberg Business News* in late November 2004, a smaller version of the heat-beam weapon could be sold to stateside law-enforcement agencies.[78]

Another weapon authorized for US government use against civilians is the Taser "stun gun," which delivers a short-term electrical charge of 50,000 volts. The Taser is marketed as a non-lethal weapon, but an increasing number of those on the receiving end of its fierce jolt are dying. In fact, in June 2006 the US government started an inquiry into 184 deaths that followed police use of Tasers and other stun weapons.[79]

TASER brand technology is deployed at more than 11,000 law enforcement agencies across the US, but the "stun gun" is of little use for crowd control or on vehicles. However, a new laser version of the gun will reportedly be able to deliver a similar 50,000-volt shock across a crowd.[80]

In other words, protest rallies could soon become much more dangerous for those with medical conditions (such as heart problems) potentially exacerbated by electric shocks.

Torturous heat-beams and electroshock guns on Main Street... what next? Makes the days of pepper spray in the eyes of protestors seem quaint.

It all boils down to this: if we allow our government to pull out of international arms control agreements and invest billions in weaponry, and if we allow ourselves to live in a mindset of perpetual war, then we lose the right to be surprised when that war and those weapons are inevitably turned against us.

Ten Easy Ways to Make a Difference Now

1. Keep updated on WMD issues

If you've got internet access, and would like to learn more about WMD, then check out these sites:

Federation of American Scientists
(www.fas.org)

Your one-stop-shop for WMD information, clearly organized under subheadings including (among others) Biological and Chemical Weapons, Nuclear Weapons, Arms Trade and Weapons in Space. The site also handily provides information on weapons systems around the world, easily accessible by country name.

Physicians for Social Responsibility
(www.psr.org)
Promotes "public policies that protect human health from the threats of nuclear war and other weapons of mass destruction, global environmental degradation, and the epidemic of gun violence in our society today."

International Physicians for the Prevention of Nuclear War
(www.ippnw.org)
Seeks to "prevent all wars, to promote non-violent conflict resolution, and to minimize the effects of war and preparations for war on health, development, and the environment."

Nuclear Threat Initiative
(www.nti.org)
Comprehensive site with everything from country profiles on nuclear, biological and chemical weapons, to tutorials and issue briefs. Sign up for its Global Security Newswire, offering "daily news updates about nuclear, biological and chemical weapons, terrorism and related issues."

If you're interested in the latest WMD and disarmament news, but prefer print publications to internet sites, then subscribe to one of the great journals in that field (*Arms Control Today, Disarmament Diplomacy, Bulletin of Atomic Scientists* and *Arms Control Reporter* are but a few out there).

2. Find out if there are WMD facilities in your area

Curious about where the nation's nuclear weapons plants are located? Then check out the Federation of American Scientists' "Where the Bombs Are" at: www.fas.org/blog/ssp/2006/11/new_article_where_the_bombs_ar.php

Is a university or military facility in your area involved in biological weapons research? One resource to help you locate biodefense projects is Project Sunshine's "Map of High Containment and Other Facilities of the US Biodefense Program," under "Biodefense" at www.sunshine-project.org.

If you live near nuclear or biological weapons facilities, chances are good that groups in your community are already busy tracking their actions. You might want to join in the fight to keep your community safe from the dangers of homegrown WMD.

3. Conduct a citizen's inspection

In late 2002, Jackie Cabasso, Inga Olson, James Long and a team of inspectors went on a mission to locate production facilities for WMD. The inspectors had heard of a lab focused on the secretive research, development, testing and production of nuclear weapons, and even worse, there were strong indications the lab was pursuing research into biological weapons too.[81]

After arriving at the lethal-weapons laboratory, the inspectors cited United Nations Security Council Resolution 1441, and asked to gain:
- "immediate, unimpeded, unconditional, and unrestricted access to any and all, including underground, areas, facilities, buildings, equipment, records, and means of transport," they wanted to inspect, as well as
- "private access to all officials and other persons" they wanted to interview "in the mode or location of" their choice

Unfortunately, all the inspectors got was a PR rep and an invitation to leave the premises; they were at the Lawrence Livermore National Laboratory in California, part of the administration's extensive program for the research, development and production of homegrown WMD.

But the 2002 "inspection" of Lawrence Livermore National Laboratory in California was widely covered in the media and raised critical awareness worldwide. As Inga Olson, Board Member of Tri-Valley CAREs (Citizens Against a Radioactive Environment) Livermore, CA, observed, "It was uncanny that at the same time weapons inspectors were returning to Iraq, we were at the gates of Livermore's nuclear weapons lab waiting to be allowed to inspect the facilities for WMD. The hypocrisy of that moment on Veterans Day, 2002 hit a nerve causing news media across the country and around the world to write about our demonstration."

If your group would like to conduct its own "inspection" of a WMD facility, check out the *Citizen Weapons Inspection Teams* site (www.cwit.org) for materials, pointers and a 5-page Citizen Inspection Team Event Checklist, covering everything from budgeting resources to issuing a declaration (For example, the CWIT checklist recommends: "Uncover your official sign, which is big enough for TV cameras, that declares: 'Warning: This facility contains weapons of mass destruction.'")

The Belgian group For Mother Earth has also put together a terrific, 42-page information package called the *Citizens' Weapons Inspections Handbook,*[82] which includes legal advice, tips on handling the media, an Inspection Report template and many other fundamentals.

4. Learn more about depleted uranium

The continued military use of depleted uranium (DU) is one of the biggest scandals of our time, yet mainstream media has ignored it. If you'd like to inform yourself about DU, and other radioactive weaponry, head over to the Traprock Peace Center site (www.traprockpeace.org). Its Depleted Uranium Resources page has a cornucopia of articles, audio and action tips. For example, you can:
- read texts of pending DU legislation in various states
- learn about the experiences of troops and civilians exposed to DU
- listen to excerpts from the World Uranium Weapons Conference

Also check out Better World Links, which provides extensive DU coverage (www.betterworldlinks.org) in its Military section. Another site worth visiting is the UK's Campaign against Depleted Uranium (www.cadu.org.uk); its Resources page is filled with books, posters, information action packs and a whole lot more. Here's an excerpt from the CADU links page:
- The International Coalition to Ban Uranium Weapons
  (www.bandepleteduranium.org)
- International Depleted Uranium Study Team
  (www.idust.net)
- Low Level Radiation Campaign
  (www.llrc.org)
- Uranium Medical Research Centre
  (www.umrc.net)
- World Information Service on Energy
  (www.antenna.nl/wise/uranium/#DU)

5. Find out what weapons your local law enforcement agencies use

It's understood that law enforcement officers need to be able to protect themselves, and if they can do so without bullets, so much the better. But what checks and balances are in place in your state to protect citizens from so-called non-lethal weapons?

For example, if Tasers are part of your local police force's arsenal you might want to ask some questions: What training do officers receive regarding how to use Tasers? In what situations is use authorized? Is it standard operating procedure to involve a medical responder to check on those who have received the Taser's strong electric jolt? Similar questions will need to be asked about the crowd-control version of the Taser, as soon as it is released.

Face it: taxpayers buy the weapons law enforcement agents use, and so have the right to find out what they are, how they're used and the relative risks.

6. Get the lowdown on nukes

How much do you really know about nuclear weapons? If you'd like to learn more, head to your local library, your local disarmament group or your computer; for starters, the International Physicians for the Prevention of Nuclear War (www.ippnw.org) has a terrific web site with features ranging from study materials to an interactive global nuclear-weapons map. The site even has a quiz that lets you test your own nuclear knowledge, with questions such as:

<u>1</u>. A "thermonuclear bomb" is the same as
a) a hydrogen bomb
b) an atom bomb
c) a fission bomb

<u>2</u>. What are long-range nuclear weapons called (reaching more than 5,500 km)?
a) tactical nuclear weapons
b) regional nuclear weapons
c) strategic nuclear weapons

Chances are good that once you discover more about the dangers of nuclear weapons you'll be inspired to push for disarmament, so the site also offers great ideas for getting involved. (Just in case you're curious, the answers are: 1. a, and 2. c)

Another online resource is GREENPEACE International's "Abolish nuclear weapons" campaign. There you'll find up-to-date information plus various ideas for anti-nuke activism.[83] Also head over to the True Majority site and check out its short video clip on nuclear stockpiles, featuring none other than Ben from Ben & Jerry's Ice Cream (www.truemajority.org/bensbbs/). Another must-see site is Nuclear Files (www.nuclearfiles.org), which offers a comprehensive history of nuclear weapons, extensive resources for educators and a free eNewsletter on global security issues.

No discussion of anti-nuclear activism would be complete without mentioning Dr. Helen Caldicott, who for 35 years, has been at the forefront of educating the public about nuclear weapons and environmental destruction. Caldicott's site archives her many articles, speeches and TV appearances, and is definitely worth a visit (www.helencaldicott.com).

For regular updates on nuclear issues, sign up for the Nuclear Age Peace Foundation's Sunflower e-newsletter and join its "Turn the Tide Campaign" action-alert network (www.wagingpeace.org).

7. Explore arms control options

CTBT? ABM? NPT? If you're not sure what to make of contemporary arms control agreements, support is available on the net. Check out The Federation of American Scientists' (www.fas.org) easy-to-use compilation of resources. You can see the projected impact a nuclear detonation would have on certain cities, search a database of US and global arms sales, and take action on promoting arms control agreements. Check out the "Take Action Now" section and sign up to receive fas.org alerts.

Another place to explore disarmament issues is the *Arms Control Association* (www.armscontrol.org), which offers fact sheets, interviews, and easily accessible information organized by country and subject area. Also check out the Acronym Institute (www.acronym.org.uk).

For some humor, head over to Control Arms and watch its spoof of a TV shopping channel selling AK-47s (www.controlarms.org/teleshop). The short video "highlights the ease with which weapons can be bought and sold due to the almost total lack of global controls on the arms trade." A must see.

8. Learn more about biological and chemical weapons

Domestically-produced anthrax was used in stateside attacks. The US military has deployed white phosphorous abroad. Billions upon billions taxpayer dollars have been diverted to expanding the US biological weapons program, often with inadequate oversight.

If any of the above makes you furious, positive action is just a mouse-click away. Visit Project Sunshine, an international non-governmental organization working on biological weapons issues, with "an intense commitment to avert the dangers of new weapons stemming from advances in biotechnology." Sign up for its mailing list (www.sunshine-project.org/).

For comprehensive yet understandable descriptions of everything from the chemical warfare agent sarin to the avian influenza virus, check out the Federation of American Scientists' Biological and Chemical Weapons section (www.fas.org). For example, did you know:

- An insecticide containing hydrogen cyanide was used in the Holocaust by the Germans.
- In 2003, the top thirteen US manufacturers of hydrogen cyanide produced over 2 billion pounds of it for use in various industries.
- In the US, prisoners were executed in gas chambers from 1924 to 1999 using cyanide.
- The toxin ricin, which can be used as a bioweapon agent, actually derives from castor beans, one million tons of which are processed each year to make castor oil.
- When anthrax was accidentally released from a lab in the Soviet Union in 1979, over 60 people died.

At the Federation of American Scientists' site, you can also learn more about legislation and treaties related to biological/chemical weapons, as well as research "in the news."

9. Keep the skies friendly

To learn more about the militarization of space, head over to the Center for Defense Information (www.cdi.org) and check out its section on Space Security. There are fact sheets, a links page, and comprehensive analyses on current hot topics. While you're out it, check out the latest version of CDI's *The Defense Monitor* magazine, available for free online. The September-October 2007 issue, for example, features juicy topics including, "The Afghan War: Which Side is DOD On?"

For background on missile defense and the Anti-Ballistic Missile (ABM) Treaty, visit GREENPEACE's Stop Star Wars site (www.stopstarwars.org). Check out its photo/video gallery, documents and links.

Finally, if you're looking for up-to-the-minute online news regarding space militarization, visit ABM Daily (www.spacewar.com/abmdaily.html) and Space War (www.spacewar.com). Both sites are business and military oriented.

10. Encourage your legislators to work against WMD

Are you a US citizen and unhappy about the amount of your taxpayer dollars being poured into destructive technologies? Contact your representatives and complain. If you aren't sure who your representatives are or how to contact them, you can find more information here: www.house.gov.

Also contact groups focused specifically on encouraging legislators to push for the elimination of weapons of mass destruction. The Council for a Livable World (www.clw.org), for example, provides financial and other support to arms-control-friendly congressional candidates. Visit the CLW Candidates Guide page, and also check out its Advocacy section to learn more about pending WMD legislation and how you can get involved.

The Physicians for Social Responsibility site (www.psr.org) additionally has an action page on Congressional legislation where you can learn more about critical bills, add your name to petition letters and much more. Sign up to receive its regular updates and urgent action alerts.

Also encourage your local leaders to join the Mayors for Peace drive to eliminate nuclear weapons by the year 2020 (www.mayorsforpeace.org). Over 1,300 cities have already joined the campaign "to work internationally to raise consciousness regarding nuclear weapons abolition."

The bottom line: Billions spent on homegrown WMD signifies a foreign policy completely out of balance. Ask yourself – and your representatives - why the US is pouring fortunes into weapons of mass annihilation when the focus should be on mutual survival.

Women's Issues

"The truth will set you free. But first, it will piss you off."
– Gloria Steinem, feminist leader and author

While Bush claims that "W stands for Woman," he tends to alienate female voters. Official tallies showed a 7-point gender gap in the November 2004 election results, with 48% of women choosing Bush, compared to 55% of men. Even more glaring, a full 75% of women of color chose Kerry over Bush.[1]

As a Republican strategist put it, "Women are sick of Bush and all the macho strutting; it's gotten pretty old."[2]

The rollbacks in women's right under the Bush administration may have seemed random at first, but collectively represent nothing less than a targeted assault – and one that must be stopped.

Back to the Kitchen, Betty

"Rail as they will about 'discrimination,' women are simply not endowed by nature with the same measures of single-minded ambition and the will to succeed in the fiercely competitive world of Western capitalism." – Pat Robertson, televangelist [3]

So long, Capitol Hill

Many of the governmental offices serving women have either been terminated or sabotaged under Bush. It started back in 2001 when he took office, and here are only two examples:

Closed the White House Women's Office
Established in 1995, the White House Office for Women's Initiatives and Outreach monitored policy initiatives, helped coordinate federal programs and served as a liaison for outside groups. One of Bush's first acts as president was to shut it down.

According to Linda Meric, spokeswoman for the Colorado chapter of the 9to5 National Association of Working Women, "It was a small office, but a very important one. It provided direct and automatic access for women's organizations to the White House ... Closing the White House women's office is just another signal that the president's pledge to be the president of all the people doesn't really include women."[4]

When asked why the women's office had been closed, a White House spokesperson said: "As far as President Bush is concerned, women's issues are very high on his priority list." High on the list of issues to get funding cuts, apparently.

Tried to axe the Department of Labor Women's Bureau regional offices

Buoyed by its success in killing off the White House women's office, in late 2001 the Bush administration proposed shutting down the ten regional offices of the Department of Labor Women's Bureau. The offices have, for example, helped women learn about their legal rights in the workplace, promoted child care and other family-friendly policies, and held conferences on domestic and workplace violence. Only after public pressure did the administration nix its plan to shut the regional offices.

Ominously, the Bush administration proposed reducing funding to the Women's Bureau itself in FY2005, and the bureau was slated to receive a crappy $9.8 million for FY 2006 – which is *less than 10% of the amount the US government was spending **per day*** on the occupations of Iraq and Afghanistan. The administration's FY 2008 budget once again slices the Women's Bureau's budget, in total by 16% compared with FY 02 funding levels.

The Bush administration has not only shut down offices for women; it's also consistently made sexist appointments to crucial governmental committees dealing with women's rights. Here's a sampler:

Food and Drug Administration's Reproductive Health Drugs Advisory Committee

Would you go to a gynecologist who:
- has refused to prescribe contraceptives to unmarried women
- believes the Bible is an antidote for premenstrual syndrome
- recommends Scripture readings to alleviate headaches[5]

If so, then you're in luck because that gynecologist, Dr. David Hager, makes house calls – in fact, for three years he made decisions for every household in America, thanks to Bush.

Appointed in 2002, Hager was one of three religious conservatives Bush put on the Food and Drug Administration's (FDA) Advisory Committee for

Reproductive Health Drugs, and only public outcry prevented him from becoming its chairperson.

In 2004, a memo which Hager wrote helped persuade the Food and Drug Administration) to overrule its advisory panel and prevent the emergency contraceptive "Plan B" from being made more easily available. Critics assailed the FDA's decision as ignoring scientific evidence, but in Hager's assessment: "Once again, what Satan meant for evil, God turned into good."[6]

A downright criminal side of Hager emerged when his former wife went public with the fact that he had been emotionally, physically and sexually abusive during their 32-year marriage, forcibly sodomizing her on a regular basis. As Hager's ex-wife told *The Nation* magazine in May 2005, "it was the painful, invasive, totally nonconsensual nature of the [anal] sex that was so horrible."[7]

Would you want that guy as your gynecologist? Do you think he's suitable to be a federal adviser on women's health issues?

Hager left the FDA committee soon after *The Nation* article was published. But you can assume that while US tax dollars were paying his salary, he wasn't exactly working towards a woman's right to reproductive choice.

National Advisory Committee on Violence Against Women
In addition to under-funding domestic violence programs, the Bush administration has planted saboteurs in the committee charged with providing advice about the Violence Against Women Act (VAWA) to both the Department of Health & Human Services and the Department of Justice. As a result, representatives of the far-right Independent Women's Forum, which has claimed VAWA "urges vulnerable women to mistrust all men" and is "apt to hurt, rather than help, women involved in dangerous relationships,"[8] were empowered to make life and death decisions for battered women.

Defense Advisory Committee on Women in the Services
Right when record numbers of women are in harm's way defending their country in the armed forces, the Department of Defense (DoD) undermined the Committee on Women in the Services by naming an appointee who opposes increasing opportunities for women in the military, and has said the Army is "a vast day-care center, full of unmarried teen-age mothers using it as a welfare home."[9] No

wonder the committee veered away from issues of equity and access for military women.

The DoD also tried to sabotage an independent commission investigating sexual assault at the Air Force Academy by appointing members hostile to women's rights.[10]

While the office closures and iffy appointees mentioned above make the blood boil, rest assured they're just the tip of the iceberg.

Erasing your right to know

Citizens in a democracy, should be able to trust that:
- the government provides accurate and trustworthy data
- religious and political ideology don't masquerade as scientific fact
- crucial information is openly available

Unfortunately, American women lost that trust when Bush became president. In addition to shutting women's governmental offices, the Bush White House has downright hidden or distorted information affecting women in critical areas ranging from pay equity, to breast cancer to HIV.

An excellent summary of these changes can be found in "Missing: Information About Women's Lives," an April 2004 report from the National Council for Research on Women (NCRW).[11] Among other rollbacks, the report notes:

National Cancer Institute
- Changed its web site to suggest a link between abortion and breast cancer, even though studies had found none existed, and only changed the site back when Congress insisted.

Centers for Disease Control
- Revised its fact sheet in late 2002 to suggest that evidence condoms prevent sexually transmitted diseases is "inconclusive."
- Seemed to apply "a political rather than educational test" to HIV health education materials.
- Moved away from science-based performance measures to "obscure the lack of efficacy of abstinence-only programs."

Department of Labor
- Has eliminated important publications on the rights of women workers, such as *Don't Work in the Dark – Know Your Rights*, and *Fact Sheets* on women workers. Has not re-released the important *Handbook on Women Workers*.

National Healthcare Disparities Report
- Downplayed "major inequities in diagnosing and treating such conditions as hypertension, diabetes and HIV – all of enormous importance to the health of women of color." Only corrected the report after public pressure.

Health and Human Services
- Distorted information on its web site to make abstinence-only programs seem more effective than evidence indicates.

According to Linda Basch, president the National Council for Research on Women, "When these instances are taken individually, perhaps we don't see the cumulative pattern of what's happening. But when we gather the information together and see the distorted or disappearing information about the economic opportunities, the situation of violence against women, health and particularly reproductive health, it is a very distressing pattern."[12]

Stacking the courts

US voters elect candidates for certain political offices, but most of the officials making crucial decisions about our daily lives aren't selected by the people at all – they're appointed. (OK, OK, Bush was also appointed, not elected, but that's another story...) Members of the Supreme Court, federal courts and governmental advisory committees come to us at the whim of whatever administration happens to be in charge, and voters trust the government in power to make fair and equitable choices.

When running for president, Bush was asked if his personal opposition to abortion rights would be reflected in his administration's judicial appointments. He replied: "Voters should assume that I have no litmus test on that issue or any other issue. The voters will know I'll put competent judges on the bench, people who will strictly interpret the Constitution and will not use the bench to write social policy."[13]

So how well has Bush fared in selecting unbiased appointees for the courts and other important positions? Look at the administration's record and judge for yourself: [14]

2000
- Installed anti-choice senator John Ashcroft as US attorney general, and anti-choice governor Tommy Thompson as Secretary of Health and Human Services

2001

- Nominated six anti-choice judges to Circuit Courts, including Professor Michael McConnell, whom Planned Parenthood describes as a "hardline opponent of Roe v. Wade who believes the US Constitution does not protect women's right to choose."[15]
- Named "abstinence-only" proponent Patricia Funderburk Ware to head the Presidential Advisory Council on HIV/AIDS
- Wanted to have John Klink, a Vatican spokesperson opposed to birth control and condom use, lead the US Global Population Program

2002

- Appointed anti-choice doctors opposed to contraception to the Reproductive Health Drugs Advisory Committee of the Food and Drug Administration
- Named "abstinence-only" supporters to the Centers for Disease Control Advisory Committee on HIV and STD (sexually transmitted disease) Prevention, as well as to lead America's family planning program
- Chose the former president of the anti-choice Harvard Law School's Society for Law, Life, and Religion to be special assistant to the US State Department Bureau of Population, Refugees and Migration
- Supported anti-choice Sen. Bill Frist (R-TN) in becoming Senate Majority Leader

2003

- Re-nominated three anti-choice judges to the Circuit Courts of Appeals; *the trio had already been rejected by the Senate.* Couldn't the administration have come up with anybody better?

2004

- Appointed two anti-choice judges to the Circuit Courts of Appeals during a congressional recess, thereby bypassing the Senate confirmation process. One of the appointees had described Roe vs. Wade (the historic 1973 decision which guaranteed abortion rights) as "an abomination."
- Named an anti-choicer to a U.S. District Court in Arkansas

2005

- Re-nominated seven anti-choice judges to federal courts; *the seven had already been rejected by the Senate.* See a pattern here? Instead of coming up with more appropriate choices, the administration just tries to recycle throwbacks.
- Put forward far-right extremist John G. Roberts to head the US Supreme Court. In Robert's illustrious career, he has fought against minority voting rights, argued against women's educational rights, and tried to limit the rights of women prisoners. A legal brief Roberts contributed to said that

Roe vs. Wade was "wrongly decided and should be overruled."[16] Roberts became Chief Justice in September 2005.
- Nominated lawyer Harriet Miers to the Supreme Court, but she was forced to withdraw when it became apparent that her main qualification for the job was slavish devotion to Bush, whom she called "cool" and "deserving of great respect." The administration's next Supreme Court nominee was far-right Third Circuit Appeal Court Judge Samuel Alito, who once wrote that "the Constitution does not protect a right to an abortion," and "I am particularly proud of my contributions in recent cases in which the government has argued in the Supreme Court ... that the Constitution does not protect a right to an abortion."[17] Alito was confirmed in late January 2006.

The agony continues. Most recently, Bush appointed birth-control opponent Susan Orr to head family planning programs at the Department of Health and Human Services. Author of a 2000 paper entitled "Real Women Stay Married," (excerpt: "To expect another human to be responsible for our personal fulfillment is too much. Only God has the capacity to complete our lives."[18]), since October 2007, anti-contraception Orr has been in charge of providing grants for low-income people to receive contraception services.[19]

This is the Bush administration's idea of open-minded appointees who will "not use the bench to write social policy."

Keep in mind that most of these appointees won't leave office when the Bush administration eventually does – they will remain in their posts working against women's rights for years to come.

Pennies on the dollar

Women still earn much less than men doing comparable work. In April 2007, the National Organization of Women (NOW) reported, "Full-time women workers are paid an average of 77 cents for every dollar men are paid. Women of color are short-changed even more, with African-American women paid only 71 cents and Latinas just 58 cents on men's dollar."[20]

Far from reflecting isolated cases, the gender wage gap spreads across age groups and educational backgrounds in the US. Female high school grads pull in $700,000 less than their male counterparts for 35 years of work, while female college grads lose $1.2 million relative to their male colleagues.

And the Supreme Court isn't helping. In May 2007, it set a shameful precedent in ruling against a woman who had experienced long-term wage discrimination. This is how NOW describes the case:[21]

"Lilly Ledbetter had worked at Goodyear for 19 years when she discovered she was being paid significantly less than every single one of her male counterparts. A jury agreed that she had been paid unfairly, and awarded her $223,776 in back pay, and over $3 million in punitive damages, but a judge cut that to only $300,000 because of a 1991 law that limited a company's liability for damages — even when found guilty of willful wage discrimination.

"In an 'off with her head' moment, the U.S. Supreme Court took away every penny of the back pay and damages awarded to Lilly Ledbetter, saying incredibly that the 180 day filing limit had begun way back when the very first paycheck showed lesser pay. Eighteen years of continuing wage discrimination against Ledbetter by Goodyear held no sway with the Roberts court."

In late July 2007, the US House of Representatives passed (225 to 199) legislation aimed at dismantling part of the Supreme Court's Ledbetter decision, by easing its newly draconian requirements on the 180-day filing requirement. Predictably, Bush vowed to veto.

Goodbye Birth Control

"I would like to outlaw contraception ... contraception is disgusting - people using each other for pleasure." - Joseph Scheidler, Pro-Life Action League [22]

"I don't think Christians should use birth control. You consummate your marriage as often as you like - and if you have babies, you have babies." - Randall Terry, Operation Rescue [23]

"We've got an issue in America ... too many good docs are getting out of business. Too many OB/GYNs aren't able to practice their love with women all across this country." - George W. Bush [24]

Keeping contraception out of reach

The overwhelming majority of US women rely on contraception for their family planning. In fact, a December 2004 study by the Centers for Disease Control reported, "Contraceptive use in the United States is virtually universal among women of reproductive age: 98 percent of all women who had ever had intercourse had used at least one contraceptive method."[25] **98 percent.**

Yet many US lawmakers are trying to cut back or eliminate this crucial component of reproductive rights.

Insurance companies aren't helping either. Birth control can be pricey, and roughly half of private indemnity insurance plans don't even cover prescription methods (such as birth control pills, IUDs, implants, injectables and diaphragms). That sorry fact contributes not only to unwanted pregnancies, but also to women of reproductive age shelling out 68% more for their health care than do men.[26]

So it's no wonder that almost 80% of privately insured adults are in favor of contraceptives being covered, even if it means paying a little more per month.[27]

Senate Minority Leader Harry Reid (D-NV) and Sen. Hillary Rodham Clinton (D-NY) added a measure to the FY 2006 congressional budget resolution which would have mandated health-insurance plans covering prescription drugs to equally cover prescription contraception. The measure also would have expanded family planning programs, supported teen pregnancy-prevention programs, and funded a public-awareness campaign about emergency contraception.

Great goals. Who could disagree? Knuckle-draggers in the Senate, that's who. They rejected the measure by a vote of 47 to 53. Why? As the chair of the Senate Budget Committee, Sen. Judd Gregg (R-NH), explained, the amendment would have reduced funding to abstinence-only education programs.

In other words, as the far-right tries to outlaw abortion, they're simultaneously working against effective solutions to reducing unwanted pregnancies. This nonsense has got to stop.

Another front in the war on birth control is your very own pharmacy counter. A small but vocal number of pharmacists is citing religious grounds for refusing to fill women's birth control pill prescriptions - and they're being supported by reactionary politicians.

This development is critical, given the overwhelming popularity of the birth control pill in the United States. Decrease access to the pill and you immediately increase the risk of unwanted pregnancies. No wonder a 2004 CBS/New York Times poll found that a full 80% of Americans think pharmacists shouldn't refuse to fill contraceptive prescriptions.[28]

But tell that to the US House of Representatives. In July 2005, a House committee held a hearing on pharmacists withholding contraception, and as the NARAL Pro-Choice America action league reports:[29]

> "Anti-choice Rep. Steve King (R-IA) told a witness, who had been denied birth control and emergency contraception by her pharmacist, that she had no 'right' to her prescriptions - she only believed she did. Anti-choice Rep. Marilyn Musgrave (R-CO) told a witness whose prescription had also been rejected by a hostile pharmacist, that her 'minor inconvenience' — that is, risking an unintended pregnancy — was nothing compared to the 'conscience' of a pharmacist."

Roughly twenty states currently protect pharmacists who refuse to fill birth control prescriptions, and the issue is shaping up to be a far-right rallying point. How ironic that the lawmakers battling birth control don't seem to have any similar problems with pharmacists handing out Viagra.

Another backdoor attack on birth control was the Bush administration's attempt to end contraceptive coverage for civil servants under the Federal Employees Health Benefit Program.

Taken as a whole, this assault on contraception is mind-boggling for anyone interested in reducing unwanted pregnancies. Women shouldn't have to deal with hassles, delays or guilt-trip lectures from extremist pharmacists every time they buy birth control. The idiocy in attacking such a fundamental platform of reproductive rights is self-evident.

There goes Plan B

We all know that condoms sometimes break, and many of us have had the horrible realization that the accident happened right during our fertile days.

So thank goodness for emergency contraception (EC), sometimes called the *morning-after pill*. EC is a high but safe dose of birth control hormones that can significantly reduce the risk of pregnancy - but only if taken within 72 hours of intercourse, and the sooner the better.

Let's say that the condom breaks late on a Friday night. Ideally, a woman would head to the pharmacy early Saturday morning to get her EC started right away, but there's a catch — if EC isn't available over the counter, a woman would have to wait for a doctor's office hours the week after to even get a prescription. Too late.

The Bush administration's Food and Drug Administration (FDA) has done all it can to keep EC out of women's hands; as a result, in 2004, Representative

Louise M. Slaughter (D–NY), a microbiologist with a master's degree in Public Health, called for the resignations of the FDA's then-Acting Commissioner Lester Crawford, and Dr. Steve Galson, acting director of the Center for Drug Evaluation and Research, on the basis of their foot-dragging over EC.[30]

But far from firing either man, Bush nominated Crawford to take over the FDA permanently.

Democratic senators initially blocked Crawford's confirmation, but gave approval in June 2005 after he promised to make a decision on EC by September 1, 2005. However, upon being confirmed, Crawford yet again delayed the decision, despite the FDA Reproductive Health Drugs Advisory Committee's having voted 23 to 4 in favor of making EC available over-the-counter.

Dr. Susan Wood, the well-respected head of the FDA Women's Health Office, resigned in protest - and that's when things got really bizarre. Weeks after Wood stepped down, the FDA Women's Health Office sent out a mass email announcing that she would be replaced by Dr. Norris Alderson, who was duly listed on the FDA site as: "Acting Director, Office of Women's Health, Associate Commissioner for Science."[31]

One small problem. Alderson is a veterinarian.

That's right. The administration appointed an animal doctor to be in charge of women's health. Speaks volumes, doesn't it?

After the predictable outcry, the FDA took a page from Orwell's playbook and tried to pretend that Alderson had never been appointed in the first place. Recipients of the initial mass emailing, of course, knew otherwise.

To make things even weirder, Crawford himself suddenly resigned as head of the FDA in September 2005 (just months after having been confirmed), amid allegations of not having properly disclosed his financial holdings to the Senate.

In August 2006, the FDA finally approved making the EC "Plan B" available over-the counter to consumers 18 years and older (those under 18 still need a prescription). An important step in the right direction.

Title X at risk

If you live in the US, chances are good that at some point in your life you've had medical services paid for by Title X of the Public Health Services Act, which among other areas covers:

- Pap tests
- Breast and pelvic exams
- STD/HIV testing
- Family planning
- Blood pressure tests

Chances are also good that you haven't heard about the Bush administration's vengeance against Title X – the media hasn't covered it.

So here are the facts: The first front in the war on Title X is funding. The administration's Title X budget for FY 2004 recommended an $8 million *decrease* from FY 2003. Adding insult to injury, Bush's FY 2005 budget proposed level funding, which was less than half the money necessary to keep pace with inflation. The FY 2006 budget also proposed level funding, and the administration's FY 2007 budget actually cut overall funding to the program.[32]

It's worth mentioning that the administration's FY2004 funding appropriations bill also allowed the Health and Human Services department to get the names of any health care providers offering abortion services with *non-Title X* dollars; many observers saw this as an attempted first step in removing governmental funding from facilities which provide abortion services.

The second assault on Title X comes from our abstinence-is-next-to-Godliness friends who have articulated "new priorities" for Title X, including "extramarital abstinence education and counseling" as well as partnering with faith-based organizations.[33]

But the nation's family planning program is far too important for any such ill-advised tinkering. Title X serves millions of people through thousands of clinics across the country, and economic downturn and welfare reform have put an increasingly critical demand on the already cash-starved program. Since more Americans are finding themselves without access to any public or private health insurance every day, Title X clinics are often the only hope for lower-income women looking for gynecological care, for example.

With that in mind, consider the fact that the entire Title X program received an amazingly crappy $283.1 million for FY 2006. Meanwhile, the administration proposed **increasing** the budget for its abstinence-only program follies by over **25%**, to $138 million.[34] Same sorry story for the FY

2007 proposed budget: cuts for Title X and big funding increases for abstinence-only education.

Exporting our insanity

As if limiting access to birth control domestically weren't enough, the Bush administration is also hell-bent on reducing family planning availability abroad. Here are some examples:

Brought back the global "gag" rule

One of Bush's first acts as president was to bring back Reagan's much-maligned "gag" rule, which prohibits healthcare providers abroad from receiving US funding even if they spend *their own money* in counseling women about abortion or in providing abortion services.

For developing countries struggling with HIV/AIDS, the gag rule's return has meant a double whammy: USAID-supplied contraceptives and condoms are no longer available, and funding cuts have led to the closure of healthcare clinics critical to local populations.

In September 2007, Congress repealed the gag rule by passing an appropriations bill which also freed up HIV prevention programs from abstinence-only constraints. Bush threatened a veto.

Defunded the United Nations Population Fund (UNFPA)

UNFPA works in over 140 countries helping people:[35]

- plan their families and avoid unwanted pregnancies
- undergo pregnancy and childbirth safely
- avoid sexually transmitted infections - including HIV/AIDS
- combat violence against women.

Since 2002, the Bush administration has withheld funding from UNFPA, ostensibly on the grounds that it was involved in coercive reproductive health practices in China – *a charge that the State Department's own investigation found false.*[36]

Obstructed a UN General Assembly Special Session on Children

At the May 2002 United Nations Special Session on Children, the US delegation tried to restrict the definition of sexual education to "abstinence-only until marriage," despite the fact that young people in HIV/AIDS ravaged nations could literally save their lives by learning about contraception such as condoms. The US delegation also fought against efforts to help young female victims of war crimes (i.e. usually rape) on the grounds that they might receive information about emergency contraception or abortion.

Sabotaged the Commission on Population and Development
In 1994, the US joined other countries in backing the so-called Cairo Consensus, "a blueprint for nations, working together, to help secure for every woman access to basic health care, a clean environment, education, and the right to make the private personal choices about childbearing that are best for her family and to have the information and means to do so."[37]

Soon after assuming office, Bush withdrew support for the agreement and even included a former Vatican negotiator in the US delegation to a related conference.

The list of Bush administration moves to limit family planning programs abroad also includes:
- opposing an endorsement of condom use to prevent AIDS at an international population conference in Bangkok
- fighting against including contraception in a population-development conference declaration in Chile

The upshot? Our politicians look like narrow-minded fools on the international stage; even worse, millions of women and children internationally are paying the ultimate price for the Bush administration's short-sightedness.

Outlawing Abortion

> "On September 11, we saw clearly that evil exists in this world, and that it does not value life ... Now we are engaged in a fight against evil and tyranny to preserve and protect life." – George W. Bush, linking abortion rights with terrorism, as he declared the 29th anniversary of Roe v. Wade to be "National Sanctity of Human Life Day."[38]

As governor of Texas, Bush signed a full 18 anti-abortion provisions into effect, and was recognized as leading the most anti-choice legislature in the country.[39]

Unfortunately, as president of the United States, Bush has had even more leeway to eliminate reproductive freedom. His administration's attack against abortion has been multifaceted, including:

- withdrawing both domestic and international funding for abortion services
- falsifying information about abortion on governmental web sites
- appointing anti-abortion extremists to key governmental positions

Bush has also been on a rampage to overturn Roe vs. Wade in the courts. Rather than taking on Roe directly, however, the administration has stealthily sliced away its legal foundation – and often with bizarre results.

Weakening Roe, one ruling at a time

You might be surprised to learn that in 2002, the administration issued regulations making fetuses eligible for prenatal care from the Children's Health Insurance Program, but not pregnant women. Here's a sampler of other bizarre steps on the far-right's legislative path to overturning Roe:

Imposed a late-term abortion-procedure ban

In early November 2003, Bush signed into law the so-called Partial Birth Abortion Ban Act of 2003, which put an end to an already rare procedure regarding late-term abortions. In a stunning photo op, Bush sat at an ornate desk signing the law into effect as nine male lawmakers happily looked on: not one woman in the bunch.[40]

Realizing the ban could mean the beginning of the end for reproductive choice, the Planned Parenthood Federation of America (PPFA) filed a lawsuit against former Attorney General John Ashcroft, who later tried to seize hundreds of confidential medical records of Planned Parenthood clients in retaliation.

In March 2004, Federal District Court Judge Phyllis J. Hamilton denied Ashcroft access to the medical records, and in June she ruled that the federal late-term abortion-procedure ban was in fact unconstitutional and therefore unenforceable. Other judges later also found the ban unconstitutional, and the Supreme Court agreed to take up the issue.

Roughly seven years earlier, the Supreme Court had ruled against a similar case, but this time, Bush's two new anti-choice Court appointees (John Robert and Samuel Alito) tipped the balance. In April 2007, the Supreme Court ruled 5-4 in support of the abortion-procedure ban. Dissenting Justice Ruth Bader Ginsburg called the decision "alarming," adding that it "tolerates, indeed applauds, federal intervention to ban nationwide a procedure found necessary and proper in certain cases by the American College of Obstetricians and Gynecologists."[41]

Declared that fertilized eggs are people

In April 2004, Bush signed the so-called "Unborn Victims of Violence Act," which granted a zygote the same legal rights as a person. Ostensibly to allow federal prosecutors more leeway in filing separate charges in case a pregnant woman and her fetus were killed, the ulterior motive was clear: another legal brick in the wall against abortion rights.

Snuck an anti-abortion provision into a crucial spending bill

In late November 2004, when lawmakers were wrapping up for the year, Republicans quietly tucked a dangerous provision into a must-pass omnibus spending bill - at the last minute and without any debate. The cynically named "Abortion Non-Discrimination Act" gives any doctor, clinic, hospital or insurer the option to refuse to perform or pay for abortions. Under the Act, which effectively legislates discrimination, providers can even refuse to tell women that they have the option for an abortion.

Reduced the options of teens in trouble

In April 2005, the House voted to make it a federal crime for an adult to help transport a minor across state lines to get an abortion without parental consent. The implications for young victims of family violence or incest are devastating, and it's worth noting that over 50 House Democrats voted for this stinker of a piece of legislation.

As Rep. Nita M. Lowey (D-NY) noted, "Thankfully, most young women involve their parents in the decision to seek an abortion. But under this legislation, those who feel they cannot turn to their parents when facing an unintended pregnancy will be forced to fend for themselves without any help from a responsible adult. Some will seek unsafe abortions close to home. Others will travel to unfamiliar places seeking abortions by themselves."[42]

And that's progress?

Denied military women their basic rights

Bear in mind that Roe vs. Wade is still the law of the land and that abortion is legal. Why then are our military women denied access to abortion services in US military hospitals, even if they pay for the procedure with their own funds? In May 2005, the House defeated an amendment that would have granted our female service members that basic right. In its infinite wisdom, Congress also denied funding for female service members who want to get an abortion after being impregnated due to rape or incest.

Given the large numbers of US military women serving today, as well as the clear risk of rape they face (including from their male colleagues) it is inexcusable to drive women away from US military hospitals and towards potentially less safe and sanitary medical facilities abroad.

Pro-choice terrorists

In early 2003, the *New York Times* ran an editorial entitled "The War against Women," which noted: "The lengthening string of anti-choice executive orders, regulations, legal briefs, legislative maneuvers and key appointments emanating from [Bush's] administration suggests that undermining the reproductive freedom essential to women's health, privacy and equality is a major preoccupation of his administration – second only, perhaps, to the war on terrorism."[43]

But the American public is fighting back. In April 2004, for example, over a million marchers in the nation's capitol sent a strong pro-choice message to the Bush administration. Yet in a *CNN Late Edition* interview that same day, former presidential adviser Karen Hughes had this to say:

"I think after September 11th the American people are valuing life more and realizing that we need policies to value the dignity and worth of every life. And President Bush has worked to say, let's be reasonable, let's work to value life, let's try to reduce the number of abortions, let's increase adoptions.

"The fundamental difference between us and the terror network we fight is that we value every life. It's the founding conviction of our country, that we're endowed by our creator with certain unalienable rights, the right to life and liberty and the pursuit of happiness.

"Unfortunately our enemies in the terror network, as we're seeing repeatedly in the headlines these days, don't value any life, not even the innocent and not even their own."

The verbal gymnastics taking Hughes from the topic of abortion rights to "our enemies in the terror network" stunned many.

Rep. Carolyn Maloney (D-NY) called for an official apology from Hughes and for Bush to "disassociate himself" from the remarks, but of course, neither ever happened.

The ultimate irony is that the administration's policies so obviously contribute to additional unwanted pregnancies in the first place. The soaring unemployment rates and plummeting incomes of many Americans these days have led potential parents to think twice before having a child; on top of that, the administration has made birth control harder to get and starved effective educational programs, choosing instead to lavish taxpayer dollars on dubious "abstinence-only" schemes.

Who has abortions?

• Fifty-four percent of women having abortions used a contraceptive method during the month they became pregnant.
• Fifty-two percent of U.S. women obtaining abortions are younger than 25
• Black women are almost four times as likely as white women to have an abortion, and Hispanic women are 2.5 times as likely.
• Forty-three percent of women obtaining abortions identify themselves as Protestant, and 27% as Catholic.
• Two-thirds of all abortions are among never-married women.
• Over 60% of abortions are among women who have had one or more children
• The abortion rate among women living below the federal poverty level ($9,570 for a single woman with no children) is more than four times that of women above 300% of the poverty level (44 vs. 10 abortions per 1,000 women).

Source: Alan Guttmacher Institute, "Facts in Brief: Induced Abortion in the United States" (2003)[44]

When one considers that the US already has one of the highest infant mortality rates in the industrialized world, thanks at least in part to relatively limited access to prenatal and postnatal care, the administration's claim to be "pro-life" looks even weaker.

The only sane approach is to fund and support tried-and-true methods of contraception and sex-education programs to avoid unwanted pregnancies, to keep abortion legal, and as a society, to make sure that the babies who are born receive proper medical care and a fair shot at a decent life.

Keeping Women in Danger

> *In the US:*
> - *1 out of every 6 women will be raped* [45]
> - *Half of the women who report rape are under 18 years old, and almost a quarter are under 12 years old* [46]
> - *Nearly 3 million children are reported abused each year, and a further 6 million cases are thought to go unreported* [47]
> - *Over three women are murdered by their intimate partners every day, and one third physically assaulted by a partner during their lifetimes.* [48]

For many women and children in the US, security is more about combating domestic violence and rape than about hunting down faceless terrorists abroad.

So, what has the Bush administration done to help? Cut funding to programs for battered women and rape victims, stacked an important committee with extremists in denial about domestic violence, and reduced housing options for victims of abuse. Gee, that should work.

Institutionalized denial

The nation's Violence Against Women Act (VAWA) was passed in 1994 and has been credited with helping institute a wide array of critical support for women and kids in danger; since VAWA passed, domestic violence incidents have been cut by half and incidents of rape have been reduced by 60%. [49]

The bill was reauthorized and expanded in 2000 to include more services for rural, disabled, immigrant, and older women. But significantly, while a full 313 members of the House and Senate cosponsored the bill in 2000, only 87 cosponsors did so when it went up for renewal in September 2005. In fact, a number of conservatives groups argued against federal money being spent on dealing with violence against women at all.

It doesn't help that the administration appointed two representatives of the far-right Independent Women's Forum (IWF) to the National Advisory Committee on Violence Against Women in 2002. IWF consistently downplays the issue of domestic violence and its web site has featured articles such as "Gun control hurts women," despite evidence that women living with a gun in the house run an over three-times greater risk of being murdered than women with no gun in the house. [50]

It would be great to say that rape, incest, spousal abuse and other forms of violence against women and children are a thing of the past in today's USA, but that's hardly the case. Despite some progress, women still are often not safe in their own homes and the law frequently works against them, for example, by favoring their abusers in child custody battles or by valuing the lives of women less than those of men (such as the 2005 Texas case in which a man was sentenced to only four months in prison for murdering his estranged wife but got a full 15 years for wounding her boyfriend).

Ironically, while Bush's FY2005 budget spent billions on beefing up the military and producing weapons of mass destruction, the budget also slashed funding for programs protecting women from harm. For example, the budget proposed reducing federal low-income housing assistance programs to help domestic violence victims find a safe place to live, and it also cut three million dollars from state grants which "improve stalking databases, encourage arrests, reduce violent crimes against women on campus, and enhance protections for older and disabled women from domestic violence and sexual assault."[51]

The administration's requested 2006 budget similarly slashed a full $19 million from Violence Against Women Act Prevention and Prosecution programs, leaving the entire VAWA area of responsibility (reducing violent crimes, providing legal assistance for victims and safe havens for women, conducting trainings on ending domestic abuse, and countless other crucial functions) with a year's funding of $363 million. Yes, $363 million for all of that.[52] Meanwhile, the Bush administration spent hundreds of times that amount in 2006 on the occupations of Iraq and Afghanistan alone. Some priorities.

As expected, the administration's FY 2007 budget made deep cuts in programs keeping women safe, such as the Community Oriented Policing Services (COPS) program, which helps put police on the streets. COPS was slated to be cut by 79% in 2007. Similarly, the Violence Against Women Act Prevention and Prosecution Programs received $39.5 million less than in FY2006, representing more than a 9% drop. Under the administration's proposed FY 2007 budget, a full 21 VAWA-authorized programs were cut, along with $35 million from domestic violence programs.

Amazingly, the administration's FY 2008 budget is even worse. In addition to the usual cuts in critical programs, Bush's new plan transfers control over anti-violence program funding to the executive branch. Specifically, the Department of Justice, rather than Congress, will be able to decide on domestic-violence program funding, conveniently allowing the administration to cut any programs it chooses - even those approved in the 2005 Violence Against Women Act reauthorization.

Adding salt to the wound, Bush also threatened to veto September 2007 legislation that expanded the definition of hate crimes to include actual or perceived gender, sexual orientation, gender identity, or disability.

The upshot? Under Bush, life has become more dangerous for American women, and help for victims has become less readily available. The administration has chosen to reduce support for VAWA when it should be expanding the program instead, by including more training for health care providers, better intervention for children at risk, and additional housing options for those fleeing domestic violence, among other measures. The administration's focus is elsewhere, leaving women at risk to fend for themselves.

Say One Thing, Fund Another

> *"President Bush's 2008 budget... continues on a troubling course. Under the President's budget, fewer low-income women and children would have access to health care, child care and early education, child support enforcement services, food assistance and other vital supports, and the education and training opportunities they need to get ahead."[63]* - National Women's Law Center, February 2007

Money talks. While Bush heaps praise on programs for women, children and impoverished families, he often turns around and slashes funding for those very same programs. Here's a sampler of programs the administration's FY 2006 budget **eliminated**:
- Women's Educational Equity Act
- Universal Newborn Hearing screening
- The Even Start Family Literacy Program
- Programs to assist victims of trafficking

And here are a few of the many programs Bush's FY 2007 proposed budget **eliminated**:
- The Community Services Block Grant - provides funding for services to low-income families as well as the elderly and disabled
- The Commodity Supplemental Food Program - gives food packages to over 400,000 low-income elderly people
- Safe and Drug Free Schools Grants
- Grants for preventive health services for underserved populations

In addition to those programs targeted for outright elimination, other critical areas affecting women and children were slated to receive drastic cuts in FY 2007. For example, Bush's budget slashed discretionary child care funding for low-income families, which translated to a loss of $1 billion over the following five years. As a result, over 400,000 *fewer* kids would be able to receive child care assistance in 2011 than did in 2005.

You get the picture.

Of course these funding cuts need to be seen in relation to Bush's tax cuts of 2001 and 2003, which overwhelmingly benefited the wealthy. According to the National Women's Law Center: "One-quarter of all households receive nothing from either the 2001 or 2003 tax cut. People with incomes below the poverty line – who are disproportionately single mothers, women of color, and elderly women living alone – are most likely to receive nothing from the tax cut. More than one-quarter (27%) of families headed by a single parent – the vast majority of whom are headed by a women – get nothing from the 2001 or 2003 tax cuts."[54]

Even worse, in order to fund tax cuts for the super-wealthy (not to mention the administration's military adventurism) Bush has starved funding from crucial programs for women and children, who get doubly hurt by increased state/local taxes and fees.

Schoolyard Scandals

> *"Women gauge their happiness and judge their success by their relationships. Men's happiness and success hinge on their accomplishments."* – excerpt from a federally-funded abstinence-only education program curriculum [55]

As if shrinking budgets for programs benefiting women and children coupled with attacks on reproductive rights weren't enough, women today also can have a hard time getting an even break in US schools.

The attack on Title IX

Title IX of the Educational Amendment aims to level the playing field for women and girls at school and in sports. The results speak for themselves: since Title IX was introduced in 1972, there has been an over 800% increase in female participation in high school sports and an over 400% increase in college sports.[56]

In spite of (or perhaps because of) this admirable outcome, the Bush administration has done all it can to weaken Title IX.

The first step came in 2002, with the Commission on Athletic Opportunity, a $700,000 boondoggle resulting in recommendations to cut back entitlements to female athletes. The verdict was unsurprising given that Title IX opponents were invited to testify before the Commission twice as often as were supporters.

According to the National Women's Law Center, if even two of the recommendations had gone through, it "could have resulted in annual losses of 50,000 athletic participation opportunities and $122 million in scholarships for women collegiate athletes, and 305,000 opportunities for female high school athletes."[57]

The Department of Education (DoE) backed down to public pressure and has not implemented the Commission's recommendations – yet.

However, in March 2005, the administration went ahead and took a backdoor approach to weakening Title IX when the DoE issued new policy guidelines making it much easier for schools to bypass the regulation. While multiple factors (such as interviews with students, coaches and faculty) had previously been used to determine the interest level in maintaining female sports teams, only one method is implemented now: surveys of female students. In other words, the onus is now on female students to **prove** that they deserve a varsity team of their own, that they are good enough athletes to sustain a team, and that there is enough potential for intercollegiate competition.[58] And somehow, all of that information is supposed to shine through in an email survey, which clearly could be written or interpreted in a biased manner.

Of course, male students in the same schools don't have to jump through similar hoops just to get a little support for their athletic activities.

But not all the news around Title IX is bad. In late-March 2005, the Supreme Court ruled in favor of Roderick Jackson, a high school girl's basketball coach who was fired when he tried to get equal funding and athletic opportunities for his team. The Court ruled that that Jackson had the right to claim retaliation under Title IX, and as the National Organization for Women noted: "The ruling is important because it protects coaches, teachers and administrators who are often more likely than female students to recognize that sex discrimination is occurring and then demand that women's and girls' rights under Title IX be upheld."[59]

So there's hope for an end to gender discrimination in US public schools, but as long as the Bush administration is in power you can assume Title IX will be in trouble. In October 2006, for example, the Department of Education weakened Title IX regulations on single-sex education in public schools, thereby sanctioning sex-segregated classrooms and school activities. Separate is seldom equal.

Some thoughts on the value of women ...

"The wife is to subordinate herself to her husband ... to place herself under the authority of the man." – Judge James Leon Holmes, nominated by the Bush administration to the U.S. District Court for the Eastern District of Arkansas[60]

"As much as when you see a blonde with great tits and a great ass, you say to yourself, Hey, she must be stupid or must have nothing else to offer, which maybe is the case many times." – Arnold Schwarzenegger, California governor[61]

"I saw this toilet bowl. How many times do you get away with this – to take a woman, grab her upside down, and bury her face in a toilet bowl? I wanted to have something floating in there." – Arnold Schwarzenegger, California governor[62]

"Women – and I don't mean to limit that to the biological sense – always become hysterical at the first sign of trouble. They have no capacity to solve problems, so instead they fret. But despite the fearful fifth columnists whiling away the war naysaying America's response, we will win this war. You just stay warm girls – the men are fixing the car." – Ann Coulter, columnist[63]

"Like communism, feminism has been a catastrophe for the people it was meant to help." – Phyllis Schafly, founder of the conservative group Eagle Forum[64]

"I know this is painful for the ladies to hear, but if you get married, you have accepted the headship of a man, your husband. Christ is the head of the household and the husband is the head of the wife, and that's the way it is, period." - Pat Robertson, religious broadcaster[65]

Academia's glass ceiling

In January 2005, Larry Summers, then-president of Harvard University, caused a stir by saying that women are under-represented in the higher levels of math and science because of "intrinsic aptitude, and particularly of the variability of aptitude" rather than "lesser factors involving socialization and continuing discrimination." In other words, forget about differing societal expectations or better opportunities for men; the real reason women don't become top mathematicians or scientists is that they just don't have what it takes.

For the record, Summers also used the "aptitude" theory to explain that "Catholics are substantially underrepresented in investment banking, which is an enormously high-paying profession in our society; that white men are very substantially underrepresented in the National Basketball Association; and that Jews are very substantially underrepresented in farming and in agriculture."[66]

And this guy was the president of Harvard.

Summers initially defended his comments, but when faced with calls to step down, he apologized and promised to "temper my words and actions in ways that convey respect and help us work together more harmoniously."

Conservative publications predictably rushed to Summer's defense, and the UK's *Economist* magazine had a particularly histrionic assessment: "For a man of his intellectual distinction, and devotion to Harvard's thriving as a centre of excellence, to be hounded out in this way would be one of the blackest acts in the history of the university."[67]

Clearer-eyed critics pointed out that Summers' controversial statements might explain why the number of higher-level positions offered to women at Harvard had *decreased* during his three years as president.

Other academics questioned how the head of such a prestigious university could be so blatantly uninformed regarding contemporary gender issues. David Targan, Dean of Science Programs at Brown University, told *Democracy Now!* that much of the variance "in terms of the difference between the numbers of men and women at the faculty levels can easily be accounted for by social factors ... [Summers] and other people have tended to minimize that if we just take some simple measures that are well-known and easy to do, relatively, we can make great strides. And the fact that he didn't seem to know this is rather striking."[68]

This is the same Larry Summers who, as Chief Economist for the World Bank, suggested that rich countries should use poor countries as toxic dumping grounds. A highly contentious memo Summers signed in 1991 stated: "Just between you and me, shouldn't the World Bank be encouraging more migration of dirty industries to the LDCs [less developed countries]? ...

I think the economic logic behind dumping a load of toxic waste in the lowest wage country is impeccable and we should face up to it."[69]

And this guy was the president of Harvard.

Summers announced his resignation from Harvard as of late June 2006, and in February 2007, Dr. Drew Gilpin Faust was named the new president. A former Radcliffe Institute dean and prominent historian, Dr. Faust became the first woman ever to lead Harvard in its 371-year history.

One down and many more to go.

"Abstinence-only" and why virgins get STDs

In Bush's 2005 State of the Union, he promised that "taxpayer dollars must be spent wisely or not at all." What a joke.

The Bush administration has made a sport of wasting taxpayer dollars, but its decision to throw money at "abstinence-only" education is definitely on the top ten list of mistakes that will come back to haunt.

Abstinence-only programs eliminate any discussion about condoms, birth control or other safe sex practices, instead teaching young people to remain virgins until marriage. As Wade Horn, the assistant secretary of Health and Human Services in charge of federal abstinence funding said, "We don't need a study, if I remember my biology correctly, to show us that those people who are sexually abstinent have a zero chance of becoming pregnant or getting someone pregnant or contracting a sexually transmitted disease."[70]

While it's not clear what Horn's been smoking, it's obvious that abstinence-only programs just don't work. By emphasizing the evils of vaginal sex, these programs have been shown to push youngsters into even riskier acts, such as anal or oral sex - and without protection. An eight-year study by Columbia's Institute for Social and Economic Research and Policy, for example, found that youngsters who had taken an abstinence pledge were six times more likely to have oral sex than those who remained abstinent without a pledge, and pledging boys were four times as likely to have tried anal sex than non-pledgers. In addition, pledgers also were less likely to use condoms during their first sexual encounter, and less likely to be tested for sexually-transmitted diseases.[71]

A second study, done by Texas A&M University, found that Texan students who'd taken abstinence-only courses became *increasingly* sexually active afterwards; 24% of the 10th grade boys in the study reported having had sex before taking the course, but a full 39% reported sexual activity afterwards. Girls also reported increased sexual activity after taking the courses - not exactly the desired outcome for programs touting virginity.[72]

Apart from being ineffective, many abstinence-only courses teach blatant lies. A 2004 report for Rep. Henry A. Waxman (D-CA), noted that 80% of the abstinence-only curricula used by grantees of the largest federal abstinence initiative "contain false, misleading or distorted information about reproductive health," such as:[73]

- **Incorrect information about contraceptives**. For example, one curriculum says that "the popular claim that 'condoms help prevent the spread of STDs' is not supported by the data." Other curricula claim that condoms are ineffective in preventing HIV transmission or pregnancy.
- **Incorrect information about abortion**. Various curricula state that the likelihood of premature birth and tubal pregnancies increase after abortion. Another curriculum states that "5%-10% of women who have legal abortions will become sterile."
- **Incorrect scientific information**. Many curricula were found to impose religious viewpoints onto scientific fact, and one curriculum even said that HIV can be spread through contact with sweat and tears.

In short, your federal taxpayer dollars are being used to teach outright lies to kids across the country.

Your taxes have also been promoting sexist gender roles. As Rep. Waxman noted, several of the abstinence-only curricula studied in his report "present stereotypes as scientific facts." Here's an example:[74]

"One book in the 'Choosing the Best' series presents a story about a knight who saves a princess from a dragon. The next time the dragon arrives, the princess advises the knight to kill the dragon with a noose and the following time with poison, both of which work but leave the knight feeling 'ashamed.' The knight eventually decides to marry a village maiden, but did so 'only after making sure she knew nothing about nooses or poison.'

"The curriculum concludes:
Moral of the Story: Occasional suggestions and assistance may be alright, but too much of it will lessen a man's confidence or even turn him away from his princess."

Can you believe this nonsense? It's being taught in public schools and you're paying for it.

Here are some other excerpts from federally funded abstinence-only program curricula, as listed in Waxman's report:
- "Men tend to be more tuned into what is happening today and what needs to be done for a secure future. When women began to enter the work force at an equal pace with men, companies noticed that women were not as concerned about preparing for retirement. This stems from the priority men and women place on past, present, and future."
- "Just as a woman needs to feel a man's devotion to her, a man has a primary need to feel a woman's admiration. To admire a man is to regard him with wonder, delight and approval."

Young women today have a hard enough time trying to forge a healthy identity out of conflicting societal expectations, and they sure don't need this sexist trash masquerading as fact in their classrooms too.

The bottom line is that most parents don't support abstinence-only programs; a 2004 survey showed that a full 94% of Americans approve of teaching young people about birth control.[75]

Regardless, the Bush administration proposed a full $38 million **increase** for abstinence-only programs in FY 2006, up to a total of $193 million for the year.

Let's put that $193 million into perspective. The administration's FY 2006 budget slashed the budgets of the Healthy Start infant mortality initiative, and the Public Health Service's Office of Minority Health, while it **eliminated funding** for the Universal Newborn Hearing program, the Even Start Family Literacy Program, and the Women's Educational Equity Act (WEEA). In fact, if you add up the administration's proposed funding for all five of those programs in FY 2006, and throw in expenditures for the Public Health Service's Office on Women's Health too, the total is roughly **$20 million less** than the administration's budget for abstinence-only programs.[76]

The FY 2007 budget proposal was even worse. The administration proposed slashing funding to Title X family planning, Violence Against Women Act Prevention and Prosecution programs, the Maternal and Child Health Block Grant, the Healthy Start infant mortality initiative and myriad other programs benefiting women and their families. In contrast, the Abstinence Education budget was increased by $89.5 million (for a total of $204 million in FY2007) on top of the $10 million already allocated in FY 2007 for a National Abstinence Education public awareness campaign.

Dangerous priorities.

Give Them Liberty, Not Death

> "In the past two and a half years, 50 million men, women, and children have been liberated in Iraq and Afghanistan, and 25 million women and girls are now free to go to school, vote in elections, and play an active role in their societies."– the far-right publication Free Republic, May 2004[77]

The Bush administration has often couched its military adventurism in terms of benefiting women abroad, but that rosy post-war assessment would no doubt come as news to the women and children of some of the countries the US has invaded.

Iraq

In the 1980s, Iraq was a wealthy country with enviable healthcare and educational systems, not to mention women's rights among the most progressive in the region. The 1980s war with Iran and the 1991 US invasion took their toll, and hard times were further exacerbated by over a decade of US-led crippling sanctions. The 2003 invasion made things much, much worse.

A July 2005 report by the United Nations Development Program and the Iraqi Ministry of Planning and Development painted a devastating picture of post-"shock and awe" Iraq. Citizens lacked access to basic utilities, chronic malnutrition was widespread among children, infant mortality rates were climbing, and infrastructure was decimated. The survey found that after the 2003 US invasion, "the situation worsened due to looting, destruction of public property, and general insecurity."[78] The report repeatedly used words such as "worsening" and "deterioration" to describe Iraqi infrastructure and civilian life – a conclusion hardly in tune with the administration's upbeat assessment.

Women have fared particularly badly under the occupation. The US Coalition Provisional Authority downplayed Iraqi women's rights from the start in order to gain support from religious conservatives; the result is empowered fundamentalist Islamic groups which, among other rollbacks, force women to wear veils, restrict educational opportunities for girls and ban women from working in certain professions.

Much of the blame falls on the former head of the US administration in Iraq, Paul Bremer. According to Yifat Susskind, associate director of the international women's human rights organization MADRE, Bremer "derailed a series of demands by Iraqi women's organizations, including calls to create a women's ministry; appoint women to the drafting committee of Iraq's interim constitution; guarantee that 40 percent of U.S. appointees were women; and pass laws codifying women's rights and criminalizing domestic violence, which has skyrocketed under U.S. occupation."[79]

As a PR smokescreen for siding with the Mullahs, the US state department set up a $10 million condescension called the "Iraqi Women's Democracy Initiative." Never mind the fact that Iraqi women have a long and proud tradition of fighting for their own rights, or that even under Hussein's vicious regime they demanded and won more liberties than most women in the region have (including government-guaranteed rights to education and employment, equal pay, universal day care, and the rights to inherit and own property, move freely, marry whom they choose, hold public office and vote).[80] Very impressive achievements, especially when compared with the relatively lacking state of affairs for women in Bush-friendly Saudi Arabia.

If the state department had really wanted to support Iraqi women after Hussein's fall, it would have worked to empower existing women's groups in Iraq and guaranteed them a meaningful seat at the negotiation table. Instead, the administration's $10 million folly funded groups such as the far-right International Women's Forum (IWF), a US Republican outfit dedicated to countering the "dangerous influence of radical feminism in the courts" and combating the "corrosive feminist ideology on campus." Dick Cheney's equally scary wife Lynne Cheney is a Director Emeritae of IWF – not exactly a role model of democratic excellence or women's rights.

Afghanistan

Afghanistan has not fared better than Iraq. Much of the post-war aid promised to the country got diverted to military spending in Iraq instead, leaving millions of Afghanis at risk. No wonder Afghanistan is once again the world's largest producer of opium.

The situation for women is especially grim. In an October 2003 report entitled "Afghanistan 'No one listens to us and no one treats us as human beings': Justice denied to women," Amnesty International detailed that forced marriage, rape and violence against women were rampant, and that the criminal justice system often subjected women to further discrimination and abuse.[81]

In a May 2005 follow-up report, Amnesty International noted that women across Afghanistan were still being "raped, murdered and abused with impunity." The report's author concluded that "on education, employment and security there is a feeling that generally things have not improved ... and in some cases have got worse."[82]

One thing is clear: the Bush administration's desperate and misguided policy of empowering dangerous warlords and the brutal Northern Alliance may have bought the Karzai puppet regime some reprieve, but has proven devastating for Afghan women. The fact that the US government opened up talks with the infamous Taliban in mid-2003 didn't help matters either.

In August 2005, the United Nations Children Fund (UNICEF) declared that women and children in Afghanistan faced a state of "acute emergency" due to extremely high maternal and child mortality rates.[83] Almost half of Afghanistan's children suffer from malnutrition, and in some regions, a stunning 6 out of 100 women die in childbirth or due to complications. The UNICEF report also noted that female illiteracy rates in Afghanistan have reached 85%, and that fewer than 10% of Afghan girls are enrolled in secondary schools.

A brief look at news headlines from the Revolutionary Association of the Women of Afghanistan (RAWA) site in November 2007 paints a clear picture: "Warlords gang-rape a woman in Badakhshan," "100 suicide attempts among women in 8 months in Kandahar," "They'd rather die: brief lives of the Afghan slave wives," "Police rapes a girl in Takhar, Women are sold in Faryab."[84]

In both Afghanistan and Iraq, the Bush administration has launched illegal invasions (ironically, partly in the name of protecting women) yet spiraling poverty, violence and despair have resulted. It's up to those of us lucky enough to live in relative freedom and financial security to make the connection between the administration's focus on achieving goals through violence and weaponry... and the inevitable suffering that approach creates for innocents abroad. It's also up to us to link the billions spent on military adventurism overseas with the inevitable cut-backs of social programs benefiting women and children domestically.

Ten Easy Ways to Make a Difference Now

1. Learn more about reproductive rights

How does your state stack up when it comes to reproductive rights? NARAL Pro-Choice America has a quick and easy way to find out via its "In Your

State" index.[85] For example, if you choose Wyoming, you'll find that as of November 2007, the Iowa legislature was considering two anti-choice bills including one requiring women to receive a "state-mandated lecture, which may include medically inaccurate information, prior to obtaining abortion services and prohibits abortion unless women wait an additional 24 hours after receiving lecture." If you choose Tennessee, you will also find three separate anti-choice bills, including one "proposing a constitutional amendment to restrict low-income women's access to abortion." The site also lets you to see your Congress members' reproductive rights voting records. Definitely worth a visit.

Would you like to meet others in your city interested in preserving reproductive rights? Then head down to your local Planned Parenthood, or other related facility, and consider donating time, money or any items it might need. You can also find a list of NARAL affiliates under the "In Your State" index mentioned above.

Since the fight for reproductive rights should also look at racism, poverty and unequal access to health care, read Pro-Choice America's excellent report called: "Breaking Barriers: A Policy Action Kit Promoting the Reproductive Health of Women of Color and Low-Income Women."[86] The January 2003 report is roughly 100 pages and covers everything from setting up culturally-appropriate training programs to increasing the number of women eligible for Medicaid.

For confidential information on pregnancy and abortion in the US, as well as referrals to funding sources, you can call the National Abortion Federation Hotline toll-free at 1-800-772-9100. The Hotline is anonymous and offers advice in both English and Spanish.

2 . Protect your right to contraception

Women across the country have run into problems when they've tried to get birth control pills and Emergency Contraception (EC); pharmacists have refused to fill prescriptions because of their personal beliefs about contraception and pharmacies have failed to keep supplies in stock. What's going on at your local pharmacy? Find out *in advance.* Thank the pharmacy if it stocks and provides birth control pills and EC with no hassle but if it doesn't, protest in whatever way you feel comfortable: write a letter to the editor, contact local officials, join others in making a mini-boycott of the store... any positive action that it takes to get the pharmacy to reconsider.

If you're interested in some internet activism then head on over to NARAL Pro-Choice America's birth control access campaign.[87] You can write a letter to your editor, download a petition, submit your own story, urge pharmacy chains such as Walgreens and Wal-mart to honor women's prescriptions, and even watch a brief educational film.

3. Support a women's group

Do you belong to any women's groups? The National Organization for Women (NOW), for example, has chapters across the country that would welcome your involvement. Check the yellow pages for other options in your town; for an internet bonanza of great possibilities, head over to the Feminist Majority Foundation's "Internet Gateway," which offers hundreds of links to groups/activities across the country (www.feminist.org/gateway/).

Are your closets bulging? Do you have a secret recipe for earth-shattering oatmeal cookies? Then why not put together a garage sale or bake sale with your friends and give the proceeds to the women's organization of your choice. Get the kids involved too! They'll learn about the power of direct positive action and also benefit by discovering more about women's issues.

If you're looking for women's groups and resources targeted on specific areas, here are some good online options:

Raging Grannies
(www.raginggrannies.com)
"Our goal is to challenge our audiences to work to bring about the social changes that are required in order to end economic oppression, particularly of women and children, and to end racial inequality, environmental destruction, human rights violations, and arms proliferation."

Women of Color Resource Center
(www.coloredgirls.org)
"Committed to organizing and educating women of color across lines of race, ethnicity, religion, nationality, class, sexual orientation, physical ability and age."

Advocate
(www.advocate.com/resources.asp)
Comprehensive resource page for gays and lesbians covering everything from Family and Parenting to Legal services. Also check out Lesbian.org (www.lesbian.org) for activism tips.

National Women's Law Center
(www.nwlc.org)

"The Center uses the law in all its forms: getting new laws on the books and enforced; litigating ground-breaking cases in state and federal courts all the way to the Supreme Court; and educating the public about ways to make the law and public policies work for women and their families."

Code Pink – Women 4 Peace
(www.codepink4peace.org/)
"A women-initiated grassroots peace and social justice movement working to end the war in Iraq, stop new wars, and redirect our resources into healthcare, education and other life-affirming activities." Fun, creative and effective.

4. Educate your school

So, about that school around the block. What is its policy regarding girls' sport programs and Title IX? Are there any sex-education classes or are they abstinence-only? How does the school deal with teen-age pregnancies? Remember, even if you left school decades ago, you still pay taxes to keep local educational facilities going, so you have the right to ask questions and express opinions.

If you're a student or faculty member and would like some tips on increasing women's rights on campus, help is a click away. Here are a few options:
NOW on Campus
(www.now.org/chapters/campus/index.html)
Good input on planning a campus action and high school organizing.

Pro-Choice America "Organizing on Campus"
(www.prochoiceamerica.org/takeaction/campus/index.cfm)
Would you like to do a voter registration drive or start a pro-choice group on your campus? Interested in learning basic organizing skills or in receiving a *Student Organizer* newsletter? It's all here.

Feminist Campus
(www.feministcampus.org)
A great resource for students and faculty, complete with daily news, e-cards, networking opportunities, actions and campaigns. Be sure to download the 225-page "Study & Action Manual" covering topics such as "Empower Women in the Workplace" and "Know the Opposition" – it's a must-read for campus feminist activists. While you're at the site, sign up for the Feminist Campus bi-monthly e-zine and campus-related alerts.

5. Connect with your "sisters" abroad

If you'd like to have an adventure, increase your knowledge and help women at the same time, then check out the international women's advocacy group Madre (www.madre.org). In addition to providing great articles and fact sheets, their site offers unique opportunities to make a difference:

> Sisters Without Borders - Arranges for bilingual, culturally competent volunteer professionals to work with women and children and provide assistance to staff and community leaders at sister organizations in Guatemala, Nicaragua, Peru and Kenya.

> Voyages with A Vision - Sponsors journeys providing first-hand knowledge of the realities of life in other countries. For example, scheduled trips will include learning about the use of medicinal plants in women's health care in Nicaragua and traveling to Kenya to meet Maasai women on their ancestral lands.

For some cyber comradeship, the Global Sisterhood Network's site (www.global-sisterhood-network.org) offers news feeds, information on upcoming events, an international community board and links to interesting women-oriented sites from around the world.

If you'd like to learn more about women in countries the US has invaded, start with the Revolutionary Women of Afghanistan (www.rawa.org), "the oldest political/social organization of Afghan women struggling for peace, freedom, democracy and women's rights in fundamentalism-blighted Afghanistan." Their multimedia offerings include "patriotic and revolutionary songs," video clips, poems and a whole lot more.

It's more difficult to communicate with women's groups in Iraq - the option at this point tends to be organizations located abroad, such as The Organization of Women's Freedom in Iraq (www.equalityiniraq.com). Also read the CODEPINK/Global Exchange report "Iraqi Women under Siege."[88]

6. Help stop violence against women and children

Rape and domestic violence thrive in environments of secrecy and denial, and often public funding is not enough to cover the expenses of community support facilities. Consider contacting your local family violence counseling center, battered women's shelter hotline or rape-crisis center to see what kind of support they need.

Stop Family Violence (www.stopfamilyviolence.org) is a great source. Join its mailing list for updates on pertinent legislation as well as positive action each of us can take to stop violence.

If you or someone you know has been the victim of violence, help is available. Here are some contacts (taken from the Stop Family Violence site):
National Domestic Violence Hotline
800-799-SAFE (7233)
800-787-3224 (TDD)

RAINN – The Rape, Abuse & Incest National Hotline
800-656-HOPE (4673)

Stalking Resource Center
800-FYI-CALL (800-394-2255)
800-211-7996 (TTY/TDD)

The Miles Foundation for victims of military sexual and domestic violence
203-270-7861

Child Help USA National Child Abuse Hotline
800-4A-CHILD (800-422-4453)
800-2A-CHILD (800-222-4453) TDD

7. Enlighten your kids

Kids today have it rough, what with destructive advertising and pop culture gender roles bombarding them 24/7. But it can be equally rough to be a parent; how do you teach good values when positive role models are few and far between?

Today's thorny issues benefit from some new approaches. For example, Take Our Daughters And Sons To Work® helps girls and boys "reach their potential by participating fully in family, work, and community." Learn more about this Ms. Foundation project at www.daughtersandsonstowork.org.

Another innovative program, Men Can Stop Rape, helps communities empower "male youth and the institutions that serve them to work as allies with women in preventing rape and other forms of men's violence." Learn more at www.mencanstoprape.org.

Of course, your own city has a variety of programs of its own, and no doubt local kids could use your support. Have you ever considered volunteering for the Girl Scouts or Boy Scouts? Helping out with children's theater? Becoming a foster grandparent? The possibilities are endless; never underestimate the powerful impact one person – YOU – can make.

For a goldmine of non-sexist books and other products for kids (and adults!), visit the Women's History Resource site (www.nwhp.org) and check out its Catalog. It's got puzzles, games, children's books and resources, curriculum and teaching kits, not to mention all kinds of multicultural resources.

8. Love your body

While it's not easy to relate to the anorexic, plastic-surgery-enhanced celebrities we're given as role models, cyber help is on the way. Here are some fun sites that bash sexist advertising, and focus on improving women's body image and self-esteem:

NOW's Love your Body
(http://loveyourbody.nowfoundation.org/oncampus.html)
A comprehensive site including positive steps each of us can take. There are additional resources for students and teachers, including an *On Campus* section which gives further ideas for actions (how about, "Invite a nutritionist to come to your group or dorm," or "Stage a mock beauty pageant").

Adios Barbie
(www.adiosbarbie.com)
It's worth a visit to the site just to play the game *Feed the Model!*

About-Face
(www.about-face.org)
There's a terrific *Making Changes* section filled with resources, activities, and a whole lot of links.

In November 2006, the Food and Drug Administration (FDA) shockingly issued approval of silicone gel-filled breast implants despite clear evidence they present health risks. As a result, campuses across the US held *Breastivals* in October 2007, informative events to coincide with Breast Cancer Awareness Month. Learn more about the dangers of breast implants and how your school or community group can hold its own *Breastival* at NOW.[89]

9. Detox

Chances are very good that if you wear cosmetics or use popular household cleaning products, you're poisoning yourself.

In the United States, 95% of the chemicals in use lack basic safety data, and Americans suffer a "body burden" of toxins picked up from everyday products. The Mount Sinai School of Medicine in New York conducted a contamination test on healthy Americans who did not work with chemicals or live near an industrial facility, and the results were staggering: an average of 91 "industrial compounds, pollutants, and other chemicals" were found in each person tested. Many of the chemicals detected were carcinogenic, brain damaging or able to cause birth defects by themselves, let alone in an untested toxic combination.[90]

For detailed information on the toxins in personal care products, visit the Environmental Working Group's excellent "Skin Deep" site.[91] You can search by type of product (cosmetics, eye care etc.), brand name or ingredient, and even build up a customized report of how the products you use are affecting your body. For example, if you happen to use Redken's Extreme Shampoo, you will find it is on Skin Deep's list of "high hazard" shampoo products, with potential dangers including cancer risks, developmental/reproductive toxicity and unassessed ingredients. You will also find an alternative list of "low hazard" shampoo products (Nurture My Body products scored well, in case you're interested) as well as safety assessment ratings for almost 700 related products.

If you're tired of having to worry about carcinogens and mutagens in your everyday products, then support The Campaign for Safe Cosmetics (www.safecosmetics.org). Over 500 companies have already signed the campaign's pledge not to use "chemicals that are known or strongly suspected of causing cancer, mutation or birth defects in their products and to implement substitution plans that replace hazardous materials with safer alternatives in every market they serve." Significantly, major brands which are probably in your household right now (including Avon, Estée Lauder, L'Oreal, Revlon, Proctor & Gamble and Unilever) have not signed the pledge.

Another great resource to protect you and your family from toxins is GreenPeace's "The Chemical Home."[92] Just input the brand name of one of your household products, such as a carpet or mattress, and you will get information on what toxins are in the product and how they put your body at risk. For example, a Fisher Price teddy bear can contain Phthalates, which harm the bladder, and a Sanyo television is likely to contain Brominated Flame Retardants and Endocrine Disrupters which affect the umbilical cord as well as the thyroid and pituitary glands. The GreenPeace site also contains a handy Get Active page with options ranging from cyber alerts to e-cards.

10. Understand women's health and development issues

Since the women's healthcare classic <u>Our Bodies, Ourselves</u> was first published in 1970, it has been translated into 18 languages and has informed readers across the globe about all aspects of women's development, ranging from birth to menopause. If you're familiar with <u>Our Bodies, Ourselves</u> and would like to expand your knowledge even further, visit the book's companion web site (www.ourbodiesourselves.org) or check out some of the other publications it recommends, including:

<u>Changing Bodies, Changing Lives</u> (for teens)
Times Books, 1998.

<u>The New Ourselves, Growing Older</u>
Simon and Schuster, 1994.

<u>Sacrificing Ourselves For Love: Why Women Sacrifice Health And Self-Esteem... And How To Stop</u>
Crossing Press, 1996.

If you prefer clicking your way to medical and health information, then visit the National Women's Health Resource Center (NWHRC) site at www.healthywomen.org. There you can find information about women's health, sexuality, aging and even alternative health-management practices such as yoga and acupuncture. NWHRC also has national public education initiatives and campaigns (often sponsored by pharmaceutical companies, unfortunately).

For an unexpected treat, visit Face the Issue (www.facetheissue.com). Subtitled "you are not alone," the site features brief animations covering topic areas ranging from eating disorders to drug abuse and alcoholism. Each animation is narrated by a different famous actress, which may make the message of taking personal responsibility more palatable for that young person in your life. Definitely worth a visit.

If you're interested in how your state compares with others regarding female health issues, the National Women's Legal Council has put together a terrific, downloadable report card which evaluates over 100 health status/policy indicators, including "key disparities in the health of women based on race, ethnicity, sexual orientation, disability status, and other facts."[93] The site is fascinating for both laypeople and researchers.

Education

"What's not fine is, rarely is the question asked, are, is our children learning?" - George W. Bush, 2000 [1]

When Bush ran for president in 2000, he vowed to bring his Texan educational "miracle" to the rest of the country.

Well, he has... and heaven help us.

Houston, We've Got Your Problem

"You teach a child to read and he or her will be able to pass a literacy test." - George W. Bush, 2001 [2]

What was behind the so-called miracle Bush imposed on Texas during his stint as governor (1994-2000)? A sham that enriched testing companies and left children scrambling far behind.

Under the auspices of "accountability," Bush pumped up the use of standardized tests to determine Texan student progress, but the stakes were high: schools whose students scored poorly could lose funding, and their principals and teachers could be fired. So Texan schools under Bush had no choice but to pour money into textbooks for standardized tests, and teachers had no option but to emphasize rote practice drills over a balanced curriculum.

Bush's "accountability" push seemed to pay off as average test scores controlled by the Texas Education Agency showed a steady annual increase. Oddly enough though, corresponding scores on nationwide standardized tests didn't increase accordingly. In fact, while Texan students scored well on their state tests, by 2002 they ranked a crummy 47th nationally on college-exam scores. [3]

You'd think that if real improvement had taken place in those Texan classrooms, it would have shown up on nationwide standardized tests too – and of course, the disparity suggests there was something bogus about the Texan tests. But why would the state spend millions implementing a testing system that wasn't valid? Who would profit from that?

Textbook producers with Bush-family ties, that's who.

As it happens, the McGraw family (of the McGraw-Hill publishing giant) has a long history with the Bush family; conveniently, Harold McGraw, Jr. has been on the board of the Barbara Bush Foundation for Family Literacy, and Harold McGraw III had a place on Bush Jr.'s transition team. It's perhaps unsurprising then that Bush Jr. gave McGraw-Hill considerable power over Texan education policy during his years as governor, allowing the company's consultants to write the Texas Education Agency's statement of principles and design its reading curriculum.[4]

As might be expected, McGraw-Hill then went on to take over the Texan textbook market. Talk about the fox guarding the henhouse.

Under Bush, Texas chose to emphasize high-stakes educational testing, which may have sold a lot of books but presented troubling choices. Say you're a teacher or principal with a job on the line and school funding at risk if your students don't score well on a standardized test. Your focus will have to be on raising the school's curve, but how can you suddenly get smarter students?

By dumping the weaker ones. According to the late Molly Ivins, the best-selling author and political commentator, Texan low-scorers are discouraged from taking the state test in the first place: "Many children – far more than 50 percent in the cities – who enroll in the first year of high school in Texas don't make it to graduation ... The low-performing students encouraged to go quietly are mostly Latino, African-American, and students with limited English Proficiency." Ivins explained that the Texas Education Agency then "cooks the books" to lower the dropout rate. In 2001, for example, the Agency reported a dropout rate of under 4%, but other groups estimated up to 52% instead. For example, a Texan education-advocacy group put the 2001 dropout rate at 40%, which would translate to over 75,000 teenagers having left school prematurely.[5]

The upshot is that Bush's "accountability" push in Texas led to bogus score results and an elevated dropout rate, especially among minorities - a result that's more criminal than miraculous. And this same nasty system has now been forced upon the whole country.

Leaving Our Children Behind

> "A results-oriented administration ... will make America what we want it to be – a literate country and a hopefuller country." - George W. Bush 2001 [6]

In his 2001 inaugural address, Bush promised to "reclaim America's schools, before ignorance and apathy claim more young lives." The culmination of Bush's glory as self-proclaimed "education president" came in 2001 with the No Child Left Behind (NCLB) Act, which among other measures advocated:

- Annual testing in reading and mathematics by school year 2005-06 for grades three through eight
- The necessity for students to reach a "proficient" level on state tests by school year 2013-14, and for schools to meet Adequate Yearly Progress (AYP) targets towards this goal
- Harsh sanctions for schools, teachers and principals whose students fail to make the required grade

On the surface, NCLB seemed like a much-needed boost for public schools, but in reality it was little more than Bush's Texan educational disaster on steroids.

You've got to question the logic of basing national school reform on a simplistic recipe including standardized tests and harsh punishments. How about issues such as educational funding, family poverty, school safety, and community involvement? Shouldn't those be factored in too?

Plus, any teacher can tell you that a single test score is hardly sufficient to measure a student's overall academic progress; a range of accountability tools at minimum is necessary, and even the best assessment tool isn't going to promote academic progress among disadvantaged students facing poor health care and nutrition, inadequate housing, and schoolyards ruled by guns. The societal causes of underperformance obviously have to be identified and addressed too.

There's also the sticky problem that the more diverse a school's population, the more likely it is that the school will fail to meet NCLB's Annual Yearly Progress demands. Why? Because NCLB breaks a school's population down into various subgroups (Hispanic, African-American, low income etc.) and **each** of those subgroups has to make progress every single year - no simple feat for one subgroup, let alone many. The fewer subgroups a school has, therefore, the easier it is to satisfy Adequate Yearly Progress demands. In essence, schools are being punished for having diversified student bodies.[7]

While one of NCLB's main goals is to close the achievement gap between groups of students, the law is so rigid and simplistic that it often serves to exacerbate the problem instead.

Don't know much about history

NCLB mandates that 100% of students be required to meet proficiency levels (which can vary from state to state) in reading and math by 2013-2014. Until then, schools and districts that don't make Annual Yearly Progress (AYP) risk punishment.

But even quality schools well-recognized for their educational proficiency are failing to meet AYP targets. A full nineteen U.S. Department of Education Blue Ribbon schools were placed on the list of low performers, as was Vandenberg Elementary of Southfield Michigan, a school which Bush himself praised as being exemplary. In the 2005-2006 school year, 22,873 public schools across the country failed to reach AYP which translates to a whopping 25.8%.[8]

That's troubling for two reasons. First, it would indicate that NCLB tests don't adequately measure student development, and second, exemplary schools will be forced to give up best-practice teaching in order to conduct rote drills for the tests. That's not progress.

An obvious drawback is that under NCLB, schools are given credit for the percent of students at or above a "proficient" level on state tests, but they aren't given credit for improvement (such as when students progress from below basic to basic, or from proficient to advanced). And then there's the subject matter. Reading and math are clearly important... but what about history? What about languages, composition, social studies and the arts? If the only important yardstick for a school is its scores on reading and math then you can assume other courses will be minimized or cut altogether.

You can also assume rote drills will devour classroom hours, which is great if you're prepping for a Trivial Pursuit game, but less effective in creating active citizens and lifelong learners. Memorization of isolated facts is not the same thing as developing higher-order thinking skills.

Faced with tough choices such as these, you've got to ask what the whole point of educational reform is anyway. Is the goal to make students see complex issues in black and white, and more likely to follow orders? If so, then we're on the right track. Who needs Aristotle's Lyceum when US youth can attend academic boot camp instead?

In a rare positive development, the administration gave in to complaints and determined that as of December 2003, the scores of students with disabilities and of students with limited English proficiency could be calculated more fairly into AYP results. But since the Department of Education refused to allow the regulations to be applied retroactively, thousands of schools that might have met AYP under the new regulations were penalized.

Senator Edward Kennedy (D-MA) and Representative George Miller (D-CA) have called the Bush administration on its hypocrisy; in June 2004, they introduced The No Child Left Behind Fairness Act of 2004, a bill mandating retroactive application of the revised regulations.[9] Small step, but at least in the right direction.

What are some of the tactics schools have been using to score high on standardized tests without actually improving the quality of their student's education? [10]

Richard Allington of the University of Florida has collected the following examples of tactics schools use to inflate their test scores:

1) Cheat: alter the answer sheets, or tell kids to answer only the questions they're sure of, and fill in the remaining (correct) answers later.
2) Encourage kids to stay home, or send them on field trips.
3) Expel, or encourage the dropping-out of, low-achieving students.
4) Identify low-achieving students as students with disabilities. In many states, their scores won't count.
5) Use irregular test accommodations for students with disabilities. For example, take dictation for the writing tests.
6) Triage: target resources away from certain groups of students. Identify likely high-scoring students and spend all your time with them.
7) Invest in test preparation materials.
8) Flunk lots of kids. It will be more expensive in the long run, but in the short term, it will raise test scores because it will remove low-scorers from any given grade.
9) Make the test easier.
10) Lower the failing grade.

Inadequate funding

Opinions may differ about the merits of NCLB, but on one point there is little disagreement: it hasn't been funded properly.

While lobbying for NCLB, Bush promised that the federal government would help schools meet the law's three main demands: putting a qualified teacher in every classroom, closing student achievement gaps and holding schools accountable for student performance.

However, soon after signing NCLB into law in early January 2002, Bush released his 2003 education budget which not only cut 40 educational programs but also came up short on funding NCLB. As US Senator Dodd (D-CT) wrote in an op-ed for the *Hartford Courant*, Bush's proposed budget allotted only 40% of the assistance that the nation's 10 million low-income school children needed; in other words, Bush's budget gave 6 million impoverished American kids the educational shaft. The budget also cut high-quality training programs for almost 20,000 teachers, forced approximately 25,000 children out of bilingual education and kicked over 30,000 children out of after-school programs.[11] Compassionate conservatism, Bush style.

Unfortunately, things have only gotten worse in the few years NCLB has been implemented. As of 2004, Bush had allocated the program $27 billion less than Congress authorized, with programs for disadvantaged students underfunded by a full $7.2 billion.[12]

For FY 2005, Bush's budget underfunded NCLB by $9.4 billion, and other crucial partner programs were cut altogether. Among those on the 2005 chopping block: Even Start (reading program for poor families), Javits Gifted and Talented Program (for gifted students who are minorities, disabled or who speak limited English), Dropout Prevention, Foreign Language Assistance, and Arts in Education.[13] All in all, the Bush administration's 2005 budget proposed cutting $1.4 billion from the education budget and axing 38 federal education programs.

Bush's proposed FY 2006 budget was even more extreme, underfunding NCLB by a full $12 billion, or roughly 33% of its authorized amount. Also slashed were programs for disadvantaged students and those with special needs.[14]

The FY 2007 proposed budget similarly underfunded NCLB by over $15 billion and eliminated numerous critical educational programs.

Factoring in the $14.8 billion underfunding slated for 2008 in Bush's budget request, NCLB is left with a 2001-2008 cumulative funding gap of $70.7 billion.

How can schools be held accountable for failing to reach NCLB goals if the federal government isn't held accountable for meeting its funding promises?

Meanwhile, the states have faced a one-two budgetary punch as the weak economy has driven down tax revenues yet simultaneously increased demand for social services. All of this has led to across-the-board cuts in education, combined with increased pressure to shell out money on standardized tests. In just one example noted by the National Education Association, "Under pressure from 'No Child Left Behind,' Yonkers, New York, is spending more on test preparation while eliminating 233 teaching positions and all athletic, visual arts, vocal, and instrumental programs, and halving the ranks of public safety officers in the high schools. Yonkers also plans to cut 41 guidance counselors, 28 librarians, and 30 social workers by the end of the following school year."[15]

Same sorry story across the country.

Propaganda, profits and NCLB

The disastrous accountability-through-high-stakes-testing formula Bush used in Texas at least profited certain textbook publishers and testing companies; the same can be said for his NCLB fiasco. In fact, one testing company CEO commented that Bush's education law for the country "reads like our business plan."[16]

Armstrong Williams made out well, too. Bush's Education Department paid the prominent pundit $240,000 to plug NCLB, in a deal that House Education Committee member Rep. George Miller (D-CA) called "a very questionable use of taxpayers' money" and "probably illegal."[17]

Williams was paid through the Ketchum PR firm, which also received Education Department funding to come up with fake news reports promoting NCLB (one Ketchum TV spot, for example, promoted Bush's educational program but failed to identify the government as the source of the report). All in all, Ketchum received $700,000 in 2003 to hype the administration's education agenda.

Put bluntly, US taxpayers paid for their own propaganda.

Also cashing in on NCLB is Bush's own brother Neil (infamous for the 1988 Silverado Savings and Loan crash, which left US taxpayers stuck with $1.3 billion in debts). Neil Bush has conveniently set up a software company specializing in academic-test preparation, and perhaps it's no surprise that middle-school students in Jeb Bush's Florida ended up using brother Neil's software in a 2002 pilot program.

Presidential brother Neil probably won't have to go knocking on many doors to push his software either; he can expect contracts from a variety of governors and others trying to curry favor with the White House. In fact, former first lady Barbara Bush earmarked the funds she donated for Katrina survivors to go through her son Neil's educational software company.[18]

In short, NCLB has been quite profitable for some administration cronies, and the future looks rosy for Neil Bush's software business venture. Meanwhile, the wealthy can still buy stock in companies profiting from NCLB and send their kids to private schools.

And for everyone else? Under Bush's education plan, they can tell their kids to expect increased class sizes, teacher layoffs, delays in school maintenance and year after year of boring rote drills.

Reading, Writing and Religion

> "Leave the matter of religion to the family altar, the church, and the private school, supported entirely by private contributions. Keep the church and state forever separate." - President Ulysses S. Grant, 1875 [19]

> "... all things equal, I would prefer to have a child in a school that has a strong appreciation for the values of the Christian community, where a child is taught to have a strong faith." - Bush's former Secretary of Education, Rod Paige, 2003 [20]

Public schools in the United States are supposed to be, well, public. They're supposed to be non-partisan, non-secular centers of learning which support all students, regardless of their beliefs or religious affiliations.

Supposed to be. Instead, US public schools have become a battleground for the separation of church and state, and in many instances, the far right is winning.

It's back-to-school time for Jesus

In 1925, a young science teacher in Dayton, Tennessee was arrested for teaching Darwin's theory of evolution in his science class. John T. Scopes had broken the so-called Butler Law which mandated teaching creationism, the biblical version of events, and his transgression set off what many considered to be the trial of the century.

Legendary criminal defense lawyer Clarence Darrow stood behind Scopes while the equally renown William Jennings Bryan, a politician and strong advocate of creationism, led the prosecution. Nicknamed the "Monkey Trial" due to the debate over evolution, the courtroom battle ended in a surprise twist when Darrow put Bryan himself on the stand.

With questions such as "Do you claim that everything in the Bible should be literally interpreted?" and "You believe the story of the flood to be a literal interpretation? When was that flood?"[21] Darrow poked holes in Bryan's fundamentalist beliefs, and tried to prove that creationism was more myth than fact.

Darrow wanted to raise the case's profile by having it sent to a higher court, so he asked the jury to return a guilty verdict, and Scopes was fined $100. A year later, the Tennessee Supreme Court reversed the guilty verdict on a technicality.

How stunning that over 80 years after young Scopes dared mention evolution in the classroom, the matter is still under debate. In fact, former House Majority Leader Rep. Tom DeLay (R-TX) blamed the 1999 student shooting massacre at Colorado's Columbine High School on the fact that "school systems teach our children that they are nothing but glorified apes who have evolutionized out of some primordial mud." According to DeLay, "Guns don't kill people; Charles Darwin kills people."[22]

In 1987, the US Supreme Court ruled that teaching creationism in schools was unconstitutional, but a number of states have already approved science-textbook disclaimers insisting that the theory of evolution is under dispute. Some states have tried omitting the word "evolution" from their textbooks, and still others have hidden the concept of biblical creationism behind the newly-coined term "intelligent design," which maintains that since life is so complex, "higher powers" must have been involved in its creation.

In August 2005, Bush joined the "intelligent design" brigade by saying that the theory should be taught in **science** classes, along with evolution.

There's a related movement to promote school prayer, a practice explicitly forbidden by the First Amendment of the US Constitution ("Congress shall make no law respecting an establishment of religion, or prohibiting the free exercise thereof.") The way it is now, if individual kids want to pray at school that's fine, but turning it into a classroom activity enforced by the state is illegal. However, that could change: a number of bills in the US House of Representatives aim to allow teachers to lead prayers during class time.

In early 2001 Bush told reporters, "...I, in the state of Texas, had heard a lot of discussion about a faith-based initiative eroding the important bridge between church and state."[23] Now there's a Freudian slip for you. Many on the far right in fact do believe that church and state should be bridged rather than separated, and US classrooms will no doubt remain center stage for that debate in years to come.

US Department of Education be damned

The Texas Republican Party's 2004 platform (which you can assume reflected Bush-administration beliefs) called for "the abolition of the US Department of Education and prohibition of the transfer of any of its functions to any other federal agency."[24]

Just out of curiosity then, who would oversee the education of America's children?

For the late televangelist Rev. Jerry Falwell, the answer was simple, "I hope to see the day when, as in the early days of our country, we don't have public schools. The churches will have taken them over again and Christians will be running them."[25]

And for many far-righters "one day" is not soon enough – they're pulling their kids out of public schools right now and encouraging others to do the same.

One person at the fight's forefront is a retired US Air Force brigadier general named T.C. Pinckney, who says, "In the Bible, God assigns the responsibility for the education of the children to the parents, not the government." In the summer of 2004, Pinckney petitioned the Southern Baptist Convention (the largest Protestant denomination in the US) to vote on a resolution urging Christians to leave public schools. The resolution calls public schools "anti-Christian" and "Godless" and says, "Just as it would be foolish for the warrior to give his arrows to his enemies, it is foolish for Christians to give their children to be trained in schools run by the enemies of God."[26]

Unsurprisingly, home schooling is on the rise among far-right fundamentalist Christians. The Home School Legal Defence Association puts the number of US kids home schooled at roughly 2 million (the Department of Education gives a lower estimate of 850,000) and while the practice is legal in all 50 states, only twenty-eight states require home-schooled children to be officially evaluated, for example through standardized tests or work portfolios.[27]

Bush has held receptions for home-schooled children in the White House, and during the 2000 campaign said: "In Texas we view home-schooling as something to be respected and something to be protected ... Protected from the interference of government." In Texas, parents don't even have to tell authorities if they decide to home school their children.

Of course, not every home-schooled child is from a far-right family, but they are more likely to support (primarily Republican) political campaigns and candidates than their peers.[28] And after "graduation," a prime spot for home-schooled kids to pursue a higher education is Virginia's Patrick Henry College, which goes by the philosophy that "God is the source of all truth, be it spiritual, moral, philosophical, or scientific ... Christian faith and genuine learning cannot be separated."[29]

According to its web site, Patrick Henry College practices a "deliberate outreach to home schooled students," and conversely, conservative politicians often practice the same deliberate outreach to Patrick Henry in filling their intern slots. The *New York Times* noted in March 2004, that 7 of the roughly 100 interns working in the White House at the time were enrolled at Patrick Henry, while an eighth was on Bush's re-election staff. In addition, a former Patrick Henry intern was on Karl Rove's staff and a full 22 Congress Members had employed at least one Patrick Henry intern for their offices since 2000.[30]

It's no small wonder that Patrick Henry College students are in such demand in D.C. – take a look at the "Civil Government" section of the school's "Statement of Biblical Worldview":

> "God himself has ordained government and commands that everyone must submit to government; moreover, there is no authority except that which God has established. (Romans 13: 1-5) Consequently, he who rebels against lawful authority is rebelling against what God has instituted, and those who do so will bring judgment upon themselves. It is necessary to submit to government, not only because of possible punishment but also because of conscience. We are to pray or all who hold public office, that we may live peaceful and quiet lives in all godliness and holiness. (Proverbs 14: 34-35, I Timothy 2: 1-2)."[31]

Not many rabble rousers in that bunch. And as for politicians who confuse themselves with God, what better assistant than an intern ready to back up that claim.

Buster Bunny and terrorist teachers

Rod Paige was superintendent of the Houston Independent School District during Bush's time in Texas, and given their success in imposing dubious standardized tests and elevating the minority dropout rate, Bush made Paige his first Secretary of Education.

Paige did not fail to please. In just a few short years he:

- **accused public schools of having no values**
  Paige told the *Baptist Press*, "The reason that Christian schools and Christian universities are growing is a result of a strong value system ... In a religious environment the value system is set. That's not the case in a public school, where there are so many different kids with different kinds of values." (April 2003)[32]
- **called the lack of educational funding "meaningless jargon"**
  In a *Wall Street Journal* op-ed, Paige wrote, "But in Washington, the land of meaningless jargon, the educational establishment in favor of the status quo says that the law is underfunded because it was appropriated at a level below what was 'authorized.'" (October 2003)[33]
- **and insulted both France and voucher opponents in one fell swoop**
  Paige compared educational voucher opponents to "the French at the United Nations, promising to veto any resolution on Iraq, regardless of what it says." (January 2003)[34]

But Paige's coup de grace came in a speech to the nation's governors in late February 2004, when he accused the National Education Association (NEA) of being a "terrorist organization." Paige later clarified that he was referring to the NEA's "obstructionist scare tactics" in opposing the No Child Left Behind law.[35]

As might be expected, the 2.7 million-strong NEA was not amused and promptly called for Paige's resignation; the American Federation of Teachers, a union with 1.3 million members, followed suit.

Few mourned when the embattled Paige stepped down at the end of Bush's first term, but his replacement has been equally glaring: Margaret Spellings, an education advisor to Bush during his days as Texas governor. Following in the homophobic tradition of James Dobson (the head of a multimillion-dollar ministry, who gained headlines in 2004 when he accused a cartoon character of being gay) Spellings immediately went on a rampage against a cartoon bunny named Buster when she took over from Paige. Apparently there were few other pressing issues for her to handle.

Spellings was peeved about an episode of the cartoon "Postcards from Buster" in which the bunny visits Vermont, learns about farm life and maple sugaring, and meets some lesbian couples. Even though Buster's show has a mandate to focus on diversity and tolerance, apparently the bunny's new friends were just too much for Spellings. She ordered the Public Broadcasting System to return federal funding used to produce the Vermont episode.

Spellings has yet to insist that Armstrong Williams and the Ketchum PR firm return the federal funds they received to support the administration's educational programs.

Selling off Public Schools

> "If all the rich and all of the church people should send their children to the public schools they would feel bound to concentrate their money on improving these schools until they met the highest ideals." – Susan B. Anthony, (1820-1906) educational reformer, labor activist, and suffragist

We're often told that our public schools are failing, and that privatization will fix them. But how do we know? Since private schools don't have the same performance pressures (i.e. rigid standardized tests), comparisons can be difficult.

One thing is clear: there's a growing trend to put public schools under private management. Only a fraction of public schools are managed by private companies, while the number tripled between 1998 and 2003 and the trend continues.[36]

The perils of privatization

If private schools really are so much better, one would expect to see superior performance at public schools that are privately managed. But an October 2003 report by the federal government's General Accounting Office found no consistent pattern of differences in scores on state tests; the report concluded that most privately-run schools in fact perform no better than publicly-run schools.[37]

Some privatization proponents insist that school districts can save a lot of money by outsourcing services away from the public sphere, but frequently the opposite is true. For example, the National Education Association cites a Kent State University study which found that Ohio districts "using private bus companies to transport students paid anywhere from 24 to 50 percent more per student than districts keeping those services in-house. The costs per mile were even greater: districts paid between 51 and 63 percent more for private transportation than district-run programs."[38]

Nonetheless, countless school boards across the country, smitten with privatization, are rushing to help companies cash in on the nearly $400 billion spent on K–12 public education annually.

One privatization pioneer is Edison Schools Inc., which handles over 285,000 public school students in 19 states across the country and in the UK. Edison's slick web site describes the company as "the nation's leading public school partner with schools and districts, focused on raising student achievement through its research-based school design, uniquely aligned assessment systems, interactive professional development, integrated use of technology and other proven program features." The company also boasts that its students are "achieving annual academic gains well above national norms."[39]

Sounds terrific, but there's a glitch. As a private school contractor, Edison is allowed to manage and release its own data on student achievement. Think about it. If a school's students make remarkable gains on a test that the school writes, administers and corrects, that doesn't necessarily have comparative validity to those students' scores on state-wide standardized tests.

According to privatization expert Heidi Steffens, "One of the true scandals of ... Edison and others is that they've been allowed to do their own accountability. I mean, that's like asking General Motors to let you know if their cars are safe or fuel efficient."[40]

Veteran public school teacher Laurie Mozlin learned about Edison the hard way. In 2001 she began teaching at an Edison-run charter school in Milwaukee, and while at first optimistic, soon became disenchanted when cost-cutting measures led to collapsing administrative support and a lack of books and curriculum materials. Mozlin quit a year later and returned to the public schools, telling *NEA Today* magazine that profit-based firms such as Edison "cut corners every chance they get because the bottom line for them is making money. They are not in it for the kids, they are in it for themselves."[41]

Charter schools

So-called charter schools, such as the one at which Mozlin taught, are at the center of the debate over privatizing education. As of 2004, there were 750,000 students attending charters, and as more public schools fail to meet the No Child Left Behind high-stakes testing demands, that number will skyrocket.

So how exactly are charter schools different? In brief, they're given a lot more autonomy over their operations and a lot less pressure to follow regulations than normal public schools. They come about through a contract (or "charter") with a state agency or local school board, and the main requirement is that they achieve the goals set out in that contract.

So far so good, but keeping charter schools accountable has proven difficult. One problem is that state laws differ over whether charters have to conform with local public-school academic standards. A second problem is charters' sometimes shoddy record-keeping, such as happened in Texas in 2001 when the closure of ten charter schools forced 600 students to repeat a grade because inadequate records had been kept of their progress.

A third problem is that charter-school students often do worse on test scores than comparable students in regular public schools. A 2004 study released by the Education Department, for example, found that fourth grade students in charter schools lagged about six months behind public school students in both reading and math.[42]

Another concern is the high turnover rate for educators in charter schools; roughly 25% quit each year – a number double the attrition rate for teachers in public schools.

But all of these drawbacks pale next to the nightmare California faced in August 2004 when the California Charter Academy, the largest chain of publicly-financed but privately-run charter schools, went belly up. Thousands of students were left with no schools to attend, and arguably even worse, thousands of their academic and immunization records were nowhere to be found.[43] Hundreds of teachers and other school employees were left scrambling for work, and since the businessperson who had set up the schools simply abandoned his office when the crisis hit, local school superintendents were left to handle the mess.

The California Charter Academy had been founded in 1999 by a former insurance executive with amazingly few educational credentials; nonetheless, his for-profit charter empire received $100 million in state financing over the following five years.

And Californian students and teachers are still paying the price.

It's important to note that the California Charter Academy is an exception rather than the rule – an egregious example of what can go wrong when taxpayer funding is not properly regulated.

It's also important to remember that charter schools can often seem like the only viable option to under-performing local public schools, and that many charter schools in fact do a very fine job of educating their students, often offering them more options than public schools.

If charters do receive public money, however, then they should be just as accountable as other public schools regarding academic achievement, student access, health/safety standards and fund allocation. Teachers and other school employees should have the same rights as in public schools, and public educators should be included in designing and running these new programs.

Salvation through vouchers

Vouchers were sold to the public as offering students "choice" regarding where they attend school. Is your kid attending a crappy school? No problem! Get a voucher and Junior can whoop it up at Harvard.

As if.

During Bush's 2000 campaign, he explained vouchers this way: "If a failing school does not change after a period of time parents should be able to take the federal money attributable to their child ... and make a choice of any school they want to send that child to." In other words, taxpayer dollars could be diverted from public schools to private schools, and Bush estimated the figure at $1,500 annually per child.[44]

Have you ever found a private school that will take a student for $1,500 per year? Good luck trying.

In *Had Enough? A Handbook for Fighting Back*, James Carville notes that the average private elementary school is over $3000 per year, the average private high school is well over $7000, and Andover, where Bush Jr. went, is more than $28,000 per year. Interestingly, while information on public school costs used to be readily available on the Department of Education's web site, it has disappeared under Bush, leading Carville to comment: "Of course, that's not surprising – given the fact that once you compare a $1,100 voucher with a $3,200 tuition, you begin to see that George Bush's voucher proposal is a bridge to nowhere."[45]

There's also the matter of accountability. Private schools don't have the same performance pressures as public schools – no need to worry about rigid standardized tests or state certification of teachers. They might receive public money (in the form of vouchers) but private schools don't have to fret much over being audited by the state. And of course, they don't need to get their curriculum approved. Good news for intelligent designers!

The National Education Association notes that lack of accountability for voucher programs has led to "rampant fraud, waste and abuse."[46] Parents are also concerned about their kids' achievement, an area in which vouchers haven't been shown to help. In fact, the strongest improvements in student achievement have been in states that don't use vouchers.[47]

Then there's the sticky issue of private schools picking and choosing kids they want and rejecting the rest; unlike public schools, private schools are under no obligation to accept all students. So religious schools will most likely recruit students of the same belief system and secular private schools will become highly competitive - for those whose parents can afford to top up their kids' vouchers with thousands of extra dollars per year. As a result, the kids left behind in public schools will mainly be low-income or "troublemakers" rejected elsewhere, and the money to deal with their special educational needs will meanwhile have been siphoned off to private schools.

Vouchers also open the door to sex discrimination in the classroom. According to the National Women's Law Center, the administration's proposed voucher program allows schools to override Title IX funding restrictions against unwarranted sex discrimination, thereby making it possible for girls to be segregated into separate schools, classes and activities.[48]

It's no wonder that for the last 30 years, voters across the country have consistently rejected vouchers.[49]

And vouchers haven't fared much better in the courts. In December 2003, a Colorado State judge overturned a statewide school voucher law, and in August 2004, a Florida District Court ruled against religious school vouchers, noting that the "'vast majority' of students with vouchers used them to enroll in the kind of 'sectarian institutions,' or religious schools, that are barred from receiving state money under the Florida Constitution."[50]

According to Samantha Smoot, director of the Texas Freedom Network: "The voucher lobby has become very clever about disguising and shielding this agenda. We have a very unholy alliance of religious political extremists who would like everyone to be taught the Bible in school, and they've linked up forces with some dangerous partners – free-market thinkers and wealthy individuals who stand to make untold amounts of money off privatizing our public schools. This is a dangerous combination."[51]

Put it all together and the Bush administration's scam seems clear: force public schools to meet impossible demands through NCLB testing, don't give them enough money to make the required changes, and then question the patriotism of anyone who disagrees. Shut down the many schools which inevitably fail and offer vouchers as the solution, thereby privatising education and mandating that taxpayers fund religion in the classroom. Nifty way to institutionalize huge corporate profits with almost no accountability.

Phi Beta capitalism[52]

While there's considerable public debate over vouchers and charter schools, other big-business inroads into education are seldom addressed.

Of course there's the occasional outrage that gains limited media attention (such as when a Georgia high school student was expelled a few years back for wearing a Pepsi T-shirt on his school's designated Coca Cola day) but for the most part, the corporate march into US public education has proceeded in relative silence.

And nowhere is that silence more profound than in colleges and universities, where shrinking budgets have led to increased dependency on corporate largesse for endowed professorships, sponsoring grants, research center funding, etc. While this development isn't necessarily harmful, it does lead to serious questions about the long-term implications of merging academia and industry.

Corporations started setting up their ivory tower playground in the early 1980s, thanks to changes in two federal laws: the 1980 Bayh-Dole Act (and a related 1983 executive order) which allowed universities to sell patent rights obtained from taxpayer-funded research, and the 1981 Recovery Tax Act which permitted corporations to increase the tax deductions they could claim for donations to universities.

Since then, industry contributions to academia have exploded. In 1984, for example, private companies contributed $26 million to university research budgets, but by 2000, that amount had increased by **9,000%** to $2.3 billion.[53]

According to the American Association of University Professors, the ensuing university-industry relationships have taken many forms, including:[54]
- tobacco companies funding biomedical research
- corporate sponsors bankrolling endowed chairs (and maintaining some control over appointments)
- a drug company funding research in which it had a vested interest and also trying to stop publication of an article that had been "rigorously vetted" by a prominent medical journal
- authors of journal articles often having a financial stake in the subject area covered

One example of the academia-industry merger is the 1998 agreement between the Department of Plant and Microbial Biology at the University of California, Berkeley, and the Novartis Corporation, a Swiss pharmaceutical company. In brief, Novartis gave the Berkeley department $25 million for research over a five-year period, and in return, Novartis got negotiating rights for licenses on a certain proportion of the department's overall research, regardless of whether the discoveries came from the specific research Novartis had sponsored.

Some would argue that it's a win-win situation: the university benefits from increased funding and the corporation benefits from cutting-edge research.

But are the scientific validity and intellectual independence that should be hallmarks of advanced education really consistent with industry demands? Should university research be aimed at short-term profit and the attainment of lucrative patents? And ultimately, should institutions of higher learning focus more on corporate gain or on the public good?

These questions will become even more profound in the next years: to cover budget deficits stemming from Bush's tax cuts and military adventurism, the proposed FY 2007 Education Department budget was slated to decrease by $3.1 billion, a 5.5% drop from already-paltry 2006 levels.[55]

No doubt a slew of sugar-daddy corporations will be more than willing to step in and pick up the tab... at a price.

Teachers in Trouble

> *"Teaching is not a lost art, but the regard for it is a lost tradition."*
> *- Jacques Barzun, writer, educator, and historian*

America has a love-hate relationship with its teachers. We praise their selfless dedication, then blame them for the educational system's failures. We entrust teachers with our nation's most precious asset – our children – then pay them lousy wages and offer little support or incentive for career development.

Low pay, low expectations

Would you like an emotionally-rewarding career based on helping others? Great, then consider becoming a teacher. But would you like decent cash, performance-based benefits and the ability to stay middle class without exhausting yourself by working extra jobs? Then avoid teaching at all costs.

That, unfortunately, defines how many of the nation's most promising grads look at a career in education. While the nation's demand for teachers is strong, the profession's perks aren't exactly seen as competitive. The Teaching Commission, a bipartisan group established and chaired by former IBM chairman Louis V. Gerstner, Jr., reports:[56]

- Almost 70% of college grads think teaching doesn't offer good possibilities for advancement and leadership.
- Almost 20% of young college graduates who end up not teaching say they would have seriously considered it as a career.
- One survey found that 85% of teachers and 72% of principals said that better financial incentives would help attract and keep good teachers.
- One out of three new teachers across the country quits within five years; turnover averages 50% within three years in some urban areas.

Over the next decade, US schools will require two million new teachers. So how can the nation get – and retain – them?

For Gerstner's Teaching Commission, the solution is clear: increase teacher pay and reward top performers. Higher salaries would go to those teachers who increase student academic gains as well as to "master and mentor teachers, to instructors who work in shortage specialties like math and science, and to teachers who embrace the challenge of working in our toughest classrooms."[57] As an incentive for accepting performance-based accountability, teachers would be given improved training and professional support services.

The Teaching Commission suggests that if America "commits an additional $30 billion annually to teacher pay, each teacher could get a 10 percent raise while the top half would receive a 30 percent increase." While $30 billion might seem like a hefty amount, it's chump change in comparison to the trillions the US government spends on weaponry and war abroad.

But the idea of performance-based benefits for teachers is not without its detractors, the main sticking point being the definition of "performance." Clearly, students' scores on standardized tests or other simplistic yardsticks can't encompass the true range of a teacher's skills or responsibilities. How do you measure empathy? How do you quantify mentoring other teachers or counseling students after hours about their personal problems?

Deregulating certification

The issue of measuring a teacher's performance takes on added urgency with the No Child Left Behind Act (NCLB), which required 100 percent of every state's teachers of core academic subjects to be "highly qualified" by the 2005-2006 school year.

What "highly qualified" means, however, is not highly clear. As might be expected, there are different requirements for new and experienced teachers, and each state has its own interpretation.

Initially, to be "highly qualified" under NCLB, teachers had to hold a bachelor's degree and a valid state teaching certificate, plus be able to demonstrate subject area competency. But as Barnett Berry of the Southeast Center for Teaching Quality observed in late 2002, the NCLB definition of teacher performance was dangerously limited:

"Guidelines issued by the U.S. Department of Education allow 'teachers' participating in an alternate route program, with just a few weeks of training, to be deemed highly qualified as long as the 'teacher' is making satisfactory progress toward full certification as prescribed by the state. This means that a novice teacher, who has just a few weeks of training and no track record of success, would be placed in the same 'highly qualified' category as an accomplished teacher, like those certified by the National Board for Professional Teaching Standards (NBPTS). But what is so disheartening about the federal guidelines is that no other profession would even consider labeling someone 'highly qualified' without their first demonstrating they have the necessary knowledge and then proving they can apply that knowledge effectively and in the best interest of their clients."[58]

This gets into the wildly political issue of how to certify teachers. Former Secretary of Education Rod Paige pumped $35 million into a program called the American Board for Certification of Teacher Excellence (ABCTE), which was set up in 2001 to identify and certify potential teachers who had not gone through traditional preparation institutions. For the first six years of the program, candidates hoping to get a *Passport to Teaching* [SM] only had to hold a Bachelor's degree or higher, pass a computer test covering the chosen subject area(s) and "professional teaching knowledge," complete a background check and voilà, they were certified. No teacher-training courses required, no internships in schools, and in fact, no experience working with kids was necessary at all – just a degree, a computer test and a background check.

One could argue it takes a bit more than that to run an effective classroom. Many educators warned about the stress on unprepared teaching candidates (let alone their students) and disagreed with what they saw as the Bush administration's transparent move to deregulate teacher certification.

As of May 2007, the *Passport to Teaching* [SM] was beefed up to include, "access to comprehensive classroom management/Professional Teaching Knowledge online coursework, which features more than 40 hours of analyzed classroom videos and 125 pages of interactive text."[59]

Major problems stem from NCLB's proposed mandate for "highly qualified effective teachers," which evaluates educators largely on the basis of improvements in their students' standardized test scores and automatically categorizes 25% of teachers in every state as not "effective."

That's not fair, and as the National Education Association has observed, "It ignores the reality that working conditions matter and impact teachers' ability to improve student learning. Teachers in schools with larger class sizes, safety problems, out-of-date textbooks and technology, and/or ineffective school leaders will be judged against teachers in schools that don't face these challenges. Thus, the mandate creates disincentives for teachers to go to and stay in such hard-to-staff schools."[60]

As the nation struggles to attract and retain great teachers, the very definition of "highly qualified" takes precedence. The impact on our children of the Bush administration's current approach remains to be seen.

Deactivating professors

What's the role of university professors today? Should they encourage students to accept the status quo or to question it? Should they follow notables such as Noam Chomsky, Howard Zinn and Edward S. Herman in spurring student activism, or should they shun taking political positions, especially any disagreeing with the current administration's?

For John Dewey (1859 -1952), arguably the most influential US educational thinker of the 20th century, the answer was simple: US classrooms were meant to actively promote democratic thinking, and educators were responsible to help students reflect on the requirements of a free and just society.

Compare Dewey's approach with that of Stanley Fish, who retired as Dean of the College of Liberal Arts and Sciences at the University of Illinois at Chicago in mid-2004. In a *New York Times* op-ed entitled "Why We Built the Ivory Tower,"[61] Fish instructed professors to "aim low and stick to the tasks we are paid to perform." Fish said academics should only "engage in politics appropriate to the enterprise they signed onto. And that means arguing about (and voting on) things like curriculum, department leadership, the direction of research, the content and manner of teaching, establishing standards – everything that is relevant to the responsibilities we take on when we accept a paycheck." In other words, professors have no business in fashioning democratic citizens or in being activists themselves.

Fish might have added another reason for professors to lay low: it's becoming increasingly dangerous for them to speak up.

In late 2003, Congress passed HR3077, the "International Studies in Higher Education Act," which aims to withhold governmental funding from international and foreign language studies programs not toeing the administration's line. Similar to 1996's Solomon Amendment, which denies federal funding to institutions of higher education that don't allow military recruiters on campus, HR3077 holds hostage $80 million in Title VI funding unless its so-called national security requirements are met, including:

- Section 6: Establishment of an advisory board, including two members from national security agencies, "to advise Congress and the Secretary on Title VI programs in relation to national needs with respect to homeland security, international education, international affairs, and foreign language training."
- Section 7: Mandating that Federal Government agency recruiters be given "access to students and student recruiting information."
- Section 8: Directing the Secretary of Education "to study and report to Congress on foreign language heritage communities of U.S. residents or citizens, particularly those that include speakers of languages critical to U.S. national security."

In short, HR3077 unabashedly inserts national security agents into universities, grants them oversight capabilities, provides them regular access to students, and authorizes "study" (i.e. surveillance) of "foreign language communities."

How creepy is that?

And can you imagine the chill it has on professors? Those who disagree with US foreign policy could risk losing their jobs, or at the very least, see their course curriculum censored.

Dewey must be spinning in his grave.

Educational Apartheid

> "With names like Shaniqua, Shaligua, Mohammed and all that crap and all of them are in jail ... Brown Versus the Board of Education is no longer the white person's problem. We've got to take the neighborhood back." - William Henry "Bill" Cosby, Jr., Ed.D [62]

In May 2004, the entertainer and activist Bill Cosby stunned a gala sponsored by the National Association for the Advancement of Colored People Legal Defense Fund by blaming the African-American community for its children's shortcomings, such as the fact that an estimated 50% of African-American males drop out of inner-city schools.

Predictably, Cosby's controversial speech was met with mixed reactions. While conservatives were quick to praise his apparent dismissal of factors normally associated with African-American academic underachievement, (poverty, prejudice, lack of school funding, etc.) detractors saw Cosby's comments as the rant of an elitist out of touch with reality in the trenches.

African-American students lag behind in academic achievement – that much is clear. While 33 percent of white kindergartners eventually obtains at least a bachelor's degree, the figure for African-American kindergartners is just 18 percent.[63] On average, African-American high school students graduate four years behind their white counterparts in basic academic skills, with most scoring "below basic" in roughly 70% of the key subjects measured by the National Assessment of Educational Progress.[64] But why does this happen, and what can be done to improve the academic performance of African-American youth?

Separate and unequal

In 1896, the US Supreme Court ruled in favor of a "separate but equal" segregation of African-American school children, but that racist imbalance changed in 1954 with Brown vs. the Board of Education. Or at least it was supposed to.

The 1954 Brown ruling (banning public school segregation as both unequal and unconstitutional) was meant to level the playing field for all American kids, regardless of race. However, while Brown served as a precedent for dismantling other Jim Crow laws, it was never properly implemented in US public schools.

Why? For starters, the Brown ruling lacked teeth, so state and local officials often just ignored it. African-Americans were told they could attend all-white schools, but the ruling didn't adequately address their difficulties and risks in doing so. Meanwhile, so-called "integrated" schools often tracked African-American students into inferior educational programs.

The situation degenerated even further in 1971 when the Supreme Court ruled that class-based discrimination in public education was constitutional; schools immediately started skirting responsibility by blaming their African-American students' poor performance on socio-economic factors, rather than on racial discrimination. A second blow came in 1974 with a decision that Brown didn't require integration across city and suburban lines; in short, the ruling gave predominantly white suburbs legal justification to protect their schools from an influx of non-whites bused in from nearby cities.

When these court decisions are seen in combination with the "white flight" out of predominantly African-American cities, it's no surprise that half a century after the historic Brown ruling, over two thirds of African-American students still attend mainly minority schools.[65]

To make matters worse, school districts with large numbers of minority students are chronically underfunded.

In a report entitled "The Funding Gap 2004 - Many States Still Shortchange Low-Income and Minority Students" the Education Trust think-tank found that each student in high-minority districts received a full $2,166 less than each student in low-minority districts in New York in 2002. Similarly, students in minority districts in Wyoming and Montana also received over $2000 less than their white-district counterparts.

All in all, 35 of the 48 states studied had a funding gap for minority students, with a nationwide average of $1,099 for every student.[66]

The Bush administration has suggested that targeting minority education with extra support is tantamount to affirmative action, a nasty concept in conservative circles. Of course, the fact that academic-underachiever Bush glided through top universities on little more than his family's name is rarely called affirmative action, just a prerogative of the super-rich.

Books or Boots?

> "It is unfair to the kids in my town that they need to risk their lives to get ahead. It is as if the rich kids go to college and the poor kids go to Baghdad." – A resident of a working-class town in Massachusetts, as told to New Statesman magazine, December 2004 [67]

The Bush fiscal 2005 discretionary budget provided $421 billion for the military and only $60 billion for education.[68] In other words, the administration's discretionary budget came up with **seven times** more money to invade hapless countries abroad than to help American students get a decent education. What kind of crazy priorities are those?

The administration's FY 2006 proposed budget priorities were even worse, with education cut back to $56 billion, compared with a five percent **increase** for the Department of Defense, to $419.3 billion.[69] For FY 2007, Bush & Co. proposed allotting $460 billion for defense, which translated to **over eight times** more money for war than for US children's educations.[70]

But there's a cruel logic behind the budget – if the playing field were more level (i.e. if all cash-strapped schools were given the support they needed and if all lower-income students saw a viable track to college) then the military would have a much harder time in recruiting. Impoverished youth looking for a decent future wouldn't see enlisting as the only option.

As it is, the Defense Department spends a full $2.6 billion per year hunting down recruits, with much of that outlay targeted towards public schools. National Guard Leadership Education programs for teens are sprouting up across the country, and the Junior Reserve Officers' Training Corps boasts a membership of over 270,000 student "cadets." Meanwhile, the Armed Services Vocational Aptitude Battery, a three-hour standardized test, is being administered to juniors and seniors across the country to help the military identify favorable prospects.

Of course, the Defense Department doesn't target all school districts equally. Relatively little attention is paid to wealthier areas, where it's assumed most kids will be heading off to college.

In November 2004, *The Boston Globe* compared recruiting tactics at a lower income school with those in a wealthier neighborhood:[71]

> "Military recruiting saturates life at McDonough High, a working-class public school where recruiters chaperon dances, students in a junior ROTC class learn drills from a retired sergeant major in uniform, and every prospect gets called at least six times by the Army alone. Recruiters distribute key chains, mugs, and military brochures at McDonough's cafeteria...

> "Meanwhile, at McLean High, a more affluent public school 37 miles away in Virginia, there is no military chaperoning and no ROTC class. Recruiters adhere to a strict quota of visits, lining up behind dozens of colleges. In the guidance office, military brochures are dwarfed by college pennants. Posters promote life amid ivy-covered walls, not in the cockpits of fighter jets."

Small wonder that McDonough students enlist six times more often than do those at McLean. And it's the same story across the country.

Some rollbacks are equal opportunity though. To supply the increasing number of military recruits needed for Bush's perpetual "war on terror," a tricky clause was placed into his NCLB educational plan: small print requiring schools that receive federal funding to turn over student's names, addresses and phone numbers to military recruiters.

Gives new meaning to the term "No Child Left Behind."

One bright spot in this march to militarize our public schools is the November 2004 ruling prohibiting the government from punishing (i.e. withholding funds from) colleges and universities that don't cooperate with recruiters. A US Court of Appeals decided that since the Pentagon refuses to admit "out" gays and lesbians into the military, colleges and universities could protest by refusing to allow recruiters on campus.

A step in the right direction, but there's still a very long way to go.

Shortchanging Students

> *"I'm Laura Bush. Education is very important to my husband. That's why he wants you to pay thousands more for your college loan. You see, if your education costs you more, you'll value it more. We're compassionate like that. Big banks helped our campaign so much, and they're expecting a big return. That's where you all come in. Everyone knows the*

kids in my family don't even have student loans like you do. And besides, it's not like you're going to send us the bill." - "No More Lip Service" 2004 webmercial parody of the plan by Bush congressional allies to increase college student loan prices by an average of $5,500.[72]

Across the board, American students are feeling the budgetary pinch:

- Only 60% of eligible preschool-age children and 3% of eligible infants and toddlers can participate in Head Start programs due to funding shortages[73]
- While the Individuals with Disabilities Act promises that the federal government will provide 40% of the national average per pupil expenditure to support special education, it actually only covers 19%[74]
- The administration has not only continually tried to weaken Title IX funding protections for female athletes and gender equity in schools, but also repeatedly tried to cut funding for the Women's Educational Equity Act, which helps schools comply with Title IX[75]

Year after year, the Bush administration has pinched pennies on student services while favoring tax cuts for the wealthy and cash boosts for the nation's lethal arsenal.

Funding our future

Some argue that military funding buys tangible, war-fighting machines, whereas money for schools just wastes precious tax dollars on a creaking and dysfunctional educational system. Public school advocate Jonathan Kozol questions the comparison: "As though it's bizarre to suggest that money would be the solution to poverty. As though it's a bizarre idea that it would really take dollars to put a new roof on Morris High School in the Bronx and get the sewage out of the schools in East St. Louis; that it would take real money to hire and keep good teachers so they would stay for a lifetime in the schools that need them most; that it would take real money to buy computers."[76]

The future of our country is only as strong as that of our kids' educations, so it's critical to provide adequate funding for our public school students, all of them. But where will the money come from?

Roughly 90% of K-12 funding is generated by the states, rather than by the federal government. And each state varies widely in how much funding it provides to local school districts. For example, in 2002, New Mexico covered a full 83.9% of local-education costs, whereas Texas covered only 43.2%, Pennsylvania only 38.7% and Nebraska only 38.2%.[77]

Since federal and state sources leave large funding gaps, school districts must raise cash locally, and property taxes are an especially popular – and especially inequitable – method of doing so.

Think about it: if a rich district with high-value homes adopts a relatively low property tax, it can still raise a bundle for its schools. Not so for an impoverished district with relatively worthless real estate. The poor district can raise property taxes through the roof and still have a hard time coming up with enough cash for its schools.

In other words, when local property taxes are a primary source of school funding, the poor part of town often gets doubly hurt: exorbitant taxes and crappy schools.

While states and local communities pick up most of the tab for education, the federal government's roughly 10% contribution is crucial, especially during economic downturns such as this one. Unfortunately, the administration has not lived up to its promises in funding the Elementary and Secondary Education Act (ESEA), known as No Child Left Behind. For example, ESEA and other federal education programs were short over $30 billion in funding for FY 2006, which meant that millions of eligible students were not served and millions of teachers were not hired for mandated educational programs, such as Head Start, Educational Technology State Grants and Safe and Drug-Free Schools and Communities, among many others.[78]

The administration's FY 2007 proposed budget cut ESEA even further (although the program was already approximately $40 billion underfunded[79]) and proposed eliminating numerous critical educational programs including Even Start, Vocational Education, and Women's Educational Equity.[80]

Unfortunately, things are slated to get even worse for US students in the long run. The nonpartisan Center on Budget and Policy Priorities (CBPP) slogged through Bush's 2006 budget to determine which long-term education cuts the administration wasn't making public. By comparing the projected cuts with expenditures necessary to track inflation, CBPP found: "Elementary, secondary and vocational education will lose out on $6.7 billion in funding in 2010, and $20.5 billion in total between 2006 and 2010. Higher education will lose $6 billion over the next five years - and $1.9 billion in 2010. Social service programs that help disadvantaged students enter school ready to learn lose $8.8 billion in this same five-year time period, and $2.5 billion in 2010 alone."[81]

In other words, education funding may be bad now, but under Bush's spending plan they're going to get much worse very soon.

Pell hell

When campaigning in 2000, Bush praised the Pell Grant program (which helps low-income students attend college) by promising to raise first-year aid from $3,300 to $5,100 per grant recipient.

Things changed once Bush entered office. He increased the maximum Pell Grant to $3850 (not the $5,100 figure flaunted on the campaign trail) and opposed Congress' move to raise the maximum to $4,000.

Then in December 2004, two days before Christmas, the administration quietly announced it would start calculating Pell Grant eligibility with a new formula, one which would eliminate funding for an estimated 85,000 low-income students, and reduce funding for over one million more.

The move was set to save the administration about $300 million in its annual budget – absolute chump change. In comparison to the proposed cuts, however, the costs of attending public 2-year and 4-year colleges rose 14% in 2003 alone; unsurprisingly, applicants to the Pell Grant program soared by over 10% in the same period.[76] The administration should have been helping those college hopefuls get a break instead of slamming school doors in their faces.

One positive development was the bipartisan Miller/Petri Direct Loan Reward Act, introduced in May 2004, which would have encouraged schools to switch from the Federal Family Education Loan program offered by private banks, to the federal government's own Direct Loan program. By cutting out middlemen bankers, the switch was slated to save taxpayers billions of dollars, half of which would be given to schools in the first year of signing up (10% in subsequent years). Each school's windfall would have been specifically earmarked for need-based financial aid programs, such as Pell Grants.

Predictably, congressional Republicans blocked consideration of the Direct Loan Reward Act, and for good measure, the Republican-controlled 109th Congress doubled student interest rates and slashed $12 billion from student aid.

Things changed when the Democrats took over. A bill sponsored by Rep. George Miller (D-CA) and Sen. Edward Kennedy (D-MA) not only increased the maximum Pell Grant from $4,300 to $5,400 by 2012, but also halved the interest rate on new Stafford loans for low-income students. The bill, which Bush signed into law in September 2007, also cut $20 billion from private-lender subsidies.

A step in the right direction, but much more is needed.

Improving NCLB

> *"All who have meditated on the art of governing mankind have been convinced that the fate of empires depends on the education of youth. "* - *Aristotle*

Few disagree on the need for accountability in public education: schools, teachers and students must be encouraged to reach and maintain high standards. But while Bush's NCLB has obviously proven counterproductive to that lofty aim, the National Education Association (NEA) has some commonsense suggestions for reform. Its *Great Public Schools for Every Child Act* says that federal education programs under NCLB should be **fully paid for**, plus:[83]

- make testing practices less punitive
- provide increased support to disadvantaged students and school districts
- budget more funds for teacher training and development
- clarify the definition of "highly qualified"
- ensure that those receiving federal education funds observe federal laws

In October 2004, over 40 organizations (ranging from the Children's Defense Fund to the National Council of Churches) joined the NEA in telling Congress that NCLB has to change. The group's detailed recommendations covered everything from proficiency targets to teacher training and concluded, "Overall, the law's emphasis needs to shift from applying sanctions for failing to raise test scores to holding states and localities accountable for making the systemic changes that improve student achievement."[84]

Then in April 2005, the NEA and school districts in Michigan, Texas and Vermont filed a federal lawsuit saying that the Department of Education hadn't provided enough funding for NCLB. Months later, Connecticut became the first state to file a federal lawsuit based on the underfunded expenses of annual testing.

A watershed event followed in September 2005, when a major study by the Education Policy Studies Laboratory at Arizona State University and the Great Lakes Center for Educational Research and Practice determined that high-stakes testing may be doing more harm than good. The study concluded: "In light of the rapidly growing body of evidence of the deleterious unintended effects of high-stakes testing, and the fact that our study finds no convincing evidence that the pressure associated with high-stakes testing leads to increased achievement, there is no reason to continue the practice of high-stakes testing."[85]

Congress is currently considering a number of bills to improve NCLB. Let's hope US politicians assign the same urgency and funding priority to domestic education as they do to foreign wars.

Ten Easy Ways to Make a Difference Now

1. Get mobilized for public schools

Interested in a citizen-led fight to ensure that every child has the right to a high-quality education? At Give Kids Good Schools you'll find everything from "10 Questions to Ask Elected Officials" to an action page on improving US public education (www.givekidsgoodschools.org). Terrific site.

Also worth a visit:
> People for the American Way – Public Education
> (www.pfaw.org/go/public_education)
> Factsheets, reports, action tips – whatever resource you're looking for involving public education, you'll find here.

> Campaign for America's Future – Revitalizing Education
> (www.ourfuture.org/issues_and_campaigns/education/index.cfm)
> Another terrific possibility. Check out the First Day of School flash animation "highlighting what kids go through on their first day of school in a time of school budget cuts and unfunded mandates."

> Parents for Public Schools
> (www.parents4publicschools.com)
> "A national organization of community-based chapters working in public schools through broad-based enrollment." Check out the site's Parent Resources and Publications and see if there is a PPS chapter near you.

> Public Education Network
> (www.publiceducation.org)

"To build public demand and mobilize resources for quality public education for all children through a national constituency of local education funds and individuals." Sign up for PEN's weekly email NewsBlast and visit the site's Taking Action section, especially the list of "50 Things You Can Do to Support Public Education in Your Community." Here's the top ten:

1. Start a Local Education Fund (LEF), a community-based nonprofit organization whose mission is to create high-quality public schools for all children.
2. Read a book aloud to a child every month for a year.
3. Visit your local public school.
4. Sit on a committee to improve your public schools.
5. Lead a team of citizens to clean up litter on school grounds.
6. Vote in your local school board elections and on bond referenda.
7. Attend your local school board meetings.
8. Donate computer equipment to a local school.
9. Invite a student to dinner in your home.
10. Tutor or mentor a student.

2. Be an Education First voter

Another Great Public Schools' aim is for citizens to become Education First Voters. Not sure how your Senators and Representatives voted on public education? Just head to the Great Public Schools site and check out its state-by-state listing of Congress members' votes on major education bills over the past few years (www.greatpublicschools.org). And, as Great Public Schools recommends, let candidates know that "you will make their commitment to education a first order factor in deciding for whom to cast your vote."

Interested in learning more about the education bills Congress is considering right now? The National Education Association has a quick and easy way: head to their "Legislative Action Center" (www.nea.org/lac/index.html) and check your Congress members' voting records or learn about current educational legislation. Sign up for the weekly newsletter.

An additional online resource is the Committee for Education Funding (www.cef.org), which not only provides legislative information, but also monthly "Hotsheets" on educational news.

3. Students, know your rights and raise your progressive voices

The American Civil Liberties Union (ACLU) web site has a terrific section dedicated to student rights (www.aclu.org/studentsrights/index.html) which explains: "Constitutional violations are far too common in public schools across the country. Teachers and administrators have a responsibility to provide a safe environment for the students that is conducive to learning. They also have a responsibility to respect each student's individual rights. Simply put, students have rights too."

The ACLU's Students Rights covers everything from drug testing to dress codes to off-campus conduct, and also has information on Becoming an Effective and Efficient Activist. You can find multimedia options, interactive features and even desktop wallpaper and E-cards. Definitely worth a visit.

Are you interested in counteracting the $35 million which conservative groups spend each year "pushing their agenda on campuses"? So is Campus Progress (www.campusprogress.org), a multilevel project including a terrific web site, a speakers' bureau, various training programs, and support for student publications. Download free MP3s, and sign up for its mailing list.

Since your local high school might be providing students with more information about the military than about post-secondary education, check out the "National Youth and Militarism Program" of the American Friends Service Committee (AFSC). The group's many offerings include a terrific bulletin (available in both English and Spanish) entitled "Do You Know Enough to Enlist?". AFSC (www.afsc.org/youthmil/) supports grassroots educational and counter-recruitment efforts across the country and may be active near you.

Also visit Leave My Child Alone!, a comprehensive site offering everything from flyers to a database that lets you input a zip code and locate school district superintendents near you (www.leavemychildalone.org). The Military Free Zone (www.militaryfreezone.org) is another great site, offering concrete examples of recruiters' misleads as well as information on how to prevent the military from obtaining students' private records.

Here's a (partial...) list of other important student activist groups:
- Idealist On Campus
  (www.idealist.org/ioc/)
- Campus Activism Network
  (http://campusactivism.org)
- Gay, Lesbian and Straight Education Network
  (www.glsen.org)

- Campus Compact
  (www.compact.org)
- Student Press Law Center
  (www.splc.org)

4. Teachers, keep informed

The National Education Association (NEA) web site offers a goldmine of possibilities for teachers.

Is your school district thinking of privatizing? Then read *Send the Privateers Packing* (www.nea.org/neatoday/0409/coverstory.html, bottom of the page) for effective ways to "show school officials and community members the public employee difference."

Do you have health questions related to education? The NEA Health Information Network (www.nea.org/health/) has a variety of interesting possibilities ranging from "Asthma and Schools" to "Teen Pregnancy Prevention" to "Kids ACT! (Act to Control Tobacco)."

Want to keep up-to-date on No Child Left Behind/ESEA? NEA has links to everything, from government sites providing "fact sheets and overview of the legislation," to a database reporting on "where states stand in regard to ESEA." The NEA site also offers downloadable publications targeted at helping educators deal with No Child Left Behind/ESEA, such as a 177-page action guide covering areas such as funding flexibility and collective bargaining, not to mention a 31-page ESEA Toolkit which helps educators "work with state and local policy makers on ESEA implementation."

Just a few of the other publications on education-oriented topics available for free download at www.nea.org include:

> **NEA Today:** "The Association's flagship publication with a circulation of 2.7 million, explores today's toughest teaching challenges--and solutions. It's an important resource that NEA members look forward to receiving eight times a year--September to May."
> **This Active Life:** "*This Active Life* is a bimonthly magazine for NEA-Retired members. It spotlights retirees and their passions, highlights upcoming events, and raises issues of particular interest to retired members, such as travel, health, Social Security, and more."
> **Tomorrow's Teachers:** "*Tomorrow's Teachers* is an annual magazine for NEA student members. It offers a wealth of resources to those new to the teaching profession. Each issue offers help with job searches, provides classroom tips for surviving the first year in the classroom,

recommends strategies for parental and community outreach, and much more."

5. Parent power

Students whose parents participate in their educations have better attendance, get higher scores on tests, are less likely to abuse drugs/alcohol, and are more likely to both graduate and receive post-secondary education.[86]

For information on how to support your kids' academic achievement, check out the Just for Parents section of the American Federation of Teachers' site (www.aft.org) and its great brochures, many of which are available in both English and Spanish. Topics cover the gamut from "What Parents & Families Can Do at Home to Help Their Children Meet High Standards" to "Helping Your Child Become a Reader" and can be downloaded free of charge.

The National Coalition for Parent Involvement in Education (www.ncpie.org) offers an extensive database on resources for Parents and Families, gleaned from dozens of outside groups. The National Education Association's site is another important source of possibilities for parents, and its *Getting Involved in Your Child's Education* page (www.nea.org/parents) is filled with helpful tips as well.

The Parent Teacher Association (www.pta.org) has a slew of resources organized around the general categories of Student Achievement, Safety, Media Technology, and Health and Fitness. For example, under Student Achievement you can find advice on helping children with homework and test performance, along with articles such as "Making a Family Museum Visit Fun for Toddlers, Teens, and In-Betweens" and "Choosing Age-Appropriate Instruments and a Good Instructor." Also visit the PTA site's active Bulletin Boards.

6. Get some good news

Tired of dreary education news? Head over to The Center on Education Policy (www.cep-dc.org) and read its excellent report from August 2005 entitled "Do You Know the Latest Good News About American Education?." The report notes that, compared to twenty years ago, more Americans are finishing high school or college, the percentage of high school students finishing advanced math and science courses has increased and some test score gaps between white and minority students have decreased.

To learn more about positive legislative developments, visit the National Education Association's Success Stories page, where you'll see concrete examples of how "the pro-public education Congress YOU helped elect has been listening to your calls and e-mails" (at www.nea.org/lac/success.html). Recent successes include Congress passing budget resolutions providing $6 billion more for education than Bush requested, and the Senate passing an amendment to "make permanent the tax deduction for educators' out-of-pocket classroom supply expenses, increase it from $250 to $400, and extend it to cover professional development expenses."

For a good laugh, check out the satire of Pastafarianism. It all started in 2005, when Oregonian Bobby Henderson wrote an open letter to the Kansas School Board. Here's an excerpt:

"Let us remember that there are multiple theories of Intelligent Design. I and many others around the world are of the strong belief that the universe was created by a Flying Spaghetti Monster. It was He who created all that we see and all that we feel. We feel strongly that the overwhelming scientific evidence pointing towards evolutionary processes is nothing but a coincidence, put in place by Him.

"It is for this reason that I'm writing you today, to formally request that this alternative theory be taught in your schools, along with the other two theories. In fact, I will go so far as to say, if you do not agree to do this, we will be forced to proceed with legal action. I'm sure you see where we are coming from. If the Intelligent Design theory is not based on faith, but instead another scientific theory, as is claimed, then you must also allow our theory to be taught, as it is also based on science, not on faith."

Henderson's open letter (available at www.venganza.org) has evolved into an internet phenomenon and marketing bonanza with T-shirts ("I was touched by His Noodly Appendage"), mugs, posters and even a book. The site's a must-visit.

7. Rank your state

How does your state fund education? What percent does it provide to local schools, and how is the difference made up? Property taxes, personal income taxes, or something else? To find out more about your state, take a look at Education Trust's "The Funding Gap 2004 - Many States Still Shortchange Low-Income and Minority Students."[87]

To learn about making high-quality pre-kindergarten programs available for all kids, visit pre[K]now (www.preknow.org) and find out how your state stacks up.

It might come as a surprise, but there are over 14 million latchkey kids in the US, including 4 million kids in grades six to eight. Do you know what kinds of afterschool programs are available in your state? The nonprofit Afterschool Alliance (www.afterschoolalliance.org) offers an excellent state-by-state breakdown of the percentage of K-12 youth responsible for taking care of themselves after school hours, the number of kids supported by current afterschool programs (as well as the number that could be if NCLB were fully funded) and other related facts. An eye-opener.

8. Relieve student debt

In early 2006, the Republican-controlled Congress approved tax breaks for the rich, yet cut $12 billion from programs supporting students - which didn't make it any easier for those struggling to meet college costs. As the advocacy group Student Debt Alert (www.studentdebtalert.org) observes, almost two-thirds of four-year college grads have educational loans and three times more students graduate owing over $25,000 than did since the early 1990s.

The Student Debt Alert site offers information on grants and loans, as well as resources and action tips. There's a running Debt Clock showing the total federal student loan debt, a Student Debt Yearbook with real-life examples of students' financial struggles, and topic-related reports. Sign up for the Student Debt Alert campaign newsletter and visit the site's More Ways to Get Involved page; creative suggestions range from setting up a campus "debtors' prison," complete with fake weights students carry around the whole day, to putting up a "debt photo gallery" where students struggling with debt can post their personal stories.

9. Learn about educational disparities

If you'd like more information about racial and economic disparities in education, visit the Children's Defense Fund (www.childrensdefense.org) and read some of its many fact sheets under "Education and Youth Development." Some examples include, "The Road to Dropping Out: Minority Students and Academic Factors Correlated with Failure to Complete High School" and "Misidentification of Minority Youth in Special Education: Quick Facts." The annual CDF Action Guides are also a must-read, focusing on the topic of "how our nation can make more just choices to *truly* Leave No Child Behind and to hold ourselves and our leaders accountable for protecting children." Also check out the CDF Activist Toolkit.

While you're at it, read the Citizens' Commission on Civil Rights' June 2006 "Days of Reckoning: Are States and the Federal Government up to the Challenge of Ensuring a Qualified Teacher for Every Student?" (at www.cccr.org/DaysofReckoning.pdf). The report details how low-income and minority students often have less-qualified teachers than their peers, and it offers concrete ways to close the "Teacher Quality Gap."

Finally, if you'd like to learn about a more equitable model of funding education, then head over to www.100percentsolution.org and discover the idea of Weighted Student Funding. Become a signatory of the proposal to "allocate dollars directly to schools on a per-student basis" and make funding systems more flexible and transparent.

10. It takes a village

If you don't have kids and haven't attended school in decades, that doesn't mean you can't get involved in improving public education. You pay taxes, right? Stop by one of your local schools, or even visit a school on the "poor" side of town and then another on the "rich" side of town and make a comparison. For example, how do the facilities/course offerings differ? What's the racial composition of each school? The student-teacher ratio? The drop-out rate? Share your observations with your friends or with your community at the next town hall meeting. Write an opinion piece for your local paper. The more that educational issues are brought out into the open, the better.

Another way to get involved is through the Adopt-a-Classroom program (www.adoptaclassroom.com), which aims to counteract the fact that "teachers are spending an average of $800 of their own money each year just to meet basic classrooms needs." Adopt-a-Classroom enables you to make a tax-deductible contribution in the form of a merchandise credit which classroom teachers can use to order necessary items.

If you're up for taking an even more active role in your community's educational system, attend school board meetings or consider running for the board yourself.

Most of all, commit to being a lifelong learner. Education isn't only for kids. Have you always wanted to learn pottery? To speak another language? To sail a boat? Check out the offerings at your local city college or adult ed facility, and invest in your own development.

Mainstream Media

"I asked them the other day, would it be okay if I cut a 30-minute tape, a piece of propaganda, no questions, just here – here it is, here's 30 minutes of me talking. Please run it, not only across your airwaves but run it internationally, if you don't mind." - George W. Bush, discussing a request to the US press corps, November 2001 [1]

Americans are said to be the most entertained and least informed people in the world. A March 2006 survey by the McCormick Tribune Freedom Museum, for example, found that over 50% of US respondents could name at least two members of The Simpsons cartoon family, but only 25% could adequately describe the First Amendment of the US Constitution. More respondents could identify the three American Idol judges than could name three First Amendment rights.[2]

An effective democracy requires informed, engaged citizens - and the US mainstream media isn't exactly helping.

McMedia Monopoly

"We're not in the business of providing news and information. We're simply in the business of selling our customer's products." – Lowry Mays, CEO of Clear Channel [3]

Due to massive deregulation, a handful of corporate media giants have diversified their holdings into a tight web around the media. Vivendi can feature one of its Universal Music artists in its *Rolling Stone* magazine, then schedule appearances on USA Networks to solidify CD sales. And Disney can ask its Miramax division to block distribution of Michael Moore's *Fahrenheit 911* lest it anger the president's brother, Florida Governor Jeb Bush, thereby threatening lucrative Disneyworld tax breaks.

While media consolidation might at first seem like a boring wonky issue, at stake are localism, diversity and media competition, not to mention the strength of our very democracy. Think about it. If Big Monopoly Corporation (BMC) based in some far-away state owns your community's newspaper, not to mention its TV and radio stations, then you can kiss local news goodbye. You'll be watching the same dumb reruns as everyone else across the country whose market BMC controls, rather than learning about matters of interest to your state or community. BMC bosses in distant towns will be able to decide what content and opinions are suitable for your hometown viewing, and local reporters, journalists and editors will be out of jobs.

Here's how a Fox executive discussed the purchase of local stations in Tampa: "We paid $3 billion for these television stations. We decide what the news is. The news is what we tell you it is."[4]

That's where the Federal Communications Commission (FCC) should come to the rescue, but unfortunately, today's FCC seems more interested in protecting media conglomerates than the public interest.

F the CC[5]

Bush is only the latest in a string of presidents tolerating, if not encouraging, undemocratic developments in mainstream media. While Reagan oversaw the end of the Fairness Doctrine, which had required broadcast stations to give opposing voices airtime, Clinton supported a dramatic weakening of US telecommunications laws.

But Bush and his first FCC Chairman, Michael Powell, took media deregulation to unprecedented levels.

Speaking to a Las Vegas convention in 1998, Michael Powell (son of former Secretary of State Colin Powell) said the FCC should handle "matters that predominantly involve the competing interests of the industry,"[6] and the same glaring screw-the-consumer mentality characterized Powell's ensuing reign as FCC chairman.

Powell set off alarm bells in late 2002 when he announced that the FCC would be looking at media ownership rules, specifically the consolidation of ownership in local markets across the country. Just one of the proposals would have allowed a single corporation to own the daily newspaper, up to eight radio stations and as many as three television stations in the same community. Not surprisingly, a full 13,000 groups and individuals met the FCC's February 2003 deadline to submit their ideas on the proposed deregulation, and the response was overwhelmingly negative.

That's where Powell ended the debate. He dismissed opposition by scheduling only one public hearing, and seemed ready to just ram the changes through.

But then a curious thing happened. Groups as diverse as the National Rifle Association and the National Organization for Women united in a groundswell of popular opposition to the proposed changes. Unions were concerned about job losses, conservatives feared media consolidation would lead to more sex and violence on television, and liberals were still reeling from the major networks' shoddy reporting on Iraq.

In early June 2003, the proposed media ownership changes came up for a vote among the five FCC Commission members, and the results were predictably split along party lines: Powell and his two Republican allies voted for deregulation while the two Democrats voted against. In short, big-business-driven media consolidation had won.

Since Powell and other Federal Communications officials had held closed-door meetings with broadcast honchos a whopping 71 times in the vote's run-up, meeting with major consumer groups only five times during the same period, the victory was no surprise. Just a month after the FCC decision, however, the House of Representatives voted 400 to 21 to roll back the new ownership cap, and months later, the Senate used a special procedure to repeal all of the new regulations, thereby putting deregulation on hold until it came up for debate again later.

Another nail in the coffin of Powell's big plan came in June 2004, a year after the original vote, when the 3rd US Circuit Court of Appeals in Philadelphia blocked implementation of the FCC's new rules on grounds that they lacked "reasoned analysis."

While Powell lost credibility with his media consolidation push, Janet Jackson's 2004 Super Bowl "wardrobe malfunction" gave him a new calling as the nation's self-appointed Prude Czar. How ironic that while he was ready to toss out regulation of media-ownership, Powell jumped at the chance to regulate Ms. Jackson's nipple. His commission slapped a record $550,000 fine on CBS for the breast display, $27,500 for each of the 20 CBS-owned television stations.

Testifying to Congress in February 2004, Powell warned of a "dramatic rise in public concern and outrage about what is being broadcast," noting that indecency complaints had jumped from 350 in 2001 to 14,000 in 2002 – and then to a full 240,000 complaints in 2003.[7]

What Powell didn't tell Congress, however, was that 99.8% of the indecency complaints the FCC received in 2003 were filed by *one* conservative activist group - the Parents Television Council. Since the FCC depends on complaints to initiate indecency proceedings, numbers count. But it's debatable whether the opinions of one conservative activist group should be enough to censor broadcast programming for the entire country.

Nonetheless, Powell continued his crusade, leveling indecency fines topping $7.7 million in 2004, whereas they'd reached only $48,000 the year before he took over at the FCC.[8] In all fairness, however, Powell's FCC alone can't be blamed for the First Amendment rollback. Congress also got into the act, with the House and Senate voting to increase the maximum indecency penalty from $27,500 per incident to between $275,000 and $500,000.

When the embattled Powell finally stepped down as chairman of the FCC in early 2005, he was replaced by Kevin Martin, a trusted Bush ally. Before being appointed to the FCC in 2001, Martin had been general council for Bush's 2000 Presidential bid and was also on the Bush-Cheney transition team. Martin's wife used to be an aide for Dick Cheney and currently serves as a Deputy Assistant to Bush.

As expected, Martin's FCC has focused on relaxing media ownership rules and favoring corporate demands over the public interest - for example, by pushing to loosen regulations so that a company could own a newspaper and multiple radio and television stations in a single city.

As Congressman Maurice Hinchey (D-NY) noted in a late-October 2007 protest rally before FCC hearings aimed at speeding up deregulation: "Chairman Martin's efforts to curtail debate and quickly advance a media consolidation proposal raise numerous warning signs that he wants to further shrink an already limited diversity of opinion found among American news outlets. His expected plan is the exact opposite of what is needed in this country."[9]

What Liberal Media?

> "I've gotten balanced coverage, and broad coverage - all we could have asked. For heaven sakes, we kid about the 'liberal media,' but every Republican on earth does that." - conservative pundit Pat Buchanan [10]

> "The liberal media were never that powerful, and the whole thing was often used as an excuse by conservatives for conservative failures." - William Kristol, conservative commentator [11]

As if stifling monopolies and a corporate-driven FCC weren't enough, the far-right has set up its own multi-billion dollar propaganda creation and distribution system which funds think tanks, creates jargon/talking points and supplies conservative media personnel with a real-time "message of the day."[12] The sad truth is that since progressives are light years behind in understanding how the media work, far-right perspectives rule the airwaves.

Terrible Tomlinson

Back in the '70s, Nixon's corrupt and paranoid regime was so intolerant of negative press that it stacked public broadcasting's oversight board with administration-friendly hacks bent on quashing dissent.

Those were the good old days. With another corrupt and paranoid regime in the White House today, the nation's Corporation for Public Broadcasting (CPB) is yet again under attack, victim of what one senior Federal Communications Commission official referred to as an "orchestrated ... right-wing coup."[13]

The CPB is a non-profit group, which was set up in the '60s to ensure that public broadcasting remained vital, fair and insulated from politics. It receives just under $400 million in federal money each year to support the nation's roughly 700 public radio stations and 350 public television stations, and is a crucial source of funding for the Public Broadcasting System (PBS), National Public Radio (NPR) and other program developers and producers.

Sounds great in theory, but the Bush administration has stacked the CPB Board of Directors with right-wing supporters, and the Board's reactionary former Chairman, Kenneth Y. Tomlinson, did his best to turn US public broadcasting into an extension of Fox.

A former editor-in-chief of *Reader's Digest*, who supported the Republican Steve Forbe's 1996 presidential run, Tomlinson used his stint as CPB Board Chairman, from 2003 to 2005, for a rampage against what he saw as a liberal bias in public broadcasting. He refused, for example, to renew the contract of the CPB Chief Executive, Kathleen Cox, replacing her with Kenneth Ferree, a former FCC head who supported weakening media-ownership regulations. In April 2005, Ferree admitted to *Times Magazine* that he rarely watched PBS, and didn't listen to much NPR either because his motorcycles ("real cruisers") were "stripped down deliberately to look cool" and had no radio access.[14]

While it's pathetic that the CEO of our nation's public broadcasting was more interested in looking cool on his cruiser than in listening to NPR or watching PBS, Feree's replacement was arguably even worse: Tomlinson filled the position with Patricia Harrison, a former co-chair of the Republican National Committee who openly supported the production and dissemination of government-produced "news" programs.

Tomlinson also joined Bush's senior advisor Karl Rove in killing legislation that would have required roughly half of the CPB's Board of Directors to have local TV or radio experience. As a result, a handful of corporate hacks with negligible journalistic experience will continue making media decisions affecting the whole country.

Tomlinson's transgressions at the CPB could fill a book. Some doozies:

- At the Bush administration's request, he hired the White House Office of Global Communications Director, Mary Catherine Andrews, to set up the CPB's new ombudsman office. Andrews ended up working at both the White House and the CPB for some time, but dismissed the blatant conflict of interest by saying she "was careful not to work on this project during office hours during my last days at the White House."[15] Sure, that clears up any questions of political bias alright.
- Tomlinson wanted an ombudsman office to "review the content of public radio and television broadcasts" and he told NPR executives that two ombudsmen would be appointed, one conservative and one liberal. In fact, both of the ombudsmen appointed in April 2005 have conservative backgrounds: William Schulz is a hard-core rightwing stalwart, and the supposed liberal, Ken Bode, is a former fellow at a conservative think tank, who endorsed Indiana's Republican gubernatorial candidate in the 2004 election. Bode had also been booted off his job at a PBS talk show, and could feasibly bear a grudge against the organization.[16]
- The CPB is supposed to keep its nose out of programming decisions, yet appointed Michael Pack - a conservative with links to Lynne Cheney - as Senior Vice President, Television Programming. Pack's former projects included "Inside the Republican Revolution: The First Hundred Days."[17]
- Tomlinson is a big fan of the reactionary Fox News, even telling the CPB Board that a Fox News anchor should be invited to "talk to public broadcasting officials about how to create balanced news programming."[18] Tomlinson ended a May 2005 Fox News interview by telling notorious host Bill O'Reilly "We love your show."[19]

Tomlinson's overriding obsession with a liberal bias was not backed up by the general public. A poll he commissioned in 2002 showed strong popular support for public broadcasting; undeterred, Tomlinson commissioned yet another poll in 2003 and got similarly favorable results. In fact, the later poll indicated that a full 80% of Americans had a positive opinion about public broadcasting. Additionally, PBS was seen as a more trustworthy news source than ABC, CBS, NBC, CNN and Fox.[20]

Very impressive results, yet Tomlinson sat on them, and in November 2004, he told a large meeting of public broadcasting officials that they should make sure their programming is *more in line with the Republican mandate*.[21] Tomlinson dismissed the ensuing outcry by saying his remarks were meant for fun.

Public broadcasting's conservative slant

When progressive talk-radio network Air America was launched in April 2004, right-wing commentators had a field day complaining that since National Public Radio (NPR) was already broadcasting a liberal perspective, introducing another network was overkill. But how liberal is NPR, really? And for that matter, how representative of the American public is its national public radio?

Launched in 1971, NPR was billed as an alternative radio network that would "promote personal growth rather than corporate gain" and "speak with many voices, many dialects."[22] If only.

NPR currently reaches 26 million listeners each week on 860 affiliated stations, and remains a favorite for those seeking an alternative to mindless chatter. But a June 2004 study found NPR doesn't exactly live up to its original lofty expectations.

The media-watch group Fairness and Accuracy in Reporting (FAIR) looked at every source quoted on four NPR news shows in June 2003, and discovered that US national public radio showed a clear bias towards elites and white, male Republicans. Some of FAIR's findings:[23]
- Three Republicans were quoted for every two Democrats
- Elite sources such as government officials, professional experts and corporate representatives dominated NPR's guest list
- When non-elite sources appeared, they tended to be unnamed "people in the street" giving one-sentences soundbites
- Corporate representatives appeared 23 times more often than labor representatives
- Women were only 21% of the sources used, and that figure tumbled further for cited experts
- Representatives of conservative think tanks outnumbered liberal think tank reps four to one
- Less than one quarter of NPR's regular commentators were women
- Only 20% of NPR's commentators were non-white, with Latinos and Native Americans particularly underrepresented

This trend has not abated. In late 2005, NPR ombudsman Jeffrey Dvorkin revealed that for 2005, NPR had strongly favored experts from right-wing think tanks over those from the left ("The score to date: Right 239, Left 141").[24]

So much for "many voices, many dialects." But even with NPR's conservative leanings, Tomlinson and other CPB board members have seemed determined to kill off public radio's ability to report the news at all.

For example, CPB board member Gay Hart Gaines (appointed by Bush during a December 2003 recess) has pushed for major programming changes, supposedly on the basis of a conversation she once had with a taxi driver. Gaines' bio describes her as "an interior designer by training ... long active in Republican Party affairs ... a trustee of the Palm Beach County Republican Party, and a board member and president of the Palm Beach Republican Club." And this woman is making programming decisions for the whole country.

Another recess appointment was Cheryl Halpern, whom the *New York Times* has described as "a former chairwoman of the Republican Jewish Coalition and leading party fund-raiser whose family has business interests in Israel." Due to Halpern's complaints, Tomlinson reportedly considered monitoring whether NPR's news coverage was sufficiently positive towards Israel.[25]

The CPB board has even recommended that NPR funding be redirected away from newscasts and towards music programs instead.

Significantly, Tomlinson was the director of Voice of America (VOA) for two years during the Reagan administration. VOA is the US government's propagandist radio station, broadcasting to over 100 million people worldwide, and is restricted in many countries due, at least in part, to its biased nature. VOA is administered through the US Broadcasting Board of Governors, which in a clear conflict of interest, Tomlinson happened to head in tandem with running the CPB.

It should then come as no surprise that Tomlinson fought against allowing NPR to be broadcast in the large Berlin market, favoring a plan to feature VOA broadcasts instead.

If right-wing propaganda masquerading as news is good enough for the folks back home in the US, it's apparently good enough for people abroad too.

Putting the BS into PBS

Just like NPR, US public television has been under fire from Tomlinson and other right-wingers seemingly determined to remake public programming in their own reactionary image – or else destroy it altogether.

During his stint at the CPB, Tomlinson particularly targeted PBS veteran Bill Moyers, and even surreptitiously monitored his popular series for liberal bias. Specifically, in late 2003, Tomlinson paid a consultant over $10,000 to conduct a three-month study of *Now with Bill Moyers* (as well as the *Tavis Smiley* show and NPR's *Diane Rehm*), labeling guests as either "liberal" or "conservative," and calling those who raised questions about Bush "anti-administration." Tomlinson kept the study secret, even telling Sen. Byron Dorgan (D-ND) that another CPB executive had approved the contract, when in fact Tomlinson had approved it himself. Sen. Dorgan later noted, "It's pretty scary stuff to judge media, particularly public media, by whether it's pro or anti the president. It's unbelievable."[26]

Tomlinson also cited the need to balance *Now* with a conservative program as justification for his pet project called *The Journal Editorial Report* – a showcase for the *Wall Street Journal*'s right-wing editorial board. Tomlinson even helped secure the $5 million in corporate financing needed to get the *Journal*'s conservative commentary program off the ground.

Remember that CPB has a mandate to keep clear of any specific programming decisions, and to insulate PBS from outside political pressure. In other words, Tomlinson was way out of line.

The conflict between CPB and PBS came to a head in early 2005, when the corporation threatened to withhold roughly $26 million in funding unless PBS changed its journalism guidelines to make "objectivity and balance" legally enforceable. PBS refused, arguing that such a move would not only limit its First Amendment rights, but also hand CPB undue editorial control over public television. An agreement was eventually reached, but many saw Tomlinson's attempt to wield funding cutbacks as a sign of things to come.

Things got so bad that by May 2005, two Democrat congressmembers (Wisconsin's David Obey and Michigan's John Dingell) called for an investigation into CPB's interference into PBS. Tomlinson welcomed the investigation, noting: "Public broadcasting is a very fragile institution. If I cause liberals to lose support for public broadcasting, I will have done the system harm."[27] But you've got to wonder if that was the administration's aim all along: use Tomlinson to kill off one of the last vestiges of non-corporate news reporting, and drive liberals away from public programming, all in one fell swoop.

Tomlinson kept quiet in June 2005 when a congressional subcommittee voted to slash funding for both the CPB and public broadcasting. He kept quiet even though children's educational programming (such as the beloved *Sesame Street)* was slated to lose a full $23.4 million. He kept quiet even though the subcommittee further voted to **end CPB funding** within two years.

Finally, in November 2005, the CPB's inspector general released a damning report accusing Tomlinson of violating "statutory provisions and the Director's Code of Ethics."[28] The report criticized Tomlinson in a number of areas, including:

- using "political tests" in recruiting top executives
- being too heavily involved in bringing right-wing programming to public television (specifically, the *Wall Street Journal's* spin-off show)
- not properly informing the CPB Board about hiring a consultant to review programming, and signing the consultant's contract without Board authorization

Under pressure, Tomlinson left the CPB and was replaced as Chairperson by the Republican fund-raiser Cheryl Halpern. Former Republican National Committee co-chair Patricia Harrison became CPB President and CEO, while Gay Hart Gaines, the interior designer "long active in Republican Party affairs," became vice chair. In late December 2006, Bush appointed conservative writer Warren Bell to the CPB Board as well.

In other words, same old biased nonsense. Tomlinson may be gone but inequity still reigns at the CPB, and public broadcasting remains in danger as a result.

Bush-league Propaganda

> *"See, in my line of work you got to keep repeating things over and over and over again for the truth to sink in, to kind of catapult the propaganda."* - George W. Bush, 2005 [29]

It's not just private and corporate money paying for far-right control over the nation's media. US taxpayer dollars are also funding propaganda.

In early 2005, news surfaced that journalists were shilling for the Bush administration. For example, Armstrong Williams, a syndicated columnist and radio commentator, admitted to having received a stunning $240,000 from the US Education Department to promote Bush's educational plan. Williams later claimed that he hadn't realized it was a conflict of interest to take the cash.

Significantly, a subsequent Education Department probe into the affair concluded that the kickback to Mr. Williams represented "poor management decisions" because "the department paid for work that most likely did not reach its intended audience and paid for deliverables that were never received."[30]

In other words, the Education Department didn't care about the ethical implications of funding propaganda; it was more concerned about not having gotten enough bang for its buck.

Weeks after the Armstrong Williams revelation, conservative "family values" media commentator Maggie Gallagher fessed up to getting $21,000 from the Health and Human Services Department to promote the administration's marriage initiative. Gallagher also had reportedly received an additional $20,000 payment from the Justice Department.

Like Williams, Gallagher was shocked, shocked that critics proceeded to question her journalistic integrity for having taken the cash. Gallagher defended herself in an article posted on her web site, insisting, "If this is the ethical standard, it is an entirely new standard." She added, "The real truth is that it never occurred to me. On reflection, I think... I should have disclosed a government contract... I would have, if I had remembered it."[31]

Can you imagine not remembering receiving a $21,000 check from the government?

One day after the revelations about Gallagher surfaced, yet another conservative commentator was found with his hand in the government till: Michael McManus, author of a syndicated column entitled "Ethics & Religion," was found to have accepted $10,000 from the Department of Health and Human Services for subcontracting work promoting Bush's marriage program. And the guy specializes in ethics...

No doubt these cases represent just the tip of the iceberg when it comes to the administration's covert propaganda program. But glaring ethical implications aside, it's pretty damn sad that the Bush administration has to pay people just to say nice things about its crappy programs.

Snow job or blow job?

The most stunning case of shilling for the administration came from a gay male prostitute and tax evader using a fake name who was given access to White House press conferences for almost two years.

Full frontal shots of James D. Guckert were featured on web sites with names ranging from Hotmilitarystud.com to Workingboys.net; his services were advertised at a rate of $200 per hour (or $1,200 for a weekend) and descriptions included "8 inches cut" and "AGGRESIVE, VERBAL, DOMINANT TOP, I DON'T LEAVE MARKS....ONLY IMPRESSIONS."[32]

Just the guy you want in White House press conferences.

In early April 2003, Hotmilitarystud Guckert changed his name to Jeff Gannon (he probably thought it rhymed with cannon...) and started working as a "journalist" at Talon News, a Republican-front news outfit, which had opened just a week earlier.

Amazingly, Guckert/Gannon was given press passes to White House briefings a staggering 196 times over the next two years – and even 39 times on days there were no press briefings. Makes you wonder what services he was providing, journalistic or otherwise, during those 39 visits.

Apart from having non-existent press credentials, there was also the untidy fact that Guckert owed the state of Delaware over $20,000 for unpaid personal taxes from 1991-1994. Given security considerations, you might ask why this guy was allowed into the White House at all.

The answer is simple: like any effective "Workingboy," Guckert/Gannon gave the client what it wanted, and in this case, it meant deflecting attention away from serious issues by delivering pro-administration statements masquerading as questions. Here's a sampler from "Gannon" during White House press conferences:[33]

> February 10, 2004: "Since there have been so many questions about what the President was doing over 30 years ago, what is it that he did after his honorable discharge from the National Guard? Did he make speeches alongside Jane Fonda, denouncing America's racist war in Vietnam? Did he testify before Congress that American troops committed war crimes in Vietnam? And did he throw somebody else's medals at the White House to protest a war America was still fighting?"

> April 1, 2004: "I'd like to comment on the angry mob that surrounded Karl Rove's house on Sunday. They chanted and pounded on the windows until the D.C. police and Secret Service

were called in. The protest was organized by the National People's Action Coalition, whose members receive taxpayer funds, as well as financial support from groups including Theresa Heinz Kerry's Tides Foundation."

May 10, 2004: "In your denunciations of the Abu Ghraib photos, you've used words like 'sickening,' 'disgusting' and 'reprehensible.' Will you have any adjectives left to adequately describe the pictures from Saddam's rape rooms and torture chambers? And will Americans ever see those images?"

White House spokesperson: "I'm glad you brought that up, Jeff, because the President talks about that often."

It's curious that Gannon's ascent to White House press corps stardom perfectly coincided with the administration's sleazy leak about the identity of a covert CIA operative.[34]

As you might recall, in early July 2003, Ambassador Joseph Wilson shot down one of the justifications for invading Iraq when he revealed that the administration had used forged documents to "prove" Hussein bought uranium yellowcake from Niger. White House retribution was swift and brutal: the very next week, conservative columnist Robert Novak wrote an article claiming that Wilson's wife, Valerie Plame, was a CIA operative and that she had been responsible for Wilson's having received the assignment of going to Niger in the first place.

"Outing" an undercover operative is illegal, and Novak's article put Plame – not to mention all of her covert contacts - in great danger. Unsurprisingly, the CIA filed a crime report with the Department of Justice, demanding an investigation.

Intriguingly, the day after Novak's scandalous article was printed, a certain Jeff Gannon made his journalistic debut on the conservative *Free Republic* site, and just ten days later, jeffgannon.com went online. The timing is rather suspect, to say the least, since Gannon quickly provided cover for Novak, Rove and a White House reeling under the Plame fiasco.

As a sideline to this sleazy tale, the grand jury investigating the Plame leak threatened two journalists (Judith Miller of the *New York Times* and Matthew Cooper of *Time Magazine*) with jail time for not revealing their sources and Miller ended up serving 85 days. Significantly, administration lackey Robert Novak, who actually had made the leaked information public, was spared such a fate.

As for Gannon, after his true identity was revealed, he "resigned" from Talon News and blamed liberals for his woes ("So feared by the left it had to take me down"), insisting that other journalists "welcomed the refreshing perspective I brought to the briefings and respected my courage for asking the questions that I did."[35]

Gannon even expressed surprise at not having been invited to the annual White House Correspondents Dinner, held at the end of April 2005. One day before the event, he told the *New York Post*, "It seems to me to be odd to exclude the one person who has brought more attention to the White House press corps than anyone else in years. Probably many who would want to extend such an invitation already assume I will be in attendance."[36] Delirious to the very end.

But it's not really fair to single out Guckert/Gannon as being an embarrassing White House shill; the press corps is filled with others who fit the same description.

The ultimate punch line to the whole tawdry Guckert/Gannon affair, however, is that even though a male prostitute tax-evader using an alias was given White House access nearly 200 times, the mainstream media paid almost no attention. You'd think there might have been a story there somewhere.

Fake news reports

Let's say you're the news director of a small TV station, and budget cuts have left you understaffed and unable to produce enough reports for your daily programs. No problem! US government agencies are only too happy to provide you with "video news release" fillers complimenting the administration's programs.

In fact, as *The New York Times* reported in March 2005, at least 20 federal agencies had produced and released "prepackaged" TV news in the previous four years, and their segments had been broadcast on local stations, often without letting viewers know the governmental link.[37]

Paid public relations experts often pose as journalists on the pieces, offering little more than generic identification, such as "In Washington, I'm Karen Ryan reporting." Local reporters can do voice-overs of the narration as well, providing instant hometown credibility.

Government-produced news is a win-win prospect for many involved: public relations companies make millions from federal contracts to produce the "news," while local stations save money on programming. International news organizations and big US networks make a bundle distributing the releases, and perhaps most importantly, the administration gets its propaganda out.

It's just the viewers who get screwed.

Video news releases don't have to lie to be misleading; it's what they leave out of the coverage that counts. Here's an excerpt from a piece which ran in the spring of 2003, covering the US Arab community's reaction to the fall of Saddam Hussein's government:[38]

Iraqi American 1: We love the United States! We love America! They help us!
Iraqi American 2: Yes!
Reporter: In this Kansas City cafe, Iraqi Americans watch the historic events on TV.
Iraqi American 3: I'm very, very happy. I said, thank you, Bush. Thank you, U.S.A. I love Bush, I love U.S.A., because they do that for Iraqi people's freedom.

Couldn't ask for better PR than that. While independent media was reporting on Iraqi civilian casualties and the devastating implications of "Shock and Awe," the State Department was releasing this gung-ho, pro-Bush silliness.

And of course, the administration's prefabricated news releases haven't been limited to covering Iraq; in just one example, the Education Department released a segment supporting Bush's No Child Left Behind program, and even hired a private firm to rank how positively different news organizations portrayed Bush's educational program.[39]

The Ketchum Inc. PR company, for example, received a cool $700,000 of US taxpayer dollars to sell the Bush administration's crappy educational plan. It also received additional funding from the Department of Health and Human Services to produce "news" releases, broadcast by at least 40 stations, praising Bush's Medicare law.

In May 2004, the congressional General Accounting Office (GAO) watchdogs finally woke up and ruled that Bush & Co.'s Medicare "news" releases were both biased and illegal. The GAO found that the segments had "notable omissions and weaknesses," were "misleading as to source," and violated federal law by using taxpayer funds for propaganda not authorized by Congress.[40]

The administration's response was predictable; it told government agency heads *just to ignore the GAO ruling* and to continue producing "news" releases at will.

For its part, the FCC has largely ignored the fake news fiasco, but under public pressure, in September 2007 finally leveled fines against Comcast for airing fake video news releases on one of its channels. Small step but in the right direction.

The upshot is that if you rely on television for your news, then expect an increasingly steady diet of Bush administration propaganda masquerading as neutral reporting. But it might be hard to tell the difference; as Karen Ryan, the reporter who fronted for many of the administration's propaganda pieces told the *New York Times*, public relations and journalism today are "almost the same thing" anyway.[41]

You can also take bitter solace in the fact that the US government is spreading fake news in other countries too. In December 2005, the *New York Times* reported that the Pentagon was not only paying a Washington-based public relations firm to get pro-US articles into Iraqi newspapers but also handing out monthly stipends to supportive Iraqi journalists.

While the administration claims to be spreading democracy across Iraq, it appears to be spreading propaganda instead.

Banging the War Drum on Cue

> *"Naturally the common people don't want war; neither in Russia, nor in England, nor in America, nor in Germany. That is understood. But after all, it is the leaders of the country who determine policy, and it is always a simple matter to drag the people along, whether it is a democracy, or a fascist dictatorship, or a parliament, or a communist dictatorship. Voice or no voice, the people can always be brought to the bidding of the leaders. That is easy. All you have to do is to tell them they are being attacked, and denounce the pacifists for lack of patriotism and exposing the country to danger. It works the same in any country."* - Herman Goering at the Nuremberg trials [42]

All the news not fit to print

In late May 2004, the New York Times (NYT) ran a quiet apology regarding its pre-invasion coverage of Iraq. At issue were six NYT articles (from

October 2001 to April 2003) dealing with alleged Iraqi terrorist training camps, hidden weapons facilities and the supposed connection to Al-Qaeda. The muted apology noted:[43]

> "The problematic articles varied in authorship and subject matter, but many shared a common feature. They depended at least in part on information from a circle of Iraqi informants, defectors and exiles bent on 'regime change' in Iraq, people whose credibility has come under increasing public debate in recent weeks ... Complicating matters for journalists, the accounts of these exiles were often eagerly confirmed by United States officials convinced of the need to intervene in Iraq. Administration officials now acknowledge that they sometimes fell for misinformation from these exile sources. So did many news organizations — in particular, this one."

The *NYT*'s mea culpa is interesting for a number of reasons, not least of which is the editors' admission that they "fell for" blatant misinformation simply because the administration had backed it up. One would think a seminal newspaper such as the *NYT* would have shown more journalistic independence.

Also indicative is the fact that the *NYT* buried this mea culpa on page A10, even though many of the offending articles cited had appeared on Page A1.

It's additionally intriguing that this apology came just a week after neo-con darling Ahmad Chalabi (cited in the article as "a favorite of hard-liners within the Bush administration") was demoted by his Pentagon handlers; makes you wonder if the *NYT* would still be printing Chalabi's lies if he hadn't fallen from grace with the administration.

To the *New York Times'* credit, however, a number of other media outlets were also guilty of acting like pro-war cheerleaders before the invasion of Iraq. They were also bamboozled by Chalabi, whose Iraqi National Congress (INC) received roughly $18 million in US funds between 1998 and 2003, ostensibly to spread pro-American propaganda in Iraq. Instead, the group appears to have focused on spreading pro-war propaganda in the US.

Here's how it worked. As early as October 2001, Chalabi began introducing prime Iraqi contacts (such as Iraqi secret service agents and a former captain in Hussein's army) to high-powered journalists working for major US publications such as the *Washington Post* and the *New York Times*. These Iraqi sources, which the Bush administration backed up as being credible, told chilling stories about everything from Hussein's terrorist training camps to his WMD stockpiles. Major newspapers ran with the informers' stories, which the administration and smaller newspapers later parroted, using the larger paper as a credible source.[44]

It later turned out that most of Chalabi's informers, many of whom the Bush administration had vouched for, were in fact bogus liars bent on getting the American public primed for an invasion of Iraq. The ultimate irony, of course, is that US taxpayer dollars paid the INC to provide US citizens with pro-war propaganda.

Now, for the punch line – although warned to keep its propagandizing out of the US, the INC sent a memo to the Appropriations Committee in June 2002, bragging that their group had been responsible for a full 108 media reports on Hussein's terrorism and WMD. Dumb move, because Congress' General Accounting Office (GAO) used that memo to start a probe into the INC's dealings, looking into whether US taxpayer money was used to persuade US citizens to support the Iraq invasion.[45]

But you've got to wonder what took the GAO so long. Why didn't somebody publicize the INC's memo when it came out in June 2002? You would think that a written document detailing propaganda efforts to lead the US public into war would be significant enough to share with American citizens right away – especially *before* the proposed invasion.

Ready, aim... invade!

Most people remember the Department of Homeland Security's (DHS) *Ready Campaign* from duct tape jokes on Letterman, but there's a more sinister side that escaped public scrutiny.

Ever wonder about the timing of those ads? And who paid for them?

The *Ready Campaign* ostensibly prepared Americans for "potential terrorist attacks and other emergencies."[46] Its fact sheet, for example, provides tips on facing biological, chemical or nuclear attacks (how about this one: "Many sick or dead birds, fish or small animals are cause for suspicion").

But while planning for the *Ready Campaign* went back as far as May 2002, the TV and radio spots didn't start until February 2003 – roughly a month before the invasion of Iraq. By DHS estimates, over 113 million people saw or read about the campaign at launch, and over 1,700 related stories were generated in media outlets.[47]

Now consider these typical *Ready Campaign* messages:

- "Terrorism forces us to make a choice: We can be afraid, or we can be ready."
- "Every family in America should prepare itself for terrorist attack."
- "To ultimately be the victor in the war against terrorism, we need all Americans to be engaged."

How convenient that scary messages about apocalyptic attacks on US soil were aired just as the Bush administration was trying to drum up public support for an invasion of Iraq. And how helpful these "We can be afraid, or we can be ready ... Go, Go, GI Joe!" messages must have been in military recruiting.

The *Ready* hype was possible because of over $200 million in donated media support from radio, print and of course, television. In fact, the *Ready Campaign* received more free advertisement benefits than any other issue in 2003.

The upshot? The Ad Council worked with major media corporations and the DHS to flood distribution channels with free ads getting you *Ready* for attack, and vicariously it would seem, *Ready* for war.

Since fake stories planted in major newspapers and paranoia-inducing media spots weren't enough to keep the war drum beating indefinitely, however, new and creative methods were needed to win US hearts and minds over to an invasion of Iraq.

Non-stop media appearances of Bush administration members warning about Hussein's catastrophic and imminent threat helped, as did network newscasts' pro-war bias; even though most Americans didn't support an invasion of Iraq without United Nation approval, only 3% of the US sources on newscasts represented an anti-war perspective.[48]

Clear Channel, which at the time owned approximately one third of US radio stations, also performed its propaganda duties when some of its local stations across the country participated in pro-war rallies, thus raising doubts about the credibility of Clear Channel's news reporting on Iraq.

It's worth noting that Clear Channel had earlier added John Lennon's *Imagine* and Cat Stevens' *Peace Train* to the list of songs its 1,200 stations should not play - presumably because lyrics such as "Imagine all the people living life in peace" or "Everyone jump upon the peace train" would not promote the optimum fighting spirit for a nation heading to war. The fact that Stevens is a Muslim convert, now known as Yusuf Islam, may have also been a factor in getting his music banned by Clear Channel.

Once "Shock and Awe" started raining down on Baghdad, US media focused on aerial shots of cool laser-guided bombs and other video game fare. In contrast, many European broadcasters and print publications showed graphic images of maimed and killed Iraqi civilians. It's no wonder that surveys found sharp differences in the transatlantic level of public support for the war.

Then came the toppling of Hussein's statue in Fardus Square, a masturbatory moment for much of the US press. Comparisons were made to the fall of the Berlin Wall; Defense Secretary Rumsfeld called the statue's destruction "breathtaking."

But while US broadcasts showed a close-up action video of the statue being brought down, which seemed to indicate massive movement against Hussein in Iraqi streets, reality on the ground was quite different. A wide-angle shot of the same event[49] showed that the square and its surroundings were almost empty, save for US troops, international journalists and relatively few Iraqis. The square had been sealed off by US tanks, and a US military vehicle was used to tear down the statue. Pivotal moment or carefully orchestrated media event?

War Is Heck

> *"The U.S is losing the war in Iraq and is increasingly isolated politically in the Arab world, so what's its response? Blame the media...There are ways that the U.S. government could legitimately reduce the negative coverage it gets on Al-Jazeera. For instance, if President Bush wants Al-Jazeera to stop airing grisly footage of dead Iraqi civilians, as commander in chief he could order U.S. troops to stop killing them."* - Reese Erlich, print/broadcast journalist [50]

As the invasion dragged on and US troops started dying in large numbers, the Pentagon banned showing the homecoming of coffins for fallen soldiers. Body bags were given the sanitized name "transfer tubes" and Bush refused to attend even one funeral for dead service members, either out of gross insensitivity or else fear the image would not play well in the media. Misleads and euphemisms turned Jessica Lynch into a US propaganda tool, while other returning wounded veterans were simply ignored by the mainstream press.

The war's impact on Iraqis was rarely covered, and the US government refused to provide estimates for the number of civilians killed. In the words of Gen. Tommy Franks, who directed the Iraq invasion, "We don't do body counts."

Transfer tubes and body counts

An October 2003 survey found that most Americans held at least one of three mistaken beliefs about why the US had invaded Iraq in the first place:[51]
- "Weapons of mass destruction have been found in Iraq"
- "Clear evidence exists of links between Iraq and al Qaeda"
- "World public opinion favored the US going to war with Iraq"

And as might be expected, people's primary media source influenced their opinions about the war. For example, 80% of those relying on Fox held at least one of the three wrong beliefs, compared to 23% relying on PBS or NPR. Not surprisingly, 86% of those who held all three mistaken beliefs backed the war, compared with only 25% of those who believed none.

A second poll in early August 2004 found that even over a year after the fall of Hussein's government, a full 35% of the Americans polled wrongly thought that Iraq possessed WMD when the US invaded, and roughly half believed that Iraq was either directly connected to the 9/11 attacks or closely linked to al Qaeda.[52]

The Iraq invasion was unique in "embedding" journalists with US military troops, essentially forbidding press members to venture outside of their assigned units. According to *Los Angeles Times* reporter David Zucchino, embedded with the 101st Airborne, "access could be suffocating and blinding ... Often I was too close, or confined, to comprehend the war's broad sweep. I could not interview survivors of Iraqi civilians killed by U.S. soldiers or speak to Iraqi fighters trying to kill Americans. I was not present when Americans died at the hands of fellow soldiers in what the military calls 'frat,' for fratricide. I had no idea what ordinary Iraqis were experiencing. I was ignorant of Iraqi government decisions and U.S. command strategy."[53]

The Bush administration has done its best to keep the rest of us ignorant, too: after getting caught altering its web site (by changing "combat" was over in Iraq to "major combat") the White House changed its Iraq directories to prevent search engines from indexing and archiving material, thus making history easier to erase.[54]

Pentagon propaganda

Psychological operations (psy-ops) are common enough in today's "war on terror." Unfortunately, it seems that the Pentagon sometimes confuses the American public with the enemy.

In February 2002, Defense Secretary Rumsfeld bowed to critics and shut down the Pentagon's Office of Strategic Influence (OSI), set up after 9/11 to win hearts and minds abroad. Turns out the OSI was providing fake news to foreign journalists instead.

Significantly, the same government operative instrumental in setting up the OSI was widely thought to have used bogus intelligence reports to build a case for war against Iraq. Douglas Feith, the former undersecretary of defense for policy, had also earlier been suspected of passing classified information to Israel.

But in late 2004, the *Los Angeles Times* revealed what many had suspected all along: Rumsfeld's OSI actually hadn't gone out of business, only relegated its propaganda duties to other governmental offices. As the *Times* put it: "Although most of the work remains classified, officials say that some of the ongoing efforts include having U.S. military spokesmen play a greater role in psychological operations in Iraq."[55]

A classic case occurred in mid-October 2004, when a marine spokesperson indicated on CNN that US troops were beginning to enter the Iraqi city of Fallujah. CNN dutifully started reporting that the Fallujah offensive had begun (and other networks fell in line with the same story), but in reality, the US military didn't enter Fallujah until three weeks later. The earlier claim had only been a psy-ops ruse by the Pentagon to see how the news would affect resistance fighters on the ground in Fallujah.

The Defense Department has propagated a slew of other half-truths and misleads about Iraq as well; retired Air Force Colonel Sam Gardiner listed these examples in a September 2004 article for *Salon.com:* "We were told of an uprising in Basra -- it did not happen. We were told Iraqis had stolen U.S. uniforms to commit atrocities -- this was not true. We were told on White House and State Department Web sites that the Iraqi military had formed units of children to attack the coalition -- untrue. We were told of a whole range of agreements between the French and Iraq before the war over weapons -- false. We were told Saddam had marked a red line around Baghdad and that when we crossed it Iraq would use chemical weapons -- completely fabricated."[56]

The linking of military psy-ops with daily news is fast becoming systemic. At the order of a top US general, public affairs was joined with combat psy-ops into one "strategic communications office" in Iraq in the summer of 2004.[57] A 2004 study by the Defense Science Board suggested giving the National Security Council a similar strategic communications structure.

But blurring the distinction between military propaganda and public affairs carries great risks, not least of which is decreased credibility for troops on the ground. It also means the American public can easily be misled whenever it suits the Pentagon.

Take the case of Pat Tillman, the football star who turned down a lucrative professional contract to join the Army Rangers after 9/11. Tillman was killed by friendly fire in Afghanistan on April 22 2004 in a botched mission characterized by miscommunication and cover-up, but that harsh reality didn't surface until months later. Instead, the U.S. Army Special Operations Command issued a made-for-TV-movie story about Tillman's heroic battle against Taliban fugitives, even going so far as to award him a posthumous Silver Star for combat valor.

The truth was kept from Tillman's grieving widow and family – not to mention the stunned American public – until weeks after a nationally-televised memorial service for Tillman had taken place. As Tillman's father later put it, "After it happened, all the people in positions of authority went out of their way to script this. They purposely interfered with the investigation, they covered it up. I think they thought they could control it, and they realized that their recruiting efforts were going to go to hell in a handbasket if the truth about his death got out. They blew up their poster boy."[58] Tillman's mother added, "If this is what happens when someone high profile dies, I can only imagine what happens with everyone else."[59]

But the Defense Department hasn't limited itself to distorting news for mainstream media to report; the Pentagon now has its very own TV channel, which broadcasts 24-7 on a complimentary basis to 2.6 million members of the US Armed Forces and is additionally available on all stateside cable and satellite providers.[60] The Pentagon Channel features vetted propaganda such as an upbeat show called "Freedom Journal Iraq," and another called "Battleground Revisited," which features historic films from previous wars.

The Pentagon Channel has competition from the Military Channel, which beams into US homes courtesy of Discovery Communications International, and provides "access to military personnel and hardware, allowing viewers to experience and understand a world full of human drama, courage, innovation and long-held traditions."[61]

Yet there's something wrong when large media companies bend over backwards to help war-glorifying TV channels enter US homes. It's creepy enough to have networks solely devoted to military pursuits cropping up everywhere, but it also raises questions about the Pentagon's influence over other media outlets too.

Abroad, the Pentagon runs a number of web sites aimed at influencing public opinion, such as a Balkans site called *Southeast European Times*. The fact that 50 journalists free-lance for the Balkans site raises ethical questions once again about the administration's use of taxpayer dollars to fund propaganda. The additional fact that only journalists who "will not reflect discredit on the U.S. government" are hired, speaks volumes about both the slanted nature of the site's reporting, and a clear fringe benefit for the administration: dangling easy money in front of moonlighting local journalists might make them think twice before writing anything negative about the Bush administration in their day jobs.[62]

In other words, we're back to the "5 o'clock follies" - the Defense Department's ridiculed daily media briefings during the Vietnam War, which lost military messengers credibility for decades. The same fate seems inevitable once again, now that the Pentagon is pushing fake news and combat psy-ops onto the mainstream – and being aided and abetted by large media companies.

Lessons from Al Jazeera

Although Al Jazeera is only 11 years old, the Qatar-based television network already has enemies in both the White House and in various Middle Eastern governments.

Good for them.

Former Defense Secretary Rumsfeld called Al Jazeera's work "vicious, inaccurate and inexcusable,"[63] and former State Secretary Powell even suggested that US-Qatari relations were suffering because of the network – which has also been shut out of Saudi Arabia, Kuwait, Iran, Egypt, Sudan, and Iraq.

So what's all the fuss about? Dubious governments in the Middle East may not appreciate the network's poking around into their misdeeds, but why is the White House so peeved? After all, Bush has repeatedly called for democracy in the Middle East, and isn't an active media part of that?

Apparently not. The problems started in late March 2004, when US-led coalition authorities shut down a small newspaper called Al Hawza; Shiite cleric Moqtada al-Sadr used the newspaper's closing to incite protest over the occupation, and days later, four US military contractors were killed and mutilated in a guerrilla ambush.

In retaliation for the killings, US forces launched an assault on the al-Sadr stronghold town of Fallujah, and of course, embedded journalists were allowed nowhere near the vicinity. However, one intrepid reporter, Ahmed Mansour of Al Jazeera, was in Fallujah during the US attack, and his live images of the civilian casualties from the siege were simultaneously broadcast by Al Jazeera.

In other words, while folks at home in the US were watching Army generals in comfortable stateside network studios discussing the evil insurgents being targeted in Fallujah, the Arab world was seeing live footage of slaughtered Iraqi women and children.

As the siege developed into a bloody stand-off, the disparity of media coverage became even more dramatic. When CNN anchor Daryn Kagan interviewed Al Jazeera's editor-in-chief, Ahmed Al-Sheik, she didn't ask for updated information from the only network on the ground during the siege. Instead, Kagan attacked Al Jazeera's right to report civilian casualties, saying it "adds to the sense of frustration and anger and adds to the problems in Iraq, rather than helping to solve them." When Al-Sheik defended his network's reporting as "accurate," Kagan asked:[64]

> "Isn't the story, though, bigger than just the simple numbers, with all due respect to the Iraqi civilians who have lost their lives-- the story bigger than just the numbers of people who were killed or the fact that they might have been killed by the U.S. military, that the insurgents, the people trying to cause problems within Fallujah, are mixing in among the civilians, making it actually possibly that even more civilians would be killed, that the story is what the Iraqi insurgents are doing, in addition to what is the response from the U.S. military?"

In other words, the number of Iraqi civilians killed by the US military isn't really important. The big story is that Iraqis should blame themselves for being bombed.

Things got even more bizarre in an Al Jazeera interview with senior US military spokesperson Brig. Gen. Mark Kimmit, who accused the network of spreading lies as he insisted that only "armed insurgents firing on our troops" were being targeted in US air attacks. When the interviewer reminded him of live coverage showing "children and women killed by the missiles, not armed insurgents" Kimmit claimed Al Jazeera "looked at things differently."[65]

Well, if that's true then thank goodness for Al Jazeera. May it continue to look at things differently for years to come.

When US military and Iraqi forces attacked Fallujah once again in November 2004, they took no chances: they allegedly targeted medical facilities first, thereby prohibiting doctors from letting people know about the heavy casualties taking place. US and Iraqi forces destroyed an emergency health clinic and medical dispensary, then arrested doctors at Fallujah general hospital, confiscating their cell phones.[66]

The media was silenced too: Al Jazeera had already been booted out of the country, and the one unembedded reporter left in Fallujah, Abdel Kader Al-Saadi of Al-Arabiya, was arrested and detained until the November siege was over.[67] As a result, viewers across the world were reduced to watching glitzy "Battle for Fallujah" reports praising the military operation, while the ongoing atrocities remained hidden.

If its detractors had their way, Al Jazeera would be booted out of business altogether. The US has leaned heavily on Qatar to shut down the network, but to no avail: in little over a decade, the Al Jazeera network has expanded from an Arabic-language channel to multiple online and television offerings, with the Al-Jazeera English channel alone reaching 80 million households.

In other words, in spite of the Bush administration's resistance, at least one avenue for an open media in the Middle East is thriving.

s-Election 04

> "It is an obscene comparison - you know I am not sure I like it - but you know there was a time in South Africa that people would put flaming tyres around people's necks if they dissented. And in some ways the fear is that you will be necklaced here, you will have a flaming tyre of lack of patriotism put around your neck. Now it is that fear that keeps journalists from asking the toughest of the tough questions, and to continue to bore in on the tough questions so often. And again, I am humbled to say, I do not except myself from this criticism." - veteran CBS News anchor Dan Rather, May 2002 [68]

In a functioning democracy, a corruption-free voting system should be complemented by balanced media coverage of election events. The US 2004 election had neither.

The fact that TV stations raked in a record $1.6 billion for political ads in the 2004 election speaks volumes about both the money-grubbing nature of the US political system, and the sleazy way media companies benefit.

Face it: broadcasters don't pay a dime to use US public airwaves, so they shouldn't charge anything to run political ads either. With such an enlightened system (in place in many countries) every candidate could get equal time and voters could make decisions based on issues rather than on the strength of campaign coffers. The US, however, clings to a corporate-driven corrupt mess instead.

And just as media companies are loath to run bad press on their favored corporate sponsors, mainstream news shies away from spilling the goods on candidates who promise deregulation and other special favors later on.

Unfair, unbalanced and undemocratic

Thanks to Michael Moore's *Fahrenheit 911*, it's common knowledge that Bush's supposed win of the 2000 presidential race came when his own first cousin, a political advisor contracted by Fox News, officially called the race in Bush's favor.

Fox's stunning conflict of interest in assigning a candidate's first cousin to monitor election results was mirrored in the network's handling of then-Governor Bush during the presidential campaign. One particularly gag-inducing scene in Robert Greenwald's 2004 documentary on Fox News (*Outfoxed: Rupert Murdoch's War on Journalism*) featured Carl Cameron, Fox's chief political correspondent, shamelessly brown-nosing Bush before an interview. Here's an excerpt:[69]

Cameron: My wife has been hanging out with your sister.
Bush: Yeah. Good. [Laughs]
Cameron: ...been all over the state campaigning, and Pauline has been constantly with her.
Bush: Yeah, [?] is a good person.
Cameron: Oh, she's been terrific! To hear Pauline tell it, when she first started campaigning for you, she was a little bit nervous. But...
Bush: Hitting her stride?
Cameron: She doesn't need notes, she's going to crowds, and she's got the whole riff down.
Bush: She's a good soul.
Cameron: She's having fun, too.
Bush: She's a really good soul.
Cameron: All right, you guys ready? All right.
Bush: [Laughing] That's great.
Cameron: Here we go governor.
[**Bush** laughs]
Cameron: See? Little things that get disclosed.
Bush: I like that.

Cameron: [Serious voice] Thank you for joining us, sir.

Bush: [Serious voice] Yes, sir. Thanks, Carl, it's good to see you.

Cameron: Just a few days away from the convention, now...

A former Fox employee had this to say about Cameron: "At Fox they didn't care. The fact that the senior political reporter whose wife was actually campaigning for the Bush campaign at a time when this guy's covering them ... didn't even register."[70]

As biased as the 2000 campaign coverage had been, Fox stooped to new lows in 2004 when Carl Cameron fabricated quotes which he attributed to the Democrat contender, John Kerry. Amazingly, the phony quotes were posted on the Fox News web site in early October 2004 – just a month before voters headed to the polls. Here are some of Cameron's fake quotes attributed to Kerry:[71]

- "Women should like me! I do manicures."
- "Didn't my nails and cuticles look great? What a good debate!"
- "I'm metrosexual — [Bush's] a cowboy."

Can you imagine? A major news channel's chief election reporter tells outright lies focused on making the opposition candidate look like a prissy idiot, then his fabrications are posted as news! Heads should have rolled when the hoax was discovered.

But, of course, at Fox no such thing happened. A terse retraction (part of which read, "We regret the error, which occurred because of fatigue and bad judgment, not malice"[72]) ran instead. The upshot: Cameron remained on the election beat despite his clear bias against Kerry, and to this day enjoys top billing as Fox's man in the White House. Yet Fox calls itself "fair and balanced."

Another outrageous news practice exposed by Greenwald's documentary is that senior Fox executives have issued instructions to their news staff indicating the right (i.e. right-wing) way to approach important stories. Fox News senior vice president John Moody seems to have been especially prolific in handing down these autocratic edicts, which one former Fox commentator described as, "talking points instructing us what the themes are supposed to be, and God help you if you stray." Here are some examples of Moody's instructions to Fox News staff: [73]

- <u>June 3, 2003</u>: "Bush's political coverage and tactical cunning ar(e) (wo)rth noting in our reporting through the day."
- <u>April 22, 2004</u>: "If, as promised, the coalition decides to take Fallujah back by force, it will not be for lack of opportunities for the terrorists holed up there to negotiate. Let's not get lost

in breast-beating about the sadness of the loss of life. They had a chance."

- April 26, 2004: "Ribbons or medals? Which did John Kerry throw away after he returned from Vietnam. This may become an issue for him today. His perceived disrespect for the military could be more damaging to the candidate than questions about his actions in uniform."
- April 28, 2004: "[L]et's refer to the US marines we see in the foreground [of pictures coming out of Fallujah] as 'sharpshooters' not snipers, which carries a negative connotation."

Doesn't say much about Fox News' democratic spirit that a senior Fox executive was blatantly coaching news staffers about negative talking points regarding Kerry during the presidential campaign. It's also well known that Fox inundated its viewers with attractive photo-ops of candidate Bush, yet featured his rival Kerry much less frequently – and with unflattering camera angles at that.

Bulgegate

Arguably the least reported yet most important story around the presidential-candidate debates in 2004 was the mysterious bulge under Bush's jacket – which photographic evidence indicated was most likely a device enabling him to be silently cued on stage.

Ironically, Fox brought the issue to light by disregarding the White House's odd request for no rear shots of the candidates during the debates.

Almost immediately after the candidates left the stage at the first debate, photos of an unusual bulge under the back of Bush's jacket began crossing the internet. As the national media watchdog group Fairness and Accuracy in Reporting put it, "The suspicion that Bush had been getting cues or answers in his ear was bolstered by his strange behavior in that first debate, which included several uncomfortably long pauses before and during his answers. On one occasion, he burst out angrily with 'Now let me finish!' at a time when nobody was interrupting him and his warning light was not flashing. Images of visibly bulging backs from earlier Bush appearances began circulating, along with reports of prior incidents that suggested Bush might have been receiving hidden cues."[74]

Salon.com's subsequent story questioning whether Bush could have been wearing a cueing device caught the eye of Dr. Robert M. Nelson, a NASA scientist specializing in photo imagery. Dr. Nelson analyzed a digital still of the first debate and could clearly make out both a "significant T-shaped object in the middle of Bush's back and a wire running up and over his shoulder."[75]

And that's when the hammer fell: no major print publication was interested in the story, despite – or perhaps because of – its clear importance for the election.

Had voters learned that Bush blatantly cheated on the debates, they might have been less inclined to see him as the beacon of moral leadership he claimed to be. Yet the *Los Angeles Times*, the *Washington Post* and Dr. Nelson's local newspapers all passed on the story. The *New York Times* looked at Dr. Nelson's photographic enhancements, prepared a corresponding investigative report, and then killed it at the last minute.

Meanwhile, the White House was issuing flimsy and contradictory excuses for Bush's bulge (including the "badly tailored suit" theory) and labeling anyone asking questions a loopy conspiracy buff. Yet when Dr. Nelson analyzed rear-shot photos in the second and third debates, the same telltale cueing device and wire could be seen under Bush's coat.

Ultimately, only *Salon.com* and *Mother Jones* ran the photos – which means that a majority of US voters were kept in the dark about that critical story.

Necklacing Dan Rather

In a rare moment of candor in May 2002, veteran CBS news anchor Dan Rather told *BBC Newsnight*:[76] "What we are talking about here - whether one wants to recognise it or not, or call it by its proper name or not - is a form of self-censorship. It starts with a feeling of patriotism within oneself. It carries through with a certain knowledge that the country as a whole - and for all the right reasons - felt and continues to feel this surge of patriotism within themselves. And one finds oneself saying: 'I know the right question, but you know what? This is not exactly the right time to ask it'."

Little did Rather know that less than two years later, he'd be out of a job, largely for having asked the right question.

In September 2004, CBS's *60 minutes* ran a story on how Bush had ducked the Vietnam draft. The story actually had been broken way back in 1999 by Greg Palast and others at the UK's *Guardian* newspaper, and in 2003, Palast did a follow-up for *BBC Television* in which he produced "a confidential letter from Justice Department files" stating that Bush Sr. had helped Bush Jr. enter the Texas Air Guard instead of being sent to Vietnam.[77]

Yet despite the UK media coverage, no major US network had seriously looked into the questions regarding Bush's time in the National Guard.

But the September 2004 broadcast, which Dan Rather reported, made a huge error - it used some memos which hadn't been properly vetted. Republicans immediately produced evidence casting doubt on the disputed documents and the entire broadcast was discredited.

Which was highly convenient for Bush. The ensuing "Rather-gate" flap meant that for the rest of the election cycle, mainstream media shied away from irrefutable proof that the "War President" had ignored mandatory duty and been otherwise AWOL during his years in the Texas Air National Guard.

The online magazine *Salon.com* did some investigating, however, and came up with over 30 examples of how Bush had ignored regulations during his National Guard service – and how his superiors had covered for him. Here's a partial list:[78]

- Bush was supposed to serve in his Guard unit for five years after finishing pilot training, but only stayed for two.
- He failed to receive discharge orders from the Texas Air National Guard adjutant general.
- He failed to take the annual physical exam required of Guard members for a full 42 months.
- Bush's unit never informed the proper authorities at Randolph Air Force Base about his absenteeism.

Yet despite the long list of obvious indiscretions, Bush still claimed that while in the Guard, "I did everything [my superiors] asked me to do."[79]

CBS assigned what it called an "Independent Review Panel" to look into the *60 minutes* "Rather-gate" uproar, but the panel consisted of only two members, neither of whom could be seen as either impartial or representing the height of journalistic integrity: Dick Thornburgh, who had helped downplay the Exxon Valdez oil spill for Bush Sr., and Louis Boccardi, who as CEO of the Associated Press, had co-operated with gun-runner Oliver North and helped suppress the Iran-Contra scandal.[80]

The "Panel" released its results in early January 2005 and came to the conclusion that the *60 minutes* program had been unfair and misleading. Four executives were fired, and much to the delight of conservatives, Dan Rather volunteered to leave his long-term post as anchor of *CBS Evening News* in March 2005, months earlier than originally planned.

The chairperson of Viacom, CBS's parent company, even got into the act by subsequently endorsing Bush for president. Sumner Redstone told a global conference in September 2004, "... the Republican administration has stood for many things we believe in, deregulation and so on ... from a Viacom standpoint, we believe the election of a Republican administration is better for our company."[81]

Interestingly, the self-censorship of "patriotism" Rather had discussed on BBC in 2002 immediately went into effect at CBS following the Rather-gate blowout, when the network chose not to run a *60 Minutes* report critical of the administration's reasons for invading Iraq.

The White House must have been ecstatic over the uproar, and indeed, many suspect Karl Rove was behind leaking the questionable memos to CBS in the first place: In one fell swoop, "Rather-gate" eliminated any questions about Bush's service, took down CBS News, and struck fear into the hearts of other networks thinking about questioning the administration. Game, set, match.

Sinclair's stolen honor

Sinclair owns or controls roughly 60 stations, reaching almost a quarter of US homes, and its executives are big-time Republican donors and promoters.[82] The Group gained headlines in April 2004 when it forbade seven of its stations from running a "Nightline" segment covering US troops killed in Iraq, and Sinclair was back in the spotlight months later with its plan to go primetime with an anti-Kerry film entitled "Stolen Honor: Wounds that Never Heal."

The documentary, in which former POWs accuse Kerry of having lengthened the Vietnam War through his anti-war activities, was scheduled to pre-empt regular programming just days before the November 2 election, but when news about the program leaked, condemnation was swift. Viewers were outraged and media analysts started complaining about the consolidation and deregulation which had allowed Sinclair to control so many markets in the first place. Advertisers went running, sending Sinclair's stock price into a tailspin. All in all, it took roughly ten days of controversy surrounding Sinclair's proposed showing of "Stolen Honor" for the Group to back down and pull the program.

The bitter irony, of course, is that none of Bush & Co.'s downright lies leading the US public into the Iraq invasion ever led to panels, firings or any other disciplinary measures for that matter. And even though the vast majority of mainstream news reports propagated the administration's misleads, they suffered no clear consequences.

In Rather's May 2002 appearance on *BBC Newsnight* he said, "I worry that patriotism run amok will trample the very values that the country seeks to defend... In a constitutional republic, based on the principles of democracy such as ours, you simply cannot sustain warfare without the people at large understanding why we fight, how we fight, and have a sense of accountability to the very top."[83]

And perhaps that's exactly why Rather was necklaced: If the US public found out that its self-proclaimed "war president" had avoided Vietnam through his family's high-powered connections, and then proceeded to make a mockery of his National Guard service, it would be understandably angered. And if the US public found out that the administration's justifications for invading Iraq were based on a pack of lies, it might demand some accountability at the very top.

In September 2007, Rather launched a $70 million lawsuit against CBS and its parent company Viacom, claiming he had been wrongly dismissed. Since the lawsuit might expose the Bush administration's intimidation of a major news organization, you have to wish Rather had fought back earlier – before the 2004 election, for example.

Press Freedom under Fire

> *"These reports follow the same unconvincing and incredible pattern: secrecy over the detail and nature of the report, a failure to examine all the evidence, paltry and cruelly insensitive shrugs of regret, and complete exoneration of responsibility of US personnel at all levels of command. It is denial of justice on a shocking scale." – Aidan White, General Secretary of the International Federation of Journalists, in an April 2005 letter to Bush discussing the 14 media workers killed in Iraq since the March 2003 invasion* [84]

Reporting on the White House for over 40 years, Helen Thomas has been highly critical of the corporate media's "herd mentality" when it comes to the Bush administration. The "first lady of the press" told CODEPINK's Gael Murphy that after 9/11, "the media really went into a coma and rolled over and played dead, just as Congress did."[85] She spoke of widespread self-censorship for fear of appearing unpatriotic and recalled Bush's press conference a few days before the Iraq invasion: "It was a fiasco, because everybody knew we were going to war and asked things like Do you pray? instead of asking the hard-news questions like: Why are we going to war?

Why haven't you done more to avoid it? Why haven't you used diplomacy? Under what justification can you go into someone else's country?"

Given the kid gloves used by the media at home, it's no wonder Bush crumbles under the weight of an interview with a real journalist, such as his unfortunate encounter with Carol Coleman of Radio and Television Ireland in June 2004. When Coleman confronted Bush's vague responses with tough follow-up questions, he squirmed like a bug dying on a windshield much of the time, repeatedly asking Coleman not to interrupt and coming out with doozies such as "My job is to do my job."[86] As might be expected, Coleman later received a phone call from the Bush camp complaining about her lack of deference to the president, and her subsequent interview scheduled with Laura Bush was abruptly canceled.

But if in "The Land of the Free and the Home of the Brave" journalists have neither the liberty nor the courage to ask their leaders tough questions, then really how strong is our democracy?

The US military and hotel journalism

CNN's former chief news executive, Eason Jordon, became a whipping boy for the right after he told a World Economic Forum audience in January 2005 that coalition forces had targeted journalists in Iraq. Although Jordan immediately backtracked, insisting that he hadn't intended to suggest that US forces killed journalists on purpose, the damage was done – he resigned weeks later, ostensibly to save CNN from being "unfairly tarnished" by the controversy.

Jordan needn't have bothered.

Before the invasion of Iraq, the Pentagon itself clearly warned journalists either to embed with troops or face grave danger. In fact, a former BBC war correspondent was told by Pentagon officials before the invasion that coalition aircraft would even fire on journalists' satellite uplinks.[87]

The threats weren't hollow. Veteran reporter Terry Lloyd was one of the invasion's first media casualties, killed in March 2003 when his clearly-marked press vehicle was strafed by an American helicopter gunship.

Weeks later, two journalists died and three were injured in Baghdad when a US tank fired on a hotel filled with media representatives covering the war. Pentagon officials at first blamed Iraqi snipers for the Palestine Hotel attack, claiming, "this desperate and dying regime will stop at nothing to cling to power," but when evidence proved a US tank was responsible, officials then said the shelling was in response to hostile fire from within the hotel. After that version of events was proven false too, the standard line became that soldiers attacked the hotel thinking they "were under direct observation from an enemy hunter/killer team."[88]

The Pentagon knew the hotel had been crowded with reporters for three weeks, yet soldiers on the ground weren't told. According to the press advocacy group Reporters Without Borders, "The US shelling of the hotel was ... the result of criminal negligence."[89]

While the Geneva Conventions clearly state that "journalists engaged in dangerous professional missions in areas of armed conflict shall be considered as civilians ... and protected as such," apparently not everyone agrees; in the view of retired Marine Lt. Gen. Bernard E. Trainor, for example, "there's nothing sacrosanct about a hotel with a bunch of journalists in it."[90]

It is perhaps no coincidence that on April 8 2003, the same day that the Palestine Hotel was hit, US forces also bombed Al Jazeera's Baghdad offices, killing one reporter.[91]

Eason Jordan is not the only media representative to have suggested that the US military targets journalists in Iraq. Others include:
- **Nik Gowing of *BBC World*:** "The trouble is that a lot of the military - particularly the American military - do not want us there. And they make it very uncomfortable for us to work. And I think that this is leading to security forces in some instances feeling it is legitimate to target us with deadly force and with impunity."[92]
- **Linda Foley, president of the 35,000-member *Newspaper Guild*:** "Journalists, by the way, are not just being targeted verbally or ... politically. They are also being targeted for real, um ... in places like Iraq. What outrages me as a representative of journalists is that there's not more outrage about the number, and the brutality, and the cavalier nature of the U.S. military toward the killing of journalists in Iraq ... They target and kill journalists ... from other countries, particularly Arab countries like Al -, like Arab news services like al-Jazeera, for example. They actually target them and blow up their studios with impunity."[93]
- **Photojournalist Molly Bingham, who spent 10 months in Iraq researching resistance to the US occupation:** "Recent actions indicate that the U.S. military will detain and/or kill any journalist who happens to be caught covering the Iraqi side of the militant resistance, and indeed a number of journalists have been

killed by U.S. troops while working in Iraq."[94]

When you add the threat of being kidnapped or murdered by insurgents, it's no wonder that journalists in Iraq are bunkering down in safe locations rather than hitting the streets to dig up facts; as of November 2007, a full 206 journalists and media assistants had been killed in Iraq with a further 14 kidnapped and two missing.[95] As veteran war correspondent Robert Fisk wrote in January 2005, "Thus, many reporters are now reduced to telephoning the American military or the Iraqi 'interim' government for information from their hotel rooms, receiving 'facts' from men and women who are even more isolated from Iraq in the Baghdad Green Zone around Saddam Hussein's former republican palace than are the journalists. Or they take reports from their correspondents who are embedded with American troops and who will, necessarily, get only the American side of the story."[96]

Fisk quotes a long-term US correspondent in Baghdad who says, "The United States military couldn't be happier with this situation. They know that if they bomb a house of innocent people, they can claim it was a 'terrorist' base and get away with it. They don't want us roaming around Iraq and so the 'terrorist' threat is great news for them."

Makes you wonder why Eason Jordan quit.

US military targeting Al-Jazeera?[97]

In November 2005, *The Daily Mirror*, a British newspaper, reported that Bush had wanted to attack Al-Jazeera's headquarters in Doha, Qatar in April 2004, but UK Prime Minister Tony Blair had talked him out of it. The revelation came via a leaked transcript of the pair's meeting in Washington D.C., and raised new questions regarding previous US military attacks on Al-Jazeera offices, including:

- 2001: Al-Jazeera's office in Kabul, Afghanistan bombed by US forces
- 2002: Al-Jazeera's office in Kabul devastated yet again when a US missile struck it. One journalist died.
- 2003: Al-Jazeera's Baghdad office struck during US bombing raid. One journalist died.

Shooting the messenger

Intrepid war correspondents who insist on getting the real story often pay with their lives, and Giuliana Sgrena of Italy's *Il Manifesto* came close. Kidnapped by insurgents in February 2005 as she interviewed refugees from

Fallujah, Sgrena spent a month in captivity, but was released after the Italian government reportedly paid millions in ransom money.

Sgrena is a seasoned journalist who has reported from Afghanistan, Somalia, Algeria and other tough locations. In Iraq, she was working to expose the dark side of the US occupation, and often explored subjects completely ignored by embedded reporters, such as the US military's alleged torture of women at Abu Ghraib prison and use of inhumane weapons.[98]

Given the nature of what she wrote, it's clear that Sgrena was not a favorite of the US occupation administrators. Before she was freed, her captors had ominously warned her to be careful, saying, "The Americans don't want you to go back."[99]

Sgrena almost didn't make it back; immediately following her dramatic rescue by Italian intelligence agents on March 4 2005, an American armored vehicle sprayed her escape car with hundreds of bullets, instantly killing Nicola Calipari, one of the agents who had secured her release. Sgrena suffered a bullet wound that punctured her lung, and would surely have died had Calipari not sheltered her with his body.

Exactly why American forces fired on Sgrena's rescue car is unclear. The official version is that the US military had no advance notice that Sgrena's car would be on that specific road, and despite the fact that troops had tried to tell the driver to stop (using arm signals, lights and warning shots) the car had approached the checkpoint at high speed, causing troops to shoot into the front of the car.

The Italian version is very different. Sgrena herself maintains that embassy officials indeed had been properly notified, the rescue car had actually been driving slowly due to poor road conditions and the US military had not given any warning signs before attacking the car. In an April 2005 interview with *Democracy Now!*, Sgrena maintained that soldiers had fired into the back of the car, and supported her claim by noting that Calipari had been seated in the back and died immediately, and she herself had been shot from the back.[100]

When asked if Calipari had received permission to drive on the road to the airport, Sgrena responded, "Of course, I was there when they called."

In an interesting twist, the US Embassy in Baghdad noted that Sgrena's car had been attacked from a temporary checkpoint set up for then-US Ambassador John Negroponte. Given Negroponte's infamous term as ambassador to Honduras during the 1980s, and his alleged support of death squads in Nicaragua and Honduras during that time, the "coincidental" Negroponte connection raised eyebrows.

Even though the Italian government owns the car Sgrebna was traveling in, *the US military initially prevented Italian authorities from examining it*, thus eliminating the possibility to determine from which angle the car had been attacked, or any other details about the attack. A subsequent Pentagon investigation found that the soldiers involved and their higher-ups had followed the appropriate "rules of engagement" and so in essence, no one was responsible.

You've got to wonder if, like the official version says, the attack on Sgrena's car was an unfortunate error - or if the real error was that she survived.

Koran-gate and anonymous sources

In May 2005, *Newsweek* journalist Mike Isikoff landed in hot water for an article he wrote detailing the mistreatment of prisoners at Guantanamo, Cuba. International condemnation resulted from the report's charges that guards had thrown the Koran, Islam's holy book, into the toilet. Anti-American demonstrations broke out in various countries, and over a dozen people died in Afghanistan when military police opened fire on a protest.

The White House went ballistic over the controversy, predictably attacking the article rather than the serious allegations behind it. The Pentagon had previously cleared Isikoff's report, but the uproar was so profound that few were surprised when the anonymous governmental source responsible for the flushed-Koran claim suddenly retracted part of the story. The upshot: *Newsweek* had no option but to make a red-faced apology, and media attention proceeded to focus on the magazine's poor journalistic ethics, rather than on the more critical issue of prisoner abuse by the US military.

The parallels between Koran-gate and Rather-gate are clear: mainstream media company gets its ass kicked for daring to address a topic which is taboo for the Bush administration. But while the document at the heart of the CBS/Dan Rather flap over Bush's military service had not been properly sourced, the Isikoff report had already been cleared by the Pentagon. As Isikoff later told the *New York Times:* "Neither *Newsweek* nor the Pentagon foresaw that a reference to the desecration of the Koran was going to create the kind of response that it did. The Pentagon saw the item before it ran, and then they didn't move us off it for 11 days afterward. They were as caught off guard by the furor as we were. We obviously blame ourselves for not understanding the potential ramifications."[101]

Notice that Isikoff doesn't say the story was factually inaccurate – just that the reaction it caused had been unexpected.

It wasn't the first time that allegations of US military members desecrating the Koran had surfaced either; reports had appeared in the international press for years prior, such as when a former detainee told Russian TV in June 2004, "They tore the Koran to pieces in front of us, threw it into the toilet."[102]

Yet the White House leaned on *Newsweek* not only to retract the allegations but also, as the Chief White House spokesperson said, "to do all they can to help repair the damage that has been done, particularly in the region."[103]

One could argue that the Bush administration has done a fine job all by itself of damaging US standing "in the region."

There's also the curious fact that the US government source at the center of the controversy didn't actually retract the entire Koran-in-toilet story; the source only expressed a lack of certainty about which military document it had appeared in. There would have been one easy way to clear up that question – release the military documents in question so that everyone could learn the truth.

Of course, the Bush administration didn't pursue that option.

As a result of the Koran-gate controversy, media outlets will be much less likely to use anonymous sources in the future. The fact that Judith Miller of the *New York Times* did jail time for not revealing her source in the Valerie Plame case only strengthened that point. Of course, that won't stop the Bush administration from continuing to hand its press corps information "off the record" – thereby eliminating any responsibility for the content.

Towards a Democratic Media

> "Our republic and its press will rise and fall together. An able, disinterested, public-spirited press, with trained intelligence to know the right and courage to do it, can preserve that public virtue without which popular government is a sham and a mockery. A cynical, mercenary, demographic press will produce in time a people

as base as itself." - Joseph Pulitzer, newspaper owner and philanthropist (1847-1911)

Beating the broadband bullies

In a functioning democracy, some things are just meant to be public property. Who owns the oceans, for example? The sky? The air? Companies or individuals shouldn't have the right to take over such *commons* as their own – they belong to everyone, plain and simple.

Airwaves are also part of the *commons;* big media corporations didn't create the airwaves, they just use them. Nonetheless, corporations are pushing for permanent copyright over parts of the airwave spectrum, a possibility that seems increasingly likely following the Supreme Court's June 2005 move to hand cable companies control over broadband, and simultaneously, the internet.

Here's some background into the Court's shameful broadband giveaway. The 1934 Communications Act, as amended by the Telecommunications Act of 1996, differentiated between "information services" and "telecommunications services" – in a nutshell, "information services" are a protected part of the commons while "telecommunications services" are not.

Naturally, the distinction has been of critical interest to the two sectors controlling the US broadband market: telephone companies, which own the high-speed wires transporting Digital Subscriber Line (DSL) service, and cable companies, which own the lines transporting cable modem service.

Common-carrier regulations have traditionally made it difficult for the cable/telephone duopoly to push out competitors or control content, so the public was guaranteed open access to communication networks. In addition, competition was intensified by giving multiple internet service providers (ISPs) access to broadband cable lines.

But in 2002, Powell's corporate-driven FCC inexplicably decided that cable modem service was actually not a "telecommunication service" after all, and as such, should be freed from FCC regulations and control. A California-based ISP subsequently sued the FCC for access to cable lines, and in October 2003, a circuit court ruled in favor of the ISP. When the FCC appealed, the so-called "NCTA v. Brand X" case ended up at the US Supreme Court.

The FCC's arguments in support of cable companies were convoluted if not downright goofy. First, the FCC reasoned that even though cable companies used telecommunications to provide modem service, that was not the same as providing telecommunications service. (Say what?) The FCC also argued that since cable companies built their own systems, they should be entitled to use the wires as they pleased.[104]

But as Dave Baker, an ISP executive, told *Internet News*, "Cable companies built their networks using government-granted monopoly franchises, access to public rights of way and discounted rates for pole attachments. Nonetheless, they now dictate what services, devices and applications companies can offer and consumers can use on those networks." Baker said that he expected the Supreme Court, "to affirm that consumers, and not cable companies, should make those choices."[105]

Unfortunately, Baker was wrong. In June 2005, the Supreme Court sided with the FCC in a 6-to-3 ruling which dumped common-carrier requirements for broadband networks.

The decision could have widespread negative consequences. For starters, telephone companies could demand the same favorable treatment as cable companies received, and bearing in mind that over 95% of broadband is controlled by the telephone/cable company duopoly, the internet could be radically transformed. The media advocacy group Free Press, for example, has predicted that the Brand X decision could threaten internet access for rural and low-income communities, destabilize the emerging Voice Over Internet Protocol (VOIP) market, and eliminate competitive broadband carriers and independent ISPs.[106]

In a related move, the House Committee on Energy and Commerce took up the issue of "net neutrality" in late April 2006, and ended up handing major telecom players the keys to the internet. In essence, the House vote inexplicably shafted consumers by allowing broadband-access providers to charge for prioritized content and services. But as SavetheInternet.com put it, "Your local library shouldn't have to outbid Barnes & Noble for the right to have its Web site open quickly on your computer."

The administration's broadband giveaway reflects a broader legal disregard for technological developments in media. Digital TV is a classic example. In 1996, Congress handed broadcasters a gift worth billions of dollars in allowing them the free use of public airwaves to develop digital TV; while today's analog broadcasting can operate, say, one channel in a given airwave "space," digital broadcasting will be able to "multicast" six or more channels of the same or higher quality in the same airwave "space."[107] In other words, the profit potential is outrageous, and broadcasters have been handed these *commons* airwaves free of charge, asked only to provide a few public service offerings in return. To make matters worse, the FCC has permitted digital TV technology to eliminate the possibility of recording programming. So toss out that VCR - the wave of the future is that the consumer pays for programming... and pays and pays.

The FCC pulled another fast one in choosing "In Band On Channel" (IBOC) for the nation's digital radio broadcasting. This technology, still under development, will enable broadcasters to grab up airwave space at will, locking out new competitors and even community radio in the process.

Once the inevitable transition to digital TV and radio is complete, you can also expect broadcasters to kick and scream about giving up the analog spectrum they've been using all along – potentially closing yet another door on alternative media.

The overriding issue in both the broadband and digital airwave giveaways is the commercialization of our *commons*. By not paying attention, we're allowing our lawmakers to permit corporate broadcasters not only to deliver more advertising and fewer perspectives in the course of normal programming, but also to determine the framework around which media technologies can develop. That's suicide for a democracy.

But all is not lost. Some interesting new technologies combined with consumer protests and good 'ole pressure on politicians can turn the tide. And the future is in low-cost public media.

Take wireless public broadband access, which promises savings for both communities and local businesses. Unsurprisingly, municipalities across the country have started looking at creating their own community internet programs, and in 2004, the mayor of Philadelphia vowed to bring low-cost public access to his city, even providing residents with a variety of wireless "HotSpots" across town that could be used free of charge.

All of this democratic progress was just a bit too much for Verizon and Comcast, though; the telephone/cable duopoly had Pennsylvanian broadband profits locked up and wasn't about to let go without a fight. As a result, the companies lobbied the state's legislature to pass a nasty law forbidding other cities in Pennsylvania to follow Philadelphia's lead **without first getting Verizon's written permission**.[108] And amazingly, the legislature went along. Can you imagine? No low-cost public access possible unless a corporation says it's OK.

So while the city of Philadelphia makes progress providing inexpensive broadband access to all 1.6 million of its residents, the rest of the state's consumers continue forking over fortunes to broadband bullies.

You might wonder why Pennsylvanian lawmakers so easily sold their citizens down the river, but given the millions telephone/cable companies can donate to politicians' re-election campaigns and the like, the answer is clear. Think tanks such as the Cato Institute and the New Millennium Research Council also stepped in to provide lawmakers with "research" warning about the dangers and downsides of community broadband. But the fact that the Cato Institute, for example, receives funding from Verizon, Comcast and other broadband bullies was conveniently left out of the research results.[109]

One way to bypass hassling with telephone/cable broadband bullies in the first place is to deliver internet through other means – such as electrical lines. While Broadband over Power Line (BPL) technology is still being developed, it holds promise for providing access to far-flung communities, as well as for breaking the telephone/cable duopoly's stranglehold on the market.

Another option is for the FCC to open up unlicensed "white spaces" (unused parts of the public airwaves) thus enabling greater broadband possibilities.

Of course, a third way to beat the broadband bullies is just to fight back. Local governments get to negotiate franchise renewals with their telephone and cable providers, and should use the opportunity first to involve the public, and second to demand that companies provide more money for the city's coffers, more public access channels, and more bandwidth for community use – at the minimum.

Recent reports of interference with online and mobile phone messages raise added concerns about the power of major phone and cable companies. In September 2007, for example, Verizon Wireless decided to block its customers from receiving text messages from NARAL Pro-Choice America, calling the group "unsavory" and "controversial" Only after concerned citizens blasted Verizon with 20,000 messages in two hours, did the company back down from its disgraceful plan.

Similar story with the progressive web sites afterdowningstreet.org and truthout.org, both of which have faced the stifling of their emails.

If a democracy is as strong as its free flow of information, the US appears to be facing some serious challenges.

Ten Easy Ways to Make a Difference Now

1. Find out who owns your local media

A comprehensive overview of "Who owns what" can be found at Columbia Journalism Review's excellent site (www.cjr.org/tools/owners). For example, if you click on News Corp., you'll find that it owns Fox Broadcasting Company as well as dozens of local stations across the United States. News Corp. also owns 19 Direct Broadcast Satellite (DBS) and cable companies, four film studios, various newspapers in the US, UK and Australia, and the vast number of imprints represented by HarperMorrow Publishers. News Corp. even has a stake in both the LA Kings and LA Lakers. (Check out the Journalism Tools and Language Corner sections of the Columbia Journalism Review site too.)

The Center for Public Integrity has a terrific search engine that lets you see exactly who owns what newspapers, radio stations and TV outlets in your community. Just type in your zip code or city name and within seconds you'll get a terrific report. Try it at www.publicintegrity.org/telecom/.

And how focused on media issues are your representatives? Rep. Bernie Sanders (I-VT) and Rep. Maurice Hinchey (D-NY) are examples of leaders who "get it" – both have been active in confronting the FCC's excesses, and both have worked to inform the American public about the importance of keeping media democratic. What's your representatives' scorecard when it comes to the media? If you're not sure, then head to Free Press (www.freepress.net/washington/) and find out how your legislators have voted on media issues. If you like what you see, then let your reps know. If you don't like it, let them know even faster.

2. Turn off the tube

The average American watches over four hours of television per day and approximately two million TV commercials by the age of 65. If you think life's too short for such a dubious addiction, you're not alone! The TV-Turnoff Network is a "national nonprofit organization that encourages children and adults to watch much less television in order to promote healthier lives and communities." They sponsor an annual TV-Turnoff Week, and their site (www.tvturnoff.org) is filled with fun tips to beat the TV habit. Definitely worth a visit.

Here are some scary statistics about kids and TV:[110]
- Time per week that parents spend in meaningful conversation with their children: 38.5 minutes
- Average number of hours per week that American one-year old children watch television: 6
- Average time per week that the American child ages 2-17 spends watching television: 19 hours 40 minutes
- Number of violent acts the average American child sees on TV by age 18: 200,000
- Percentage of Hollywood executives who believe there is a link between TV violence and real violence: 80

Add the scourge of childhood obesity to these warning signals and you've got ample reason to help the kids in your life buck the TV habit. Not sure how? Take a trip to the zoo, a walk in the park, or read a book together - the fun possibilities are endless. For more ideas, head back to the TV-Turnoff Network and check out their Online Activity Book, and its fun activities for kids of all ages.

3. Check out some cool media sites

Would you like to learn more about the press and keep up-to-date with changes in the media? Here are some great places to start:

Fairness & Accuracy in Reporting (www.fair.org)
"FAIR, the national media watch group, has been offering well-documented criticism of media bias and censorship since 1986." It has a mailing list and a Women's Desk too.

Free Press (www.freepress.net)
Free Press is "working to increase informed public participation in crucial media policy debates, and to generate policies that will produce a more competitive and public interest-oriented media system with a strong nonprofit and noncommercial sector." Sign up for the mailing list, and explore the site's comprehensive resources.

MediaChannel (www.mediachannel.org)
"MediaChannel is concerned with the political, cultural and social impacts of the media, large and small." It has a mailing list too.

Media Matters (www.mediamatters.org)
"Not-for-profit progressive research and information center dedicated to comprehensively monitoring, analyzing, and correcting conservative misinformation in the U.S. media."

Reporters sans Frontières (www.rsf.org)
"Reporters Without Borders, kept on constant alert via its network of over 100 correspondents, rigorously condemns any attack on press freedom world-wide by keeping the media and public opinion informed through press releases and public-awareness campaigns."

The Center for Digital Democracy (www.democraticmedia.org)
"The Center for Digital Democracy is committed to preserving the openness and diversity of the Internet in the broadband era, and to realizing the full potential of digital communications through the development and encouragement of noncommercial, public interest programming."

Stop Big Media (http://stopbigmedia.com)
"An alliance of consumer, public interest, media reform, organized labor and other groups that have joined together to fight runaway media consolidation and urge the FCC to put public service before the self-interest of large media corporations."

4. Support public broadcasting and alternative media

Bored with mainstream news magazines? Pick up a copy of *Global Outlook, Ms., The Progressive, Harper's, Mother Jones, The Nation, In These Times, Covert Action Quarterly* or some other great alternative news source. Subscribe or insist that your local magazine shop and/or public library keep your favorite in stock.

While you're at it, fight against the US Postal Regulatory Commission's June 2007 hike of postal rates for small and independent publications. Many of your favorite progressive political magazines face postal rate increases of 20%-30% and risk being run out of business because of this blatant give-away to large publishers. Take action at www.freepress.net/postal.

Not happy with the incessant drone of right-wing commentators? Do you want more from news than Clear Channel can offer? Then tune into Air America, Democracy Now!, Meria Heller, Lizz Brown, Stephanie Miller, David Barsamian, Talk Nation Radio, Peter B. Collins, Jeff Farias, Peter Werbe, Counterspin, Working Assets, Diane Rehm, Pacifica, Guy James or any of the other fine alternative radio options out there (for a comprehensive listing of offerings, try Unconservative Listening at www.makethemaccountable.com). While you're at it, check out Free Speech TV (www.freespeech.org) or Al Gore's IndTV for a refreshing change.

And if you're one of the many who believe that public broadcasting shouldn't have to rely on corporate underwriting and Congress just to survive, then support the movement to make noncommercial public broadcasting truly independent. Write a letter to the editor, donate to groups fighting for public broadcasting, and if you're so inclined, volunteer for the cause. If you're not sure how to find like-minded folks in your area, the Free Press "Action Squad" (www.freepress.net/action/squad/signup.php) will hook you up with a local group fighting for public broadcasting through "public education and outreach, letter writing, grassroots organizing, lobbying and research." Also head over to the Hands Off Public Broadcasting site and sign up for its mailing list too (http://mediamatters.org/handsoff).

5. Keep a critical eye on programming and content

You've got a lot more power to influence local media content than you might realize. As Free Press reminds us, "Most people do not even know that they can challenge the renewal of a local radio or television license if a broadcaster is not serving the public interest. Activism must be directed at the hometown level, where such licenses can be challenged. Renewals of cable franchise agreements in local communities must be seen as opportunities to hold cable companies accountable to the public interest."[111]

So let networks and stations know when there's room for improvement. Do you think there's too much violence in your programming? Has the local voice been lost from your community's TV and radio channels? Do you hear political opinion masquerading as fact on news shows? Contact the broadcasters and let them know. And while you're at it, find out when their licenses expire.

If you're concerned about how much the public relations industry is infiltrating your news and programming, then subscribe to the Center for Media & Democracy's quarterly *PR Watch*. It "specializes in blowing the lid off today's multi-billion dollar propaganda-for-hire industry, naming names and revealing how public relations wizards concoct and spin the news, organize phony 'grassroots' front groups, spy on citizens, and conspire with lobbyists and politicians to thwart democracy." Or sign up for its "Weekly Spin" mailing list (at www.prwatch.org).

6. Make your own media

The "citizen journalism" movement, which began in the late 80s, has picked up steam as the general public loses faith in mainstream media. Citizen journalism (or citJ, as it's nicknamed) empowers ordinary people to be more active in collecting, reporting and analyzing the news, while reaching out to demographic groups often left out of news reporting, such as minorities, youth and low-income women.

So how does it work? On the web, citJ means blogs, message boards and wikis (an application that lets users add content, i.e. to a forum, permitting anyone to edit the content). The Independent Media Center (http://indymedia.org) is a classic example of citizen journalism at work, with branches all across the world inviting users to instantly upload audio, video, photo or text directly from their browsers. The resulting vibrant mix often scoops big stories weeks ahead of mainstream news outlets.

The South Korean phenomenon OhmyNews (http://english.ohmynews.com/) set up shop in 2000, and gets "up to 70% of its copy from some 38,000 'citizen reporters.'"[112] 150 stories are published on the site each day, vetted by editors, and its traffic is roughly half a million people daily.

If you're a Democrat and concerned about the way the party is going, then check out the "Aggressive Progressives" at www.democrats.com. Petitions, blogs, forums, polls, "Protest and Organize!" possibilities, it's all there and waiting for your input.

In these days of simplified self-publishing, citizen journalism can also mean print publications produced by and for a local audience, and covering issues that local communities care about most. The citJ movement has additionally led to some newspapers, such as the *Rocky Mountain News*, adding citizen editors to their staff lists.[113]

For more information on the citJ movement, visit "I, Reporter" a site dedicated to "Inspiring, guiding, and educating citizen journalists and the news organizations that work with them" (www.ireporter.org). Sign up for its web feed... and start reporting!

7. Learn more about diversity in the media

Women still make up just roughly a third of full-time journalists in mainstream media, a figure which hasn't changed since 1982.[114] And they represent little more than a quarter of senior-level management positions in the communications industry.[115]

The International Women's Media Foundation (www.iwmf.org) aims to change that sorry fact by strengthening "the role of women in the news media around the world, based on the belief that no press is truly free unless women share an equal voice." The IWMF site is filled with goodies including an online training center and a slew of interesting publications and program initiatives. For example, IWMF offers these online *Tips and Guides*, free of charge:

Journalism Skills:
- Accuracy and Fairness Checklist
- Broadcast Writing
- Business Reporting
- Good Internet Sites for Background Information
- Investigative Reporting
- Organizing an Article
- Pitching Your Story
- Using Statistics in a Story
- Writing Compelling Leads

Media Awareness Skills:
- Conducting a Front-Page Study
- Starting a Women's Media Association

These *Online Training Courses* are available too:
- Leadership Development
- Building Your Influence in the Newsroom
- Developing Radio Skills

Since "no press is truly free unless women share an equal voice, " the IWMF site features articles from/interviews with inspiring women journalists from across the world. But the site's educational resources are a goldmine for anyone interested in learning more about journalism, or in developing their professional capabilities. So head on over to IWMF; sign up for its mailing list while you're at it.

Also check out SheSource.org, which is "dedicated to closing the gender gap in news media" by providing journalists with "a database of women who are distinguished experts in their fields and experienced spokespeople."

Diversity doesn't bode much better for people of color working in the US media. A 1990-2005 analysis of the American Society of Newspaper Editors' census data showed that staffing at 73% of large US papers has become **less** racially diverse in recent years.[116] And the problem is systemic. People of color comprise roughly a third of the US population, yet own less than 4% of all radio stations and less than 2% of all TV stations. Minorities represent only:[117]
- 7.4% of TV news managers
- 4.2% of radio news managers
- 11.8% of radio news staffs

- 13.4% of the 2005 newsroom workforce

If facts like that make you cringe, visit the Ethnic Majority's Media section (www.ethnicmajority.com/media_home.htm) where you'll find everything from statistics on the "level of diversity on the journalistic staffs of the newspapers" to a report on "the casting of people of color for roles in films." Sign up for the newsletter, contribute to the Newsblog and use the Shout Out! page to contact decision-makers about media-diversity hot topics.

UNITY: Journalists of Color (www.unityjournalists.org) is another one-stop-shop with a wide range of publications, resources and even information on trainings and events related to media diversity. UNITY partners with: Good Internet Sites for Background Information
- Asian American Journalists Association (www.aaja.org)
- The National Association of Black Journalists (www.nabj.org)
- National Association of Hispanic Journalists (www.nahj.org)
- Native American Journalists Association (http://naja.com)

8. Get wonky

Chances are good that, if you're like most Americans, issues such as interconnectivity, media consolidation, and broadband over power line may seem wonky and off-putting. But truth told, it's media issues like those that will make or break our democracy.

So, get your feet wet. If you've got access to the Internet, then visit the Free Press site (www.freepress.net) and download any of its comprehensive library; under Activist Issues, for example, you'll find scores of topics organized under eight major headings such as "Internet and Broadband" and "Intellectual Property." Everything is laid out clearly and explained so easily that even a novice can understand.

While you're at it, take time to learn about the governmental organizations controlling your media. What is the Federal Communications Commission responsible for anyway? Check out its site (www.fcc.gov) with subheadings ranging from "Consumer Center" to "Strategic Goals." Then head over to the Corporation for Public Broadcasting (www.cpb.org) and compare its Mission Statement to its actions. Be sure to share with them any compliments, complaints or suggestions. Your opinion counts!

If you prefer print material to web surfing, then head to the library or bookstore and dig into any number of the great books available on the media. Here are some starters:

- Our Media, Not Theirs, The Democratic Struggle Against Corporate Media, by Robert W. McChesney, John Nichols (Seven Stories Press, 2002)
- A Citizen's Guide to the Airwaves, by J.H. Snider, (New America Foundation, 2003)
- Manufacturing Consent, The Political Economy of the Mass Media, by Edward S. Herman and Noam Chomsky, (Pantheon 2002)
- The Media Monopoly, (6th Edition) by Ben H. Bagdikian, (Beacon Press 2000)

9. Be a champion of community radio

Just as the Greek mythological character Prometheus stole fire from the heavens and gave it to the people, the Prometheus Radio Project is focused on taking radio out of the grips of commercial monopolies and handing it back to communities.

At the center of the struggle is low-power FM radio (LPFM), an important component of community-based, noncommercial radio. Although LPFM broadcast licensing was approved by the FCC in 2000, heavy lobbying by broadcasters has held it at bay, in part due to disproven claims that LPFM signals would interfere with their signal receptions. But activist groups, such as Philadelphia's Prometheus Radio Project (www.prometheusradio.org) have taken matters into their own hands, literally, by holding "radio barnraisings" across the country for those stations which have obtained a construction permit. In early April 2005, for example, Prometheus volunteers descended on Nashville, Tennessee with soldering irons and a mission - and they got local station WRFN-LP up and running in just one weekend!

So what are the options for community radio where you live? One easy way to find out is by inviting a Prometheus Radio Project staff member or volunteer to speak to your community group or school. You might also consider donating your time or money to the project, or even just stopping by the site and introducing yourself. As Prometheus says, "We never know when we might need a couch to sleep on in Iowa, a local volunteer to organize a hearing in San Antonio, or a persuasive citizen to contact their senator in Alaska. If you sign up, we will know that we have a friend in your town when we need one!"

10. Take action on media reform

If you're truly hardcore about media reform, then check out the Free Press' 68-page "Media Reform Action Guide: tools, tips and techniques for promoting change," available for complimentary download or print purchase at $2.50 each.[118] This handy booklet covers everything from hosting a media reform house party to filing comments on FCC rule changes. The Action Guide also includes comprehensive appendices with such topics as "10 Questions to Ask Every Candidate and Elected Official" and "Talking Points for a Presentation on Media Reform," in addition to a sample letter to the editor and a sample newspaper article. Look no further for ideas on how to impact media reform – it's all there!

Also visit the Center for Digital Democracy (www.democraticmedia.org), dedicated to "ensuring that the public interest is a fundamental part of the new digital communications landscape." The CDD site has myriad resources including an Activist Library, videos on topics ranging from net neutrality to media policy, and of course, a Get Involved page. Definitely worth a visit.

To fight for net neutrality, head over to SavetheInternet.com. You'll find background information on this crucial topic, a blog, and various activism opportunities (http://savetheinternet.com).

Final Thoughts

"When we can't dream any longer we die." – Emma Goldman,
author and revolutionary (1869-1940)

As **The Progressives' Handbook** series details, the rollbacks under Bush have been neither random nor isolated. Billions spent on producing weapons of mass destruction, for example, have meant funding cuts for education and domestic social programs, increased environmental dangers, new threats to national security – and of course, more reason to start fresh wars.

Bottom line: since the administration's assaults have been both across the board and interconnected, the progressive response must be as well. That means finding our political voice and using our collective power to make a positive impact. And it means crossing party lines, ditching blue-red rhetoric and reaching out to others who also want peace, justice and a decent future for their kids.

You're personally invited to drop by **The Progressives' Handbook** Action Center and share your ideas for positive change. And if you're looking for an antidote to apathy, join Heather's blog/podcast mailing list.

Visit The Progressives' Handbook Action Center
www.progressiveshandbook.com

Sign up for Heather's blog and podcast:
www.heatherwokusch.com

Notes

Introduction

1. *The New York Times*, "Without a Doubt," by Ron Suskind (October 17 2004) archived at www.truthout.org/docs_04/101704A.shtml
2. *US Census Bureau,* 'Household Income Rises, Poverty Rate Declines, Number of Uninsured Up" at www.census.gov/Press-Release/www/releases/archives/income_wealth/010583.html

US Weapons of Mass Destruction

1. *TheTruthAboutGeorge.com*, "Bushisms, Foot-in-Mouth Disease Strikes Again" citing *The Chicago Sun-Times*, October 13 2003 as its source at www.thetruthaboutgeorge.com/bushisms/index.html
2. *The Pipa/Knowledge Networks Poll*, "Americans on WMD Proliferation," (April 15 2004) at www.pipa.org/OnlineReports/WMDProliferation/WMD_Prolif_Apr04/WMDProlif_Apr04_pr.pdf
3. *Take Them At Their Words*, by Bruce J. Miller, (Academy Chicago Publishers, 2004, p. 113), citing as its source: "Rush Limbaugh, on the proposed ban on chemical weapons, 4-7-97."
4. *Los Angeles Times*, "Bioterrorism, hyped," by Milton Leitenberg (February 17 2006) archived at http://tinyurl.com/cdjul
5. *Salt Lake City Weekly*, "Just Testing: Is the US Government making anthrax bombs in Utah?" by Ted McDonough (February 23 2006) at www.slweekly.com/article.cfm/justtesting
6. This section adapted from *The Baltimore Sun,* "Deceit, Danger Mark U.S. Pursuit of New WMD," by Heather Wokusch (July 29 2003) at www.heatherwokusch.com/columns/column48.html
7. *The Guardian*, "US finds evidence of WMD at last - buried in a field in Maryland," by Julian Borger (May 28 2003) at www.guardian.co.uk/international/story/0,3604,965231,00.html
8. *The Sunshine Project*, "Biosafety Bites #1 - US Army Builds Biodefense Lab, Neglects to Inspect It" (June 28 2004) at www.sunshine-project.org/biodefense/bb.html#1
9. *The Sunshine Project*, "Joint News Release - Institute Responsible for Anthrax Accident in California, in Charge of Safety and Security at Chicago Biodefense Laboratory," (June 22 2004) at www.sunshine-project.org
10. *The National Academies,* "Balanced Approach Needed to Mitigate Threats From Bioterrorism Without Hindering Progress in Biotechnology," (October 9 2003) archived at www.wi.mit.edu/news/archives/2003/gf_1009.html
11. *The New York Times*, "U.S. anti-bioterrorism effort stumbles," by

Scott Shane (January 25 2005) at
www.iht.com/articles/2005/01/24/news/germs.php

12. *Associated Press*, "U.S. labs mishandling deadly germs, " (October 2 2007) at www.msnbc.msn.com/id/21096974/

13. *Office of Management and Budget*, "Health and Human Services," at www.whitehouse.gov/omb/budget/fy2007/hhs.html

14. *Gulf News*, "Bush's bioterror defence plan could trigger arms race," (April 30 2004) at www.gulf-news.com/Articles/World2.asp?ArticleID=119679

15. *The Sunshine Project*, "Earth Calling NSABB: Voluntary Compliance Won't Work," (April 18 2007) at www.sunshine-project.org

16. *Sydney Morning Herald*, "US admits to 50 secret tests of bio weapons on troops," (July 1 2003) at www.smh.com.au/articles/2003/07/01/1056825376086.html. For more information, check out the blog at http://testvets.blogsource.com/

17. *U.S. Code collection § 1520a*, "Restrictions on use of human subjects for testing of chemical or biological agents," archived at www.law.cornell.edu/uscode/html/uscode50/usc_sec_50_00001520---a000-.html

18. *U.S. Code collection § 1515*, "Suspension; Presidential authorization," archived at www.law.cornell.edu/uscode/html/uscode50/usc_sec_50_00001515----000-.html

19. *Associated Press*, "Intel chief changing 1981 security order," by Katherine Shrader (June 12 2007) at www.usatoday.com/news/washington/2007-06-12-4038583883_x.htm

20. *Wikipedia*, "Napalm," at http://en.wikipedia.org/wiki/Napalm

21. *Inter Press Service*, "'Unusual Weapons' Used in Fallujah," by Dahr Jamail (November 26 2004)

22. *Aljazeera*, "Humanitarian aid barred from Falluja," (November 14 2004) at http://english.aljazeera.net/NR/exeres/443C3B4E-C2D2-4B18-9C5C-7C9B657A8DCF.htm

23. *Wikipedia*, "White phosphorus use in Iraq," at http://en.wikipedia.org/wiki/White_phosphorus_use_in_Iraq#endnote_refbot.485

24. *CNN*, "Cheney: 'Reasonable' to assume anthrax cases linked to terrorists," (October 12 2001) at www.cnn.com/2001/US/10/12/gen.cheney/

25. *Judicial Watch*, "FBI & Bush Administration Sued Over Anthrax Documents," (June 7 2002) at www.judicialwatch.org/1967.shtml

26. *The White House*, "Radio Address by the President to the Nation," (November 3 2001) at www.whitehouse.gov/news/releases/2001/11/20011103.html

27. *World Socialist Web Site*, "Bush protects drug giant's patent on anthrax medicine," by Jerry White (October 20 2001) at www.wsws.org/articles/2001/oct2001/cip-o20.shtml

28. *Mother Jones*, "The Next Worst Thing," by Michael Scherer (March/April 2004 Issue) at www.motherjones.com/news/outfront/2004/03/02_400.html

29. *AFP*, "US Senate leader urges 'Manhattan Project' against bio-terror threat," (January 27 2005) archived at www.politicalgateway.com/news/read.html?id=2685

30. *Grist*, "No Nukes Is Good Nukes, An interview with longtime anti-nuclear activist Helen Caldicott," by Gregory Dicum (May 3 2005) at www.helencaldicott.com/grist.pdf

31. *Arms Control Today*, "Nuclear Weapons Activity Surges in Energy Department Budget," (March 2003) at www.armscontrol.org/act/2003_03/nuclearweapons_mar03.asp

32. *NRDC*, "Bush Administration Wasting Billions on Nuclear Weapons Stockpile Research and Production, Report Charges," (April 13 2004) at www.nrdc.org/media/pressReleases/040413.asp

33. *Department of Energy Appropriation Account Summary* www.nukewatch.org/economics/FY06Budget/Content/appropsum.pdf

34. *The Albuquerque Tribune*, "Commentary: Weapons budget boost, DOE continues funding nuclear weapons programs while cutting environmental cleanup funds," by Jay Coghlan (March 8 2005)

35. *White House*, "Office of Management and Budget - Department of Energy," at www.whitehouse.gov/omb/budget/fy2007/energy.html

36. Adapted from *In These Times* (*issue 28/11*) "Nuke Nation: Putting Profits Before Safety," by Heather Wokusch (March 13 2004) at www.heatherwokusch.com/columns/column60.html

37. *Wired*, "U.S. Uranium Stock in Peril," (January 27 2004) at www.wired.com/news/politics/0,1283,62052,00.html?tw=newsletter_topstories_html

38. *Guardian*, "Halt Ordered to Classified Los Alamos Work," by Leslie Hoffman (July 15 2004) at www.guardian.co.uk/worldlatest/story/0,1280,-4314863,00.html

39. *Reuters*, "Data on Nuclear Agency Workers Hacked: Lawmaker," by Chris Baltimore (June 10 2006) archived at www.truthout.org/docs_2006/061106X.shtml

40. *The Associated Press*, "U.S. facing $553.9 million payout for plutonium leaks," by Catherine Tsai (February 16 2006) archived at http://seattletimes.nwsource.com/html/nationworld/2002808447_rockyflats16.html

41. Adapted from "Destroying the Village to Save Weapons Manufacturers" by Heather Wokusch (January 24 2003) at www.heatherwokusch.com/columns/column41.html

42. *BBC*, "UK considers DU testing," (January 12 2001) at http://news.bbc.co.uk/2/hi/uk_news/1112942.stm

43. *International Physicians for the Prevention of Nuclear War (IPPNW)*, "Depleted Uranium Weapons and Acute Post-War Health Effects: An IPPNW Assessment," at www.mapw.org.au/nuclear/du/01ippnw.html

44. *Uranium Medical Research Center*, "Afghan Field Trip # 2 Report –

Precise Destruction – Indiscriminate Effects," (September/October 2002) at http://www.umrc.net/os/downloads/destruction_effects.pdf

45. *Russian News & Information Agency NOVOSTI*, "Iraqis blame U.S. depleted uranium for surge in cancer," (July 23 2007) at http://en.rian.ru/world/20070723/69509899.html

46. *The Independent / UK*, "Are the Governments of Nato Guilty of Committing a Heinous War Crime?" by Robert Fisk (January 17, 2001) archived at www.commondreams.org/views01/0117-01.htm

47. *Campaign Against Sanctions on Iraq*, "Hamburg: World Uranium Weapons Conference," (September 17 2003) at www.casi.org.uk/discuss/2003/msg04325.html

48. *United States Department of Defense*, "Nuclear Posture Review Report," (January 8 2002) archived at www.globalsecurity.org/wmd/library/policy/dod/npr.htm

49. *The Guardian*, "The two faces of Rumsfeld," by Randeep Ramesh (May 9 2003) at www.guardian.co.uk/korea/article/0,2763,952289,00.html

50. *Editor and Publisher*, "One in Four Americans Would Use Nukes Against Terrorists, Gallup Finds," by Greg Mitchell (March 01 2005) at www.editorandpublisher.com/eandp/news/article_display.jsp?vnu_content_id=1000819252

51. *American-Arab Anti Discrimination Committee*, "Members of Congress Should Not Advocate for Nuclear War Against Any Country," (March 2 2005) at www.adc.org/index.php?id=2450

52. *San Jose Mercury News*, "U.S. ponders resumption of nuke-weapons test," (November 15 2002) archived at www.nukewatch.org/media2/postData.php?id=133

53. *The Guardian*, "China and Iran threaten test ban treaty," by Julian Borger and John Gittings (March 26 2002) at www.guardian.co.uk/iran/story/0,12858,893557,00.html

54. *Center for Arms Control and Non-Proliferation*, "House Energy & Water Appropriations FY 2007 Nuclear Non-Proliferation Summary," (June 06 2006) at www.armscontrolcenter.org/archives/002258.php

55. *Center For Defense Information*, "On Eve of Key Defense Authorization Vote, 31 Former Government Officials Call Missile Defense Deployment 'Sham'," (May 7 2004) at www.cdi.org/program/document.cfm?DocumentID=2203&StartRow=1&ListRows=10&appendURL=&Orderby=D.DateLastUpdated&ProgramID=6&from_page=index.cfm

56. *Center for Arms Control and Non-Proliferation*, "FY'05 Discretionary Budget Request ($ in Billions)," archived at www.oldamericancentury.org/fy05.gif

57. *Nieman Watchdog*, "Missile defense costs $10 billion a year. What do we get for that?" by Philip E. Coyle (January 24, 2006) at www.niemanwatchdog.org/index.cfm?fuseaction=ask_this.view&askthisid=00163

58. *Windsor Star,* "Canada won't fund missile shield: PM," (December 15, 2004) archived at
www.cndyorks.gn.apc.org/yspace/articles/bmd/canada85.htm

59. *Centre for Research on Globalisation,* "Washington's New World Order Weapons Have the Ability to Trigger Climate Change," by Michael Chossudovsky (January 4 2002) at
www.globalresearch.ca/articles/CHO201A.html

60. Ai*r Force Chief of Staff,* "Air Force 2025 - Weather as a Force Multiplier: Owning the Weather in 2025," (December 11 1996) at
www.au.af.mil/au/2025

61. *High Frequency Active Auroral Research Program,* "HAARP Fact Sheet," (January 21 2003) at www.haarp.alaska.edu/haarp/haarpFactSheet.html

62. *Earthpulse Press,* "Ground-Based 'Star Wars' Disaster Or 'Pure' Research?" at www.earthpulse.com/haarp/ground.html

63. *DARPA,* "FALCON Technology Demonstration Program Fact Sheet," (November 2003) at archived at www.cesaroni.net/falcon_fs.pdf

64. *Landmine Survivors Network* and the *Mines Advisory Group,* Keynote Address "Responding to Landmines: A Modern Tragedy and its Solutions," by Diana, Princess of Wales (June 12 1997) at
www.landminesurvivors.org/news_feature.php?id=38

65. Quotes taken from *International Campaign to Ban Landmines,* "What's the problem?" at www.icbl.org/problem/what

66. *Department of Defense,* "Global Message" (March 2 2004) at
www.whitehouse.gov/news/releases/2004/03/20040302.html

67. *Human Rights Watch,* "New U.S. Landmine Policy: Questions and Answers What is new about this policy? "at
http://hrw.org/english/docs/2004/02/27/usint7678.htm

68. *Democracy Now,* "U.S. a No-Show At International Anti-Landmine Conference," Amy Goodman, (November 30th, 2004) at
www.democracynow.org/article.pl?sid=04/11/30/1525250

69. *Biological Weapons Convention,* "Remarks to the 5th Biological Weapons Convention RevCon Meeting," John R. Bolton, Under Secretary for Arms Control and International Security (November 19 2001) at
www.state.gov/t/us/rm/janjuly/6231.htm

70. *San Francisco Chronicle,* "Pentagon has lost track of exported missiles Terrorists could use anti-aircraft Stinger missiles, critics say," by Paul J. Caffera (June 2 2004) http://sfgate.com/cgi-bin/article.cgi?file=/chronicle/archive/2004/06/02/MNGT26VCPB1.DTL

71. *ABC,* "Video Suggests Explosives Disappeared After U.S. Took Control," by Martha Raddatz and Luis Martinez (October 28, 2004) at
http://abcnews.go.com/WNT/story?id=206847

72. *The Guardian,* "Nuclear materials from Iraq 'missing'" by Ian Traynor (October 13 2004) at
www.guardian.co.uk/Iraq/Story/0,2763,1325814,00.html

73. *New York Times,* "Lockheed and the Future of Warfare LOCKHEED MARTIN doesn't run the United States. But it does help run a breathtakingly big part of it," by Tim Weiner (November 28 2004) archived at www.corpwatch.org/article.php?id=11731
74. Ibid.
75. *Los Angeles Times,* "America -- the world's arms pusher," by Frieda Barrigan (May 21 07) archived at www.informationclearinghouse.info/article17744.htm
76. *New York Times,* "Lockheed and the Future of Warfare," op. cit.
77. *The Sacramento Bee,* "Invisible beam tops list of nonlethal weapons," by Greg Gordon (June 1 2004) at www.sacbee.com/content/news/story/9499345p-10423294c.html
78. *Boston Business Journal,* "Report: Raytheon 'heat beam' weapon ready for Iraq" (December 1, 2004) at http://boston.bizjournals.com/boston/stories/2004/11/29/daily30.html
79. *NewScientist.com,* "Taser deaths to be investigated," (June 27 2006) at http://technology.newscientist.com/channel/tech/weapons/mg19025576.300 -taser-deaths-to-be-investigated.html
80. *New Scientist,* "Sweeping stun guns to target crowds," by David Hambling (June 16 2004) at www.newscientist.com/article.ns?id=dn6014
81. *Citizen Weapons Inspection Teams,* "Who Will Disarm America?," (November 11 2002) at www.wslfweb.org/docs/citinspletllnl.htm
82. *For Mother Earth,* "Citizens' Weapons Inspections Handbook," at www.motherearth.org/inspection/inspectbook_en.pdf
83. GREENPEACE, "Abolish Nuclear Weapons," at www.greenpeace.org/international/campaigns/abolish-nuclear-weapons

Women's Issues

1. *"No Mandate from Women of Color,"* by Linda Burnham (January 8 2005) at www.commondreams.org/views05/0108-27.htm
2. *MSNBC, Capitol Hill Letter (Newsweek)* "The Gender Gap: Bush is falling further behind among women and it could cost him come election time," by Eleanor Clift (May 14 2004) at www.msnbc.msn.com/id/4980895/
3. *Take Them At Their Words,* by Bruce J. Miller, (Academy Chicago Publishers, 2004, p. 77), citing as its source: "Pat Robertson, newspaper column, 11-22-83. USA Today, 2-22-96."
4. *Denver Business Journal,* "Women's groups blast Bush's policies," by Lyn Berry, (April 13 2001) at http://denver.bizjournals.com/denver/stories/2001/04/16/story6.html
5. *Time Magazine,* "Jesus and the FDA," by Karen Tumulty (October 25 2002) at www.time.com/time/nation/article/0,8599,361521,00.html
6. *Washington Post,* "Memo May Have Swayed Plan B Ruling FDA Received 'Minority Report' From Conservative Doctor on Panel," by Marc Kaufman

(May 12 2005) at www.washingtonpost.com/wp-dyn/content/article/2005/05/11/AR2005051101812.html

7. *The Nation*, "Dr. Hager's Family Values," by Ayelish McGarvey (May 13 2005) at www.alternet.org/rights/21990/

8. *National Women's Law Center*, "Justice Department Policies Undermine Women's Rights," by Judith C. Appelbaum and Virginia Davis (April 30 2004) at www.watchingjustice.org/reports/article.php?docId=220#_ednref16

9. *National Women's Law Center*, "Slip-Sliding Away: The Erosion of Hard-won Gains for Women under the Bush Administration and an Agenda for Moving Forward," (April 2004), pg. 43, at www.nwlc.org/pdf/AdminRecordOnWomen2004.pdf

10. Ibid. pg. 43

11. *National Council for Research on Women*, "Missing: Information About Women's Lives,"(April 2004) www.ncrw.org/misinfo/report.htm#report

12. *Salon.com* "Making women's issues go away," by Rebecca Traister, (April 28 2004) at www.salon.com/mwt/feature/2004/04/28/womens_report/index_np.html

13. *Transcript, Commission on Presidential Debates*, "The first 2000 Gore-Bush Presidential Debate" (October 3 2000) at www.cnn.com/ELECTION/2000/debates/transcripts/u221003.html

14. *Planned Parenthood*, "The War on Women: A Pernicious Web" at www.plannedparenthood.org/pp2/portal/files/portal/medicalinfo/femalesexualhealth/report-030114-rights.xml#1098156639426::-8009202803831991695

15. Ibid.

16. *CNN*, "Bush nominates Roberts to Supreme Court," (July 20 2005) at http://edition.cnn.com/2005/POLITICS/07/19/scotus.main/index.html

17. *CNN*, "Alito denied that Constitution protected abortion," by Bill Mears (November 15 2005) at http://edition.cnn.com/2005/POLITICS/11/14/alito/

18. *Washington Watch*, printed by the Family Research Council, "Real Women Stay Married," by Susan Orr (June 2000) archived at www.doesgodexist.org/MayJun01/RealWomenStayMarried.html

19. *Washington Post*, "Birth-Control Foe To Run Office on Family Planning," (October 17, 2007) at www.washingtonpost.com/wp-dyn/content/article/2007/10/16/AR2007101601762.html?hpid=moreheadlines

20. *National Organization for Women*, "Women Lose Millions Due to Wage Gap, NOW Calls for Passage of Pay Equity Legislation," (April 24, 2007) at www.now.org/press/04-07/04-24.html

21. *National Organization for Women*, "House Passes 'Ledbetter' Fair Pay Act But Too Soon to Declare Victory, *Statement of NOW President Kim Gandy* (July 31, 2007) at www.now.org/press/07-07/07-31.html

22. *AlterNet*, "The Christian Taliban," by Stephen Pizzo (March 28 2004) at www.alternet.org/story/18259/

23. Ibid.

24. *The Washington Post*, "A New Problem, or the Wrong Word?" by Dana Milbank, (September 7 2004) as cited at www.thetruthaboutgeorge.com/bushisms/index.html

25. *Centers for Disease Control and Prevention*, "Use of Contraception and Use of Family Planning Services in the United States: 1982-2002," by William D. Mosher et al. (Number 350 December 10 2004) at www.cdc.gov/nchs/data/ad/ad350.pdf

26. *The Alan Guttmacher Institute*, "U.S. Policy Can Reduce Cost Barriers to Contraception" at www.guttmacher.org/pubs/ib_0799.html

27. Ibid.

28. *National Organization for Women*, "Testimony of Kim A. Gandy, President National Organization for Women, Submitted to the House Committee on Small Business Hearing on Freedom of Conscience for Small Pharmacies," (July 25 2005) at www.now.org/issues/abortion/testimony7-25-05.html

29. *NARAL Pro-Choice America*, "Birth Control under Attack in Congress," at http://prochoiceaction.org/campaign/house_alpha_072605/suunk64y5e6b6j?

30. *Women's Enews*, "Heads Should Roll at FDA," by Rep. Louise Slaughter, (June 16 2004) at www.womensenews.org/article.cfm/dyn/aid/1864/context/archive

31. *Think Progress*, "Google Cache Thwarts Bush Spin Machine," at http://thinkprogress.org/2005/09/20/google-bush

32. *Child Welfare League of America*, "FY2007 Funding for Selected Children's Programs Chart," at www.cwla.org/advocacy/budgetdetails07.htm

33. *The Guttmacher Report on Public Policy*, "Title X Program Announcement Articulates New Priorities for Nation's Family Planning Programs, (December 2003) at www.guttmacher.org/pubs/journals/gr060513.pdf

34. *Child Welfare League of America*, "FY2006 Funding for Selected Children's Programs Chart," at www.cwla.org/advocacy/budgetdetails06.htm

35. *United Nations Populations Fund*, "About UNFPA" at www.unfpa.org/about/index.htm

36. *United Nations Populations Fund*, "34 Million Friends of UNFPA" at www.unfpa.org/support/friends/34million.htm

37. *Planned Parenthood*, "U.S. citizens reaffirm commitment to mothers and children, U.S. government refuses," (March 26 2004) at www.plannedparenthood.org/pp2/portal/files/portal/international/pressroom/news-040326-cairo-consesus.xml

38. *The White House*, "National Sanctity of Human Life Day, 2002," (January 18, 2002 press release) at www.whitehouse.gov/news/releases/2002/01/20020118-10.html

39. *National NOW Times*, "George W. Bush: What Does the 'W' Stand For?" by Patricia Ireland (Spring 2000) at www.now.org/nnt/spring-2000/georgewp.html

40. The photo can be seen at www.whitehouse.gov/news/releases/2003/11/20031105-1.html

41. *The Associated Press*, "Top Court Upholds Abortion Ban," (April 18 2007) archived at www.truthout.org/docs_2006/041807B.shtml

42. Congresswoman Nita M. Lowey (D-Westchester/Rockland) "Lowey Speaks Out Against Child Interstate Abortion Notification Act," (April 27 2005) at www.house.gov/list/press/ny18_lowey/ciana042705.html

43. *New York Times*, "The War against Women," Editorial (January 12 2003) archived at www.umich.edu/~umsfc/nytimes.html

44. Quotes taken from *Alan Guttmacher Institute,* "Facts in Brief: Induced Abortion in the United States," (2003) at www.guttmacher.org/pubs/fb_induced_abortion.html

45. *10 for Change*, "Violence against Women," at www.10forchange.org/issues/violence_brief.html

46. Ibid.

47. Ibid.

48. *AlterNet*, "Domestic Violence Not a Problem?" by Judith Kahan (July 21 2005) at www.alternet.org/story/23641/

49. *700women.org*, "About the Violence Against Women Act," at www.700women.org

50. *Violence Policy Center*, "Women and Firearms Violence Factsheet," at www.vpc.org/fact_sht/womensfs.htm

51. *National Women's Law Center,* op. cit., "Slip-Sliding Away," p. 39

52. *Women's Policy*, "FY2006 Budget Summary Introduction," (Volume 10, No. 39 -- ISSN 1526-8713) at www.womenspolicy.org/thesource/article.cfm?ArticleID=1570

53. *National Women's Law Center*, "Increasing Inequality, Increasing Insecurity for Women and Their Women and Their Families: An Analysis of the President's FY 2008 Budget," (February 2007) at www.nwlc.org/pdf/NWLCBudgetAnalysis.pdf

54. *National Women's Law Center,* op. cit., "Slip-Sliding Away," p. 25

55. *United States House of Representatives Committee on Government Reform – Minority Staff Special Investigations Division*, "The Content of Federally Funded Abstinence-Only Education Programs," (December 2004) at www.democrats.reform.house.gov/Documents/20041201102153-50247.pdf

56. *National Coalition for Women and Girls Education (NCWGE)*, "Questions and Answers on the Department of Education's 'Clarification' of Title IX Policy" at www.savetitleix.com/questions.html

57. *National Women's Law Center* "Slip-Sliding Away," op. cit., p. 18

58. *National Organization for Women*, "Good News and Bad News for Title IX," by Katy Litwak (March 31 2005) at www.now.org/issues/title_ix/033105titleix.html

59. Ibid.

60. Miller, op. cit., p. 70, citing as its source: "*The New Yorker*, 'The Back Page,' Paul Slansky" (December 4 2003)

61. Miller, op. cit., p. 67, citing as its source: "*San Francisco Chronicle*, 'Schwarzenegger's 2 sides when it comes to women: Macho actor exhibits disdain and respect for the opposite sex,' Robert Salladay," (August 14 2003)

62. Miller, op. cit., p. 70, citing as its source: "*Entertainment Weekly* interview (July 11 2003)"

63. Miller, op. cit., p. 71, citing as its source: *Townhall.com*, "The Eunuchs are Whining," (November 1 2001)

64. Miller, op. cit., p. 73, citing as its source: Phyllis Schafly, Feminist Fantasies, (jacket copy) Spence 2003.

65. *The 700 Club*, Pat Robertson (January 8 1992) as quoted at www.religioustolerance.org/quotes1.htm

66. *Harvard University*, "Remarks at NBER Conference on Diversifying the Science & Engineering Workforce," Lawrence H. Summers (January 14 2005) at www.president.harvard.edu/speeches/2005/nber.html

67. *The Economist*, "Harvard's Disgrace," (March 19 2005 issue)

68. *Democracy Now!*, "Women and Science: A Look at Harvard Pres. Larry Summers" (January 25 2005) at www.democracynow.org/article.pl?sid=05/01/25/1458243

69. *The Whirled Bank Group*, "Lawrence Summers The Bank Memo," at www.whirledbank.org/ourwords/summers.html

70. *Associated Press*, "Bush Seeks Funds for Abstinence Education," (November 28 2004) archived at www.newsmax.com/archives/articles/2004/11/27/124442.shtml

71. *The Washington Post*, "Depends what you mean by abstinence Study: Pledge-takers engage in riskier acts," by Ceci Connolly (March 19 2005) archived at www.concordmonitor.com/apps/pbcs.dll/article?AID=/20050319/REPOSITORY/503190352/1013/NEWS03

72. *The Associated Press*, "Study finds abstinence programs haven't influenced TX teens," (January 31 2005) archived at www.aegis.com/news/ads/2005/AD050197.html

73. *United States House of Representatives Committee on Government Reform Minority Staff Special Investigations Division*, op. cit.

74. Ibid.

75. *Planned Parenthood*, "What You Should Know about Sexuality Education," at www.plannedparenthood.org/pp2/portal/files/portal/educationoutreach/sexualityeducation/education-REAL-WhatYou.pdf

76. *Women's Policy*, op. cit.

77. *Free Republic*, "The Honorable Elaine Chao, Doro Bush Koch and Liz Cheney Announce the Bush-Cheney '04 National 'W Stands for Women' Leadership Team," (May 14 2004) at www.freerepublic.com/focus/f-news/1135716/posts

78. *United Nations Development Program (UNDP) and the Iraqi Ministry of Planning and Development*, "Iraq Living Conditions Survey 2004, Volume 1: Tabulation Report" at www.iq.undp.org/ILCS/PDF/Tabulation%20Report%20-%20Englilsh.pdf

79. *TomPaine.com*, "Iraq's Second-Class Citizens," by Yifat Susskind, at www.tompaine.com/articles/20050818/iraqs_secondclass_citizens.php

80. Ibid.

81. *Amnesty International*, "Afghanistan 'No one listens to us and no one treats us as human beings': Justice denied to women," (October 2003)

82. *Scotsman.com*, "The Taleban may be gone, but the abuse of women goes on," by Jeremy Lovell (May 30 2005) archived at www.rawa.org/ai-wom05-2.htm

83. *The United Nations Children Fund (UNICEF)*, "Afghanistan's maternal and child mortality rates soar KABUL," (August 4 2005) at www.unicef.org/media/media_27853.html

84. *Revolutionary Association of the Women of Afghanistan*, "Afghan Women under the Tyranny of Fundamentalists," at www.rawa.org/women.html

85. *NARAL Pro-Choice America*, "In Your State," at www.prochoiceamerica.org/choice-action-center/in_your_state/

86. *NARAL Pro-Choice America*, "Breaking Barriers, A Policy Action Kit Promoting the Reproductive Health of Women of Color and Low-Income Women," at www.prochoiceamerica.org/issues/women-of-color/breaking-barriers.html

87. *NARAL Pro-Choice America*, "Choice Action Center," at www.prochoiceamerica.org/choice-action-center/

88. *CODEPINK/Global Exchange*, "Iraqi Women under Siege," by Marjorie P. Lasky, at www.codepinkalert.org/downloads/IraqiWomenReport.pdf

89. *National Organization for Women*, "NOW's Work on Breast Implants," at www.now.org/issues/health/implants/index.html

90. *Environmental Working Group and Commonweal*, "Body Burden, The Pollution in People," at www.ewg.org/reports/bodyburden1/es.php

91. *Environmental Working Group*, "Skin Deep," at www.ewg.org/reports/skindeep/

92. *Greenpeace*, "The Chemical Home," at www.greenpeace.org.uk/Products/Toxics/chemicalhouse.cfm

93. *National Women's Law Center*, "Making the Grade on Women's Health: A National and State-by-State Report Card 2004," at www.nwlc.org/details.cfm?id=1861&section=health

Education

1. George W. Bush, January 2000, as quoted in *The Bush Dyslexicon*, by Mark Crispin Miller, (W.W. Norton & Company Inc., 2001, p. 138), citing the *Los Angeles Times*, January 14, 2000 as its source.

2. As quoted in *The Nation*, "Mangler-in-Chief" by Ken Silverstein (March 13 2001) at www.thenation.com/doc/20010326/silverstein20010313

3. *Bushwhacked*, by Molly Ivins and Lou Dubose (Allison & Busby Ltd., 2004, p. 78)

4. Ibid., p. 94-95

5. Ivins and Dubose, op. cit., p. 79

6. Silverstein, op. cit.

7. *National School Boards Association*, "The Why Report: NCLB Series - NSBA RECOMMENDATION #5," at www.nsba.org/site/docs/37800/37729.pdf

8. *National Education Association*, "More Schools Are Failing NCLB Law's 'Adequate Yearly Progress' Requirements" at www.nea.org/esea/ayptrends0106.html

9. *Committee on Education and the Workforce*, "Miller, Kennedy Introduce Bill to Require Department of Education to Play by its Own Rules on No Child Left Behind," by Representative George Miller (D-CA) and Senator Edward Kennedy (D-MA) (June 17 2004) at http://edworkforce.house.gov/democrats/releases/rel61704.html

10. Quotes taken from *FairTest*, ""How to Improve High-Stakes Test Scores Without Really Improving," by Richard L. Allington, Ph.D. at www.fairtest.org/k12/allington.html

11. *Hartford Courant*, "Bush has left education reform behind," by US Senator Christopher J. Dodd (D-CT), (May 13 2002) archived at www.senate.gov/~dodd/press/Speeches/107_02/0512.htm

12. *Mother Jones*, "Left Behind," at www.motherjones.com/news/feature/2004/05/left_behind.html

13. Ibid.

14. *American Prospect*, "Failing Grade," by Robert Gordon, (February 14 2005) at www.prospect.org/web/page.ww?section=root&name=ViewWeb&articleId=9169

15. *National Education Association*, "Cuts Leave More and More Public School Children Behind," (December 2003/January 2004) at www.nea.org/esea/storiesfromthefield.html

16. Ivins and Dubose, op. cit., p. 81

17. *USA Today*, "Education Dept. Paid Commentator to Promote Law," by Greg Toppo (January 7 2005) at www.usatoday.com/news/washington/2005-01-06-williams-whitehouse_x.htm

18. *Houston Chronicle*, "Former first lady's donation aids son, Katrina funds earmarked to pay for Neil Bush's software program," by Cynthia Leonor

Garza (March 23 2006) at
http://chron.com/cs/CDA/printstory.mpl/headline/metro/3742329
19. "The President's Speech at Des Moines, Iowa (1875)," cited at
www.kqed.org/topics/news/perspectives/youdecide/pop/schoolpray/3yes.html
20. As quoted in *AP/Fox News,* "Education Secretary States Preference for
Christian Schools," (April 10 2003) at
www.foxnews.com/story/0,2933,83708,00.html
21. Excerpt from Loren Baritz ed., *The Culture of the Twenties* (NY 1970)
cited at "The Monkey Trial" at
http://chnm.gmu.edu/courses/hist409/scopes.html
22. As quoted in *New York Times,* "Gotta Have Faith," by Paul Krugman
(December 17 2002) archived at www.pkarchive.org/column/121702.html
23. "Remarks by the President in Question and Answer Session with the
Press - The Oval Office," (January 29 2001) at
www.whitehouse.gov/news/releases/20010129-7.html
24. *Theocracy Watch,* "The Rise of the Religious Right in the Republican
Party – Abolish the U.S. Department of Education?" at
www.theocracywatch.org/schools2.htm#Abolition
25. *America Can Be Saved!* by Jerry Falwell, (Sword of the Lion Publishers,
1979, p. 52-53) as quoted at
www.theocracywatch.org/schools2.htm#Abolition
26. *Education Week,* "Vote Sought on Public School 'Exodus,'" by Mary Ann
Zehr (May 26 2004) archived at http://edpolitics.blogspot.com/2004/05/vote-
sought-on-public-school-exodus.html
27. *Economist,* "George Bush's secret army," (February 26 2004) at
www.economist.com/printedition/displayStory.cfm?Story_ID=2459411
28. Ibid.
29. *Patrick Henry College,* "Christian Philosophy of Education - Adopted by
the Board of Trustees September 28, 2002" at
www.phc.edu/about/ChristianPhilosophy.asp
30. *New York Times,* "College for the Home-Schooled Is Shaping Leaders for
the Right," by David D. Kirkpatrick (March 8 2004) archived at
www.hslda.org/docs/news/hslda/200403/200403080.asp
31. *Patrick Henry College,* "Statement of Biblical Worldview - Adopted by the
Board of Trustees September 28, 2002" at
www.phc.edu/docs/statementbiblicalworldview.pdf
32. *CNN,* "Education leader defends Christian comments," (April 10 2003) at
www.cnn.com/2003/EDUCATION/04/10/paige.religion.ap/index.html
33. *Wall Street Journal,* "It's Not About the Money," by Rod Paige (October
29 2003) at www.ed.gov/news/pressreleases/2003/10/10302003.html
34. *New York Times,* "Union Urges Bush to Replace Education Chief Over
Remark," by Sam Dillon and Diana Jean Schemo (February 25 2004) at
www.nytimes.com/2004/02/25/education/25PAIG.html?ex=1093320000&en
=7d8b5454189f0fdc&ei=5070

35. *Seattle Post-Intelligencer*, "Rub of a bad joke," Editorial Board (February 25 2004) at http://seattlepi.nwsource.com/opinion/161884_seceded.html

36. *General Accounting Office*, "Comparison of Achievement Results for Students Attending Privately Managed and Traditional Schools in Six Cities," Report submitted to the U.S. House of Representatives Committee on Education and the Workforce (October 2003) at www.gao.gov/new.items/d0462.pdf

37. Ibid.

38. *National Education Association (NEA)*, "Cash Cow - ESPs on the Front Lines," by Kristen Loschert, John O'Neil, and Dave Winans at www.nea.org/neatoday/0409/coverstory.html

39. *Edison Schools* at www.edisonschools.com/home/home.cfm

40. *National Education Association (NEA)*, "Cash Cow - At the Classroom Door," by Kristen Loschert, John O'Neil, and Dave Winans at www.nea.org/neatoday/0409/coverstory.html

41. *National Education Association (NEA)*, "Cash Cow – It Was the Videotape That Sold Her," by Kristen Loschert, John O'Neil, and Dave Winans at www.nea.org/neatoday/0409/coverstory.html

42. *New York Times*, "Education study finds weakened charter results Public school students often do better -- data bode ill for Bush's philosophy," by Diana Jean Schemo (August 17 2004) archived at www.sfgate.com/cgi-bin/article.cgi?file=/c/a/2004/08/17/MNGCT89CA51.DTL

43. *New York Times*, "Collapse of 60 Charter Schools leaves Californians Scrambling," by Sam Dillon (September 17 2004) at www.nytimes.com/2004/09/17/education/17charter.html

44. *CNN*, "Bush pushes for school vouchers," by Ian Christopher McCaleb (April 12 2001) at www.cnn.com/2001/ALLPOLITICS/04/12/bush.speech/

45. Quote taken from James Carville's 2003 book (with Jeff Nussbaum) *Had Enough? A Handbook for Fighting Back*, from Simon & Schuster, p. 150

46. *National Education Association (NEA)*, "Five Talking Points on Vouchers," at www.nea.org/vouchers/talkingpoints.html

47. Ibid.

48. *National Women's Law Center*, "Slip-Sliding Away: The Erosion of Hard-won Gains for Women under the Bush Administration and an Agenda for Moving Forward." (April 2004) at www.nwlc.org/pdf/AdminRecordOnWomen2004.pdf

49. *National Education Association (NEA)*, "Voters repeatedly reject vouchers," at www.nea.org/vouchers/vouchervotes.html

50. *New York Times*, "Florida Court Rules Against Religious School Vouchers," by Greg Winter (August 17 2004) archived at http://pewforum.org/news/display.php?NewsID=3827

51. *Theocracy Watch*, "School Vouchers," quoting "Samantha Smoot, director of the Texas Freedom Network" as its source at www.theocracywatch.org/schools_voucher.htm

52. Title taken from *Covert Action Quarterly*, "Phi Beta Capitalism:
Universities in Service to Business," by Lawrence Soley (Spring 1997)
53. *Washington Monthly*, "Doctors Without Borders – Why you can't trust
medical journals anymore," by Shannon Brownlee (April 2004) at
www.washingtonmonthly.com/features/2004/0404.brownlee.html
54. *American Association of University Professors*, "Statement on Corporate
Funding of Academic Research," at
www.aaup.org/statements/Redbook/CorporateFunding.htm
55. *Stateline.org*, "Bush budget cuts education," by Kavan Peterson
(February 06 2006) at
www.stateline.org/live/ViewPage.action?siteNodeId=136&languageId=1&con
tentId=86486
56. *The Teaching Commission*, "Press Center – Key Facts" at
www.theteachingcommission.org/press/key-facts.html
57. *The Teaching Commission*, "Teaching at Risk: A Call to Action," (2004)
pg. 17, at www.theteachingcommission.org/press/FINAL_Report.pdf
58. *Southeast Center for Teaching Quality*, "What It Means To Be A "Highly
Qualified Teacher," by Barnett Berry (October 2002) at
http://www.teachingquality.org/pdfs/definingHQ.pdf
59. Memo from ABCTE's former Communications Director Andrew
Campanella entitled "Changes to ABCTE's Passport to Teaching Program
Effective May 1" at
http://certification.dadeschools.net/pdf/Changes%20to%20ABCTE%E2%80
%99s%20Passport%20to%20Teaching%20Program.pdf
60. *National Education Association (NEA)*, "NEA Position on 'Highly Qualified
Effective Teacher' Mandate," at www.nea.org/lac/esea/hqetposition.html
61. *New York Times*, "Why We Built the Ivory Tower," by Stanley Fish (June
1 2004) archived at www.sa.utah.edu/bennion/welch/sfish.htm
62. *Eight Cities Media*, "Dr. Bill Cosby Speaks at the 50th Anniversary
commemoration of the Brown vs. Topeka Board of Education Supreme Court
Decision," (May 2004) at www.eightcitiesmap.com/transcript_bc.htm
63. *The Teaching Commission*, "Teaching at Risk: A Call to Action," op. cit.,
p. 13
64. *Economist*, "Lexington - The Cosby Show," (July 8 2004) at
www.economist.com/printedition/displayStory.cfm?Story_ID=2910178
65. Ibid.
66. *The Education Trust*, "The Funding Gap 2004 - Many States Still
Shortchange Low-Income and Minority Students," by Kevin Carey at
www2.edtrust.org/NR/rdonlyres/30B3C1B3-3DA6-4809-AFB9-
2DAACF11CF88/0/funding2004.pdf
67. As quoted in: *New Statesman*, "Rich kids go to college, poor ones to
Baghdad," by Tom Woodward (December 6 2004) archived at
http://207.44.245.159/article7429.htm

68. *The Center for Arms Control and Proliferation.* "FY'05 Discretionary Budget Request" at www.oldamericancentury.org/fy05.gif

69. *Office of Management and Budget,* "FY 2006 Budget," at www.whitehouse.gov/omb/budget/fy2006/budget.html

70. *WAND Education Fund,* "Proposed FY07 federal budget" at www.wand.org/news/fy07chart.htm

71. *Boston Globe,* "Military recruiters target schools strategically," by Charlie Savage (November 29 2004) archived at http://tinyurl.com/65f5n

72. *Campaign for America's Future and MoveOn.org,* "Send Bush Your Student Loan Bill," archived at http://archive.democrats.com/preview.cfm?term=Education

73. *National Women's Law Center,* op. cit., p. 21

74. *Committee for Education Funding,* "Myth vs. Reality: The Facts Behind Education Funding Myths" (February 2, 2004) at www.cef.org/News/articlefiles/1288-Myth%20vs.%20Reality--Press%20Release.pdf

75. *National Women's Law Center,* op. cit.

76. *Educational Leadership,* "On Savage Inequalities: A Conversation with Jonathan Kozol," interview with Marge Scherer, (Dec92/Jan93, Vol. 50 Issue 4, p4) archived at www.whitman.edu/education/EdWebCourses/Web360/downloads/Kozol_Interview.pdf

77. *The Education Trust,* op. cit., p. 12

78. *National Education Association,* "Final Appropriations (HR 3010) Fiscal Year 2006," at www.nea.org/lac/fy06edfunding/images/fifty.pdf

79. *National Education Association,* "Schools Lack Funding to Comply with No Child Left Behind, According to New Report from Center on Education Policy Report's Release Follows News That More Schools Have Failed to Meet Law's Standards," *at* www.nea.org/newsreleases/2006/nr060329.html

80. *National Women's Law Center,* "*Women and Children Last – Again: An Analysis of the President's FY 2007 Budget,"* at www.nwlc.org/pdf/FY07_BudgetAnalysis.pdf

81. *Tom Paine,* "A Hidden Budget Blow," by Earl Hadley, (February 25 2003) at www.tompaine.com/articles/a_hidden_budget_blow.php

82. *Committee for Education Funding,* op. cit.

83. *National Education Association,* "Improving the Law," at www.nea.org/esea/eseaamend.html

84. *National Education Association,* "Joint Organizational Statement on 'No Child Left Behind' Act" at www.nea.org/presscenter/nclbjointstatement.html

85. *Great Lakes Center,* "High-Stakes Testing and Student Achievement: Problems for the No Child Left Behind Act," by Sharon L. Nichols, Gene V. Glass and David C. Berliner (September 2005), Executive Summary at www.greatlakescenter.org/g_l_new_doc/EPSL-0509-105-EPRU-ExSum.pdf

86. *National Parent Teacher Association,* "National Standards for Parent/Family Involvement Programs," at www.pta.org/archive_article_details_1118251710359.html

87. *The Education Trust,* op. cit.

Mainstream Media

1. *White House,* "News Conference with U.S. President George W. Bush and Russian President Vladimir Putin, The East Room of the White House," (November 13 2001) at www.whitehouse.gov/news/releases/2001/11/20011113-3.html

2. *Associated Press,* "Simpsons Outpace U.S. Constitution Poll: More People Know Homer & Bart Than Know First Amendment," (march 1, 2006) at www.cbsnews.com/stories/2006/03/01/politics/main1356854.shtml?cmp=EM 8705

3. *AlterNet,* "The Power of People's Media," by Jim Hightower (June 16 2003) at www.alternet.org/module/printversion/18966

4. *Extra! Update,* "We Paid $3 Billion For These Stations. We'll Decide What the News Is," (June 1998) at www.fair.org/extra/9806/foxbgh.html

5. Track from Steve Earle's 2004 "The Revolution Starts Now" (Artemis Records)

6. *Columbia Journalism Review,* "Tripping up Big Media," by Gal Beckerman at www.cjr.org/issues/2003/6/media-beckerman.asp

7. *Media Week,* "Activists Dominate Content Complaints," by Todd Shields (December 6 2004) archived at www.parentstv.org/PTC/news/2004/indecency_mediaweek.htm

8. *Associated Press,* "Powell to Step Down as FCC Chairman," (January 21 2005) archived at www.editorandpublisher.com/eandp/news/article_display.jsp?vnu_content_id =1000769315

9. *Free Press,* "Public Urges the FCC to Listen to Broad Outcry Against Big Media" (October 30, 2007) at www.freepress.net/press/release.php?id=295

10. As cited in *San Francisco Bay Guardian,* "Politics: What is Disinformation?" by Norman Solomon (August 8 1996) as quoted at www.buzzflash.com/contributors/2002/02/020402_Liberal_Bias_A_Myth.html

11. Ibid.

12. BUZZFLASH, "David Brock, Author of "The Republican Noise Machine: Right Wing Media and How it Corrupts Democracy"(June 14 2004) at www.buzzflash.com/interviews/04/06/int04029.html

13. *Democracy Now!,* "A 'Right-Wing Coup' at PBS & the CPB? A Roundtable Discussion on the Future of Public Broadcasting," (May 12 2005) at www.democracynow.org/article.pl?sid=05/05/12/1426203

14. *Times Magazine,* "Questions for Ken Feree Recasting PBS? - Interview" by Deborah Solomon (April 24 2005) at

www.nytimes.com/2005/04/24/magazine/24QUESTIONS.html?ex=11167344
00&en=2cfde9026e918fea&ei=5070&ex=1115179200&en=bcdd7803b7c8fb
a7&ei=5070

15. *Media Matters*, "As O'Reilly let CPB's Tomlinson deny White House contacts, Tomlinson gushed, 'We love your show'" (May 13 2005) at http://mediamatters.org/items/printable/200505130006

16. *Democracy Now!*, "A 'Right-Wing Coup' at PBS & the CPB? A Roundtable Discussion on the Future of Public Broadcasting," (May 12 2005) at www.democracynow.org/article.pl?sid=05/05/12/1426203

17. *Real Screen Summit*, "Meet the Conference Speakers" Michael Pack Senior Vice President, Television Programming Corporation for Public Broadcasting, at www.realscreensummit.com/2006/speakers.html?a=563830&_c=1

18. *Media Matters*, "Media Matters launches Hands Off Public Broadcasting," by Jamison Foser (Week ending May 27 2005) at http://mediamatters.org/items/200505270003#3

19. *Media Matters*, "As O'Reilly let CPB's Tomlinson deny White House contacts, Tomlinson gushed, 'We love your show,'" op. cit.

20. *Salon*, "Pushing PBS to the right," by Eric Boehlert, (May 10 2005) archived at www.freepress.net/news/8109

21. *New York Times*, "Republican chairman exerts pressure on PBS, alleging biases," by Stephen Labaton, Lorne Manly & Elizabeth Jensen (May 2 2005) archived at www.freepress.net/news/7995

22. *Fairness & Accuracy in Reporting*, "How Public Is Public Radio?" (June 2004) at www.fair.org/extra/0405/npr-study.html

23. Ibid.

24. NPR Ombudsman, Jeffrey A. Dvorkin NPR: Mysteries of the Organization, Part I www.npr.org/templates/story/story.php?storyId=5053335

25. *New York Times*, "NPR Conflict with Overseer is Growing," by Stephen Labaton, (May 16 2005) at www.nytimes.com/2005/05/16/business/media/16radio.html

26. *CommonDreams.org*, Blacklist Isn't New to CPB's Tomlinson Public Broadcasting Chair Misrepresented Link to 1984 USIA Blacklist, by Michael Winship (June 28 2005) at www.commondreams.org/views05/0628-26.htm

27. *Los Angeles Times*, "The Leaning Tower of PBS Liberals see a conservative bent and vice versa. Meanwhile, station officials are getting nervous," by Matea Gold (May 9 2005) archived at www.commondreams.org/headlines05/0509-07.htm

28. *Corporation for Public Broadcasting*, "Office of Inspector General Report of Review, Review of Alleged Actions Violating The Public Broadcasting Act of 1967, as Amended," at www.cpb.org/oig/reports/602_cpb_ig_reportofreview.pdf

29. *White House*, "President Participates in Social Security Conversation in New York" (May 24 2005) at

www.whitehouse.gov/news/releases/2005/05/20050524-3.html

30. *New York Times*, "Inquiry Finds Radio Host's Arrangement Raised Flags," by Anne E. Kornblut (April 16 2005) at www.nytimes.com/2005/04/16/politics/16armstrong.html

31. *Independent*, "Bush administration paying independent commentators," by Andrew Buncombe (January 27 2005) archived at www.apfn.net/Messageboard/01-28-05/discussion.cgi.23.html

32. *Americablog.com*, "A man called Jeff," by John Aravosis, (February 14 2005) at http://americablog.blogspot.com/2005/02/man-called-jeff.html

33. *Washington Post*, "Scandal in the Press Corps," by Dan Froomkin (February 10 2005) at www.washingtonpost.com/ac2/wp-dyn/A14148-2005Feb10?

34. A great timeline is provided by *Daily Kos*, "Plame Leak Timeline II... the case is made (Gannon)" by Spiderleaf (February 5 2005) at www.dailykos.com/story/2005/2/5/212837/3714

35. *JeffGannon.com*, "Fear and Loathing in the Press Room," by Jeff Gannon, (column posted in May 2005) at www.jeffgannon.com/Column%20archive/fear_and_loathing_in_the_press_r.htm

36. *New York Post*, "ANYBODY HAVE A TICKET?" (April 29 2005)

37. *New York Times*, "Under Bush, a New Age of Prepackaged Television News," by David Barstow and Robin Stein (March 13 2005) archived at www.truthout.org/cgi-bin/artman/exec/view.cgi/37/9592

38. *Democracy Now!*, "State Propaganda: How Government Agencies Produce Hundreds of Pre-Packaged TV Segments the Media Runs as News," (March 14 2005) at www.democracynow.org/article.pl?sid=05/03/14/152202

39. *Associated Press*, "Bush education ads eyed," by Ben Feller, (October 11 2004) at www.boston.com/news/politics/advertising/articles/2004/10/11/bush_education_ads_eyed?mode=PF

40. *New York Times*, "White House's Medicare Videos Are Ruled Illegal," by Robert Pear (May 19 2004) at http://www.nytimes.com/2004/05/20/politics/20medicare.html?ex=1105419600&en=3476510de88506c0&ei=5070&ei=5070&en=1c4cc7e0718ea1f2&ex=1105246800&pagewanted=print&position=

41. Barstow and Stein, op. cit.

42. Quote accessed at www.snopes.com/quotes/goering.htm

43. *New York Times*, "The Times and Iraq," From the Editors (May 26, 2004) archived at www.commondreams.org/headlines04/0526-15.htm

44. *Le Nouvel Observateur Hebdomadaire*, "How the Press Was Manipulated by Ahmed Chalabi," Vincent Jauvert (July 24 2004)

45. *Democracy Now!*, "Congress Probes INC's Lobbying Efforts" (April 27 2004) at www.democracynow.org/article.pl?sid=04/04/27/1434258

46. *Department of Homeland Security*, "Fact Sheet: 'Ready' Campaign Update," at www.dhs.gov/dhspublic/display?content=3502

47. Ibid.

48. *Fairness & Accuracy in Reporting*, "FAIR study finds democracy poorly served by war coverage," (May/June 2003) at www.fair.org/extra/0305/warstudy.html.

49. *Information Clearing House*, "The photographs tell the story...," (April 10 2003) at www.informationclearinghouse.info/article2842.htm

50. *Inter Press Service*, "Washington pushes freedom – but not for Al-Jazeera," by Emad Mckay (May 26 2004) at www.antiwar.com/ips/mekay.php?articleid=2666

51. *PIPA/Knowledge Networks*, "Misperceptions, The Media and The Iraq War," (October 2 2003) at www.pipa.org

52. *Editor & Publisher*, "Public Remains Poorly Informed On Reasons for War," by Greg Mitchell (August 26, 2004) citing poll conducted by the Program on International Policy Attitudes (PIPA)

53. As quoted in "They Shoot Journalists Don't They?" by Norman Solomon (March 12 2004) archived at www.antiwar.com/solomon/?articleid=2117

54. *The Sydney Morning Herald*, "White House site prevents Iraq material being archived," by Sam Varghese (October 28 2003) at www.smh.com.au/articles/2003/10/28/1067233141495.html?from=storyrhs

55. *Los Angeles Times*, "PR Meets Psy-Ops in War on Terror," by Mark Mazzetti, (December 1 2004) archived at www.commondreams.org/headlines04/1201-01.htm

56. *Salon*, "The enemy is us," by Sam Gardiner, (September 22 2004) at www.salon.com/opinion/feature/2004/09/22/psychological_warfare/index_np.html

57. *New York Times*, "The Reach of War: Hearts and Minds; Pentagon Weighs Use of Deception in a Broad Arena," by Thom Shanker and Eric Schmitt (December 13, 2004) archived at www.commondreams.org/headlines04/1213-03.htm

58. *Washington Post*, "Tillman's Parents are Critical of Army," by Josh White, (May 23 2005) at www.washingtonpost.com/wp-dyn/content/article/2005/05/22/AR2005052200865.html

59. Ibid.

60. *Pentagon Channel*, at www.pentagonchannel.mil

61. *Mediachannel.org*, "Militainment Gone Amok," by Rory O'Connor, (December 3 2004) at www.mediachannel.org/views/dissector/affalert294.shtml

62. *CNN*, "Pentagon sites: Journalism or propaganda?" by Barbara Starr and Larry Shaughnessy (February 5 2005) at www.cnn.com/2005/ALLPOLITICS/02/04/web.us/index.html

63. *Institute for Public Accuracy*, "Al-Jazeera: Blaming the Messenger?" (April 30, 2004) as archived at www.commondreams.org/news2004/0430-05.htm

64. *Fairness & Accuracy In Reporting*, "CNN to Al Jazeera: Why Report Civilian Deaths?" (April 15 2004) at www.fair.org/activism/cnn-aljazeera.html

65. *Al-Jazeera*, "U.S. Forces want Aljazeera out of Fallujah" (April 9 2004)

archived at www.islamonline.net/English/News/2004-04/09/article06.shtml

66. *The Guardian*, "In Iraq, the U.S. does eliminate those who dare to count the dead," by Naomi Klein (December 4 2004) archived at www.truthout.org/docs_04/120604V.shtml

67. Ibid.

68. *BBC Newsnight*, "Veteran CBS News Anchor Dan Rather speaks out on tonight," (May 16 2002) at www.bbc.co.uk/pressoffice/pressreleases/stories/2002/05_may/16/dan_rather.shtml

69. Transcript archived at *Daily Kos*, "Carl Cameron DESTROYED in Outfoxed Video Clip," by Michael D. (posted July 10 2004) at http://michael-d.dailykos.com/story/2004/7/11/24252/0443

70. Ibid.

71. *Talking Points Memo*, "Is Fox News literally making stuff up out of whole cloth about John Kerry?" by Joshua Micah Marshall, (October 1 2004) at www.talkingpointsmemo.com/archives/week_2004_09_26.php#003551

72. *Fox News*, "Trail Tales: What's That Face?," (October 1 2004) at www.foxnews.com/story/0,2933,134166,00.html

73. *MediaMatters.org*, "33 internal FOX editorial memos reviewed by *MMFA* reveal FOX News Channel's inner workings," (July 14 2004) at http://mediamatters.org/items/200407140002

74. *Extra!*, "The Emperor's New Hump, The New York Times killed a story that could have changed the election—because it could have changed the election," by Dave Lindorff (January/February 2005) at http://fair.org/index.php?page=2012

75. Ibid.

76. *BBC Newsnight*, op. cit.

77. *GregPalast.com*, "I'd rather not say good-bye, Dan," by Greg Palast, (March 9, 2005) at www.gregpalast.com/detail.cfm?artid=416&row=0

78. *Salon*, "Bush in the National Guard: A primer. The flap over dubious documents has obscured the real story. Here it is," by Eric Boehlert (September 20, 2004) at www.salon.com/news/feature/2004/09/20/bush_guard_records/print.html

79. Ibid.

80. *GregPalast.com*, "CBS' cowardice and conflicts behind the purge. Network's craven back-down on Bush draft dodge report sure to get a standing Rove-ation at White House," by Greg Palast, (January 11 2005) at www.gregpalast.com/detail.cfm?artid=407&row=0

81. *The Asian Wall Street Journal*, "Guess Who's a GOP Booster? The CEO of CBS's parent company endorses President Bush," (September 24 2004) www.opinionjournal.com/extra/?id=110005669

82. *Washington Post*, "Sinclair Retreats on Kerry Film," by Elizabeth Jensen, (October 20 2004) archived at www.freepress.net/news/5052

83. *BBC Newsnight*, op. cit.

84. *International Federation of Journalists*, "Impunity, Justice Denied and Media Killings That Haunt the United States," (April 8 2005) at www.ifj.org/default.asp?index=3057&Language=EN

85. *AlterNet.org*, "The Guards Are Sleeping," by Gael Murphy, (May 2 2005) at www.alternet.org/mediaculture/21904/

86. *Interview of the President by Radio and Television Ireland*, by Carole Coleman, (June 24 2004) at www.whitehouse.gov/news/releases/2004/06/20040625-2.html

87. *Television Week*, "Independent Press Was a Target in Iraq," by Danny Schechter (February 28, 2005) archived at www.mediachannel.org/views/dissector/affalert331.shtml

88. *Reporters sans Frontières*, "Two murders and a lie" (January 2004) at www.rsf.org/IMG/pdf/iraq_report.pdf

89. *Reporters sans Frontières*, "Two murders and a lie: An investigation of the US Army's firing at the Palestine Hotel in Baghdad on 8 April 2003" (January 15 2004) at www.rsf.org/article.php3?id_article=9045

90. *Reporters sans Frontières*, op. cit. (full report)

91. Klein, op. cit.

92. Danny Schechter, op. cit.

93. *World Net Daily*, "U.S. troops killing journalists," (May 19 2005) archived at www.globalresearch.ca/articles/WOR505A.html

94. *The Courier-Journal*, "Home from Iraq Journalist urges Americans to search for truth, freedom" by Molly Bingham (May 8 2005) at www.courier-journal.com/apps/pbcs.dll/article?AID=/20050508/OPINION04/505080346/1054/OPINION

95. *Reporters sans Frontières*, "War in Iraq," (accessed November 1 2007) at www.rsf.org/special_iraq_en.php3

96. *The Independent*, "Hotel Journalism Gives American Troops a Free Hand As the Press Shelters Indoors," by Robert Fisk (January 17 2005) archived at www.truthout.org/docs_05/011805B.shtml

97. *Mirror*, "EXCLUSIVE: BUSH PLOT TO BOMB HIS ARAB ALLY Madness of war memo," by Kevin Maguire and Andy Lines (November 22 2005) at www.mirror.co.uk/news/tm_objectid=16397937&method=full&siteid=94762&headline=exclusive--bush-plot-to-bomb-his-arab-ally-name_page.html

98. Two examples of Giuliana Sgrena's reporting from Iraq can be found here: *Il Manifesto*, "Napalm Raid on Falluja? 73 charred bodies -- women and children -- were found," (November 23 2004) at http://ilmanifesto.it/pag/sgrena/en/420dd721e0ff0.html, and *Il Manifesto*, "Interview with an Iraki woman tortured at Abu Graib," (July 1 2004) at www.ilmanifesto.it/pag/sgrena/en/420dc5a37ba4d.html

99. *Il Manifesto*, "My Truth," by Giuliana Sgrena (March 6 2005) at http://ilmanifesto.it/pag/sgrena/en/422c903151e6f.html

100. *Democracy Now!*, "Giuliana Sgrena Blasts U.S. Cover Up, Calls for U.S.

and Italy to Leave Iraq," (April 27th, 2005) at
www.democracynow.org/article.pl?sid=05/04/27/1350235&mode=thread&ti
d=25

101. *New York Times*, "Reporter on Retracted Newsweek Article Put Monica
on the Map," by Charles McGrath (May 17 2005) as quoted at
http://en.wikipedia.org/wiki/Qur'an_desecration_controversy_of_2005

102. *Washington Post*, "Desecration of Koran Had Been Reported Before," by
Carol D. Leonnig (May 18 2005) at www.washingtonpost.com/wp-
dyn/content/article/2005/05/17/AR2005051701315.html

103. *Associated Press*, "*Newsweek* limits use of anonymous sources," (May
23 2005) archived at www.fac.org/news.aspx?id=15297

104. *Internet News*, "Supreme Court Questions FCC Cable Modem Regs," by
Roy Mark (March 29 2005) at
www.internetnews.com/infra/print.php/3493741

105. Ibid.

106. *Free Press*, "Free Press responds to Supreme Court rulings in Brand X
and Grokster cases High Court decisions could 'change the face of the
Internet as we know it.' (June 27 2005) at
www.freepress.net/press/release.php?id=80

107. *Free Press*, "Digital and HD TV," at www.freepress.net/issues/newtv

108. *MasterNewMedia.org*, "The US Struggle For Broadband Community
Internet," by Robin Good (May 17 2005) at
www.masternewmedia.org/news/2005/05/17/the_us_struggle_for_broadban
d.htm

109. Ibid.

110. Quotes taken from *TV-Turnoff Network*, "Facts and Figures about Our
TV Habit," at www.tvturnoff.org/images/facts&figs/factsheets/FactsFigs.pdf

111. *Free Press*, "Beginner's Guide, 10 Policies to Fix Our Media" at
www.freepress.net/guide/fix2.php

112. *TIME*, "The People's News Source" by Donald Macintyre (May 29 2005)
archived at
http://english.ohmynews.com/articleview/article_view.asp?article_class=8&n
o=153109&rel_no=2

113. *Editor & Publisher*, "New Desk in the Newsroom: The Citizen Editor's,"
by Steve Outing, (May 26, 2005)

114. *Poynter.org*, "Finding 2: The American Journalist Survey
Women Journalists Aren't Increasing Overall," (citing a *Project for Excellence
in Journalism* study) at
www.poynter.org/content/content_view.asp?id=28784

115. *WomensENews.org*, "In TV Anchor Land, Time Stands Still for Women,"
by Caryl Rivers (December 8 2004) at
www.womensenews.org/article.cfm/dyn/aid/2100/context/archive

116. *National Association of Black Journalists*, "NABJ Expresses Dissatisfaction Over Setbacks in Newsroom Diversity," (June 2 2005) at www.nabj.org/newsroom/news_releases/2005/story/15225p-20614c.html
117. These facts came from: *Unity Journalists*, "Increasing Newsroom Diversity: It's Time to Make It Personal," (April 12 2005) at www.unityjournalists.org/news/news041205.html and *Free Press*, "Diversity in Staffing," at www.freepress.net/issues/staffing
118. *Free Press*, "Activist Tools," at www.freepress.net/action/tools

Made in the USA